# EVENING BY EVENING

# EVENING BY EVENING

*A New Edition of the Classic Devotional Based on*
*The Holy Bible, English Standard Version*

## Charles H. Spurgeon

REVISED AND UPDATED BY

### Alistair Begg

## CROSSWAY BOOKS
### WHEATON, ILLINOIS

*Evening by Evening*

Copyright © 2007 by Alistair Begg

This book was formerly part of *Morning and Evening*, copyright © 2003 by Alistair Begg.

Published by Crossway Books
       a publishing ministry of Good News Publishers
       1300 Crescent Street
       Wheaton, Illinois 60187

Unless otherwise indicated, Scripture quotations are taken from *The Holy Bible: English Standard Version,*® copyright © 2001 by Crossway Bibles, a publishing ministry of Good News Publishers.

Scripture quotations indicated KJV are taken from the King James Version.

Cover design: Luke Daab

First printing, 2007

Printed in Belgium

---

**Library of Congress Cataloging-in-Publication Data**
Spurgeon, C. H. (Charles Haddon), 1834–1892.
    Evening by evening : a new edition of the classic devotional based on the Holy Bible, English standard version / Charles H. Spurgeon ; revised and updated by Alistair Begg.
      p. cm.
    "This book was formerly part of Morning and Evening, copyright 2003 by Alistair Begg."
    ISBN 978-1-58134-982-5 (trutone)
    1. Devotional calendars—Baptists. 2. Bible—Meditations. I. Begg, Alistair. II. Spurgeon, C. H. (Charles Haddon), 1834–1892. Morning and evening. III. Title.
BV4811.S6669      2007
242'.2—dc22                       2007033106

| SP | | 17 | 16 | 15 | 14 | 13 | 12 | 11 | 10 | 09 | 08 | 07 |
|----|----|----|----|----|----|----|----|----|----|----|----|----|
| 15 | 14 | 13 | 12 | 11 | 10 | 9 | 8 | 7 | 6 | 5 | 4 | 3 | 2 | 1 |

*"Morning by morning he awakens; he awakens my ear to hear as those who are taught."*

ISAIAH 50:4

*"My soul will be satisfied as with fat and rich food, and my mouth will praise you with joyful lips, when I remember you upon my bed, and meditate on you in the watches of the night."*

PSALM 63:5-6

# Introduction

Spurgeon's daily devotional readings have stood the test of time and are unrivaled as an example of deep theological insight and warm pastoral concern. They are so classic that one hesitates to tamper with them.

In revising and updating the material, I have tried to make them more readable without spoiling the splendor of the language. Most of the changes are minor and will go largely undetected. On a few occasions, because of the difference between the King James Version and the English Standard Version, I was forced to take more liberty.

My goal throughout has been to fashion the material in such a way that it will be accessible to a far wider audience than before. Spurgeon's vocabulary is so vast that the reader may still find himself reaching for a dictionary, but this will surely be an added benefit!

Since I did not have the opportunity to ask Spurgeon's permission, when I meet him I will seek his forgiveness if in attempting to bring clarity I have clouded the issue. The reader must judge. My prayer is that another generation will emerge thankful to God for the work of Spurgeon, whose memory we revere and whose example of godly devotion we seek to follow.

*Alistair Begg*

## *We will exult and rejoice in you.*

SONG OF SOLOMON 1:4

We will be glad and rejoice in You. We will not open the gates of the year to the sorrowful notes of the organ, but to the sweet strains of the harp of joy and the high-sounding cymbals of gladness. "O come, let us sing to the LORD; let us make a joyful noise to the rock of our salvation."[1] We, the called and faithful and chosen, will drive away our griefs and set up our banners of confidence in the name of God. Let others lament over their troubles; we with joy will magnify the Lord. Eternal Spirit, our effectual Comforter, we who are the temples in which You dwell will never cease from adoring and blessing the name of Jesus. Jesus must have the crown of our heart's delight; we will not dishonor our Bridegroom by mourning in His presence. We are ordained to be the minstrels of the skies; let us rehearse our everlasting anthem before we sing it in the halls of the New Jerusalem. We will exult and rejoice: two words with one sense, double joy, blessedness upon blessedness. Need there be any limit to our rejoicing in the Lord even now? Do not men of grace find their Lord to be the sweetest of incense even now, and what better fragrance have they in heaven itself? We will be glad and rejoice in You. That last word is the meat in the dish, the kernel of the nut, the soul of the text. What heavens are laid up in Jesus! What rivers of infinite bliss have their source, aye, and every drop of their fullness in Him! Since, O sweet Lord Jesus, You are the present portion of Your people, favor us this year with such a sense of Your preciousness that from its first to its last day we may be glad and rejoice in You. Let January open with joy in the Lord, and December close with gladness in Jesus.

[1]Psalm 95:1

## *Let the peoples renew their strength.*

ISAIAH 41:1

All things on earth need to be renewed. No created thing continues by itself. "You renew the face of the ground,"[1] was the psalmist's utterance. Even the trees, which wear not themselves with care, nor shorten their lives with labor, must drink of the rain of heaven and draw from the hidden treasures of the soil. The cedars of Lebanon, which God has planted, only live because day by day they are full of sap freshly drawn from the earth. Neither can man's life be sustained without renewal from God. As it is necessary to repair the body by the frequent meal, so we must repair the soul by feeding upon the Book of God, or by listening to the preached Word, or by the soul-fattening table of the ordinances. How depressed are our graces when means are neglected! What poor starving souls they are who live without the diligent use of the Word of God and secret prayer! If our piety can live without God it is not of divine creating; it is but a dream; for if God had begotten it, it would wait upon Him as the flowers wait upon the dew. Without constant restoration we are not ready for the perpetual assaults of hell, or the stern afflictions of heaven, or even for the strife within. When the whirlwind shall be loosed, woe to the tree that has not sucked up fresh sap and grasped the rock with many inter-twisted roots. When tempests arise, woe to the mariners that have not strengthened their mast, nor cast their anchor, nor sought the haven. If we suffer the good to grow weaker, the evil will surely gather strength and struggle desperately for the mastery over us; and as a result a painful desolation and a lamentable disgrace may follow. Let us draw near to the footstool of divine mercy in humble entreaty, and we shall realize the fulfillment of the promise, "They who wait for the LORD shall renew their strength."[2]

[1]Psalm 104:30   [2]Isaiah 40:31

## *"The voice of one crying in the wilderness: 'Prepare the way of the Lord, make his paths straight.'"*

LUKE 3:4

The voice crying in the wilderness demanded *a way for the Lord, a way prepared, and a way prepared in the wilderness.* I would be attentive to the Master's proclamation and give Him a road into my heart, cast up by gracious operations, through the desert of my nature. The four directions in the text[1] must have my serious attention.

*Every valley must be exalted.* Low and groveling thoughts of God must be given up; doubting and despairing must be removed; and self-seeking and carnal delights must be forsaken. Across these deep valleys a glorious causeway of grace must be raised.

*Every mountain and hill shall be laid low.* Proud creature-sufficiency, and boastful self-righteousness, must be ·leveled, to make a highway for the King of kings. Divine fellowship is never promised to haughty, high-minded sinners. The Lord has respect to the lowly and visits the contrite in heart, but the lofty are an abomination unto Him. My soul, beseech the Holy Spirit to set you right in this respect.

*The crooked shall be made straight.* The wavering heart must have a straight path of decision for God and holiness marked out for it. Double-minded men are strangers to the God of truth. My soul, take heed that in everything you are honest and true, as in the sight of the heart-searching God.

*The rough places shall be made smooth.* Stumbling-blocks of sin must be removed, and thorns and briers of rebellion must be uprooted. So great a visitor must not find miry ways and stony places when He comes to honor His favored ones with His company. Oh, that this evening the Lord may find in my heart a highway made ready by His grace, that He may make a triumphal progress through the utmost bounds of my soul, from the beginning of this year even to the end of it.

[1]Isaiah 40

11

## *And Joseph recognized his brothers,*
## *but they did not recognize him.*

GENESIS 42:8

This morning our desires went forth for growth in our acquaintance with the Lord Jesus; it may be well tonight to consider a kindred topic, namely, *our heavenly Joseph's knowledge of us.* This was most blessedly perfect long before we had the slightest knowledge of Him. "Your eyes saw my unformed substance; in your book were written, every one of them, the days that were formed for me, when as yet there were none of them."[1] Before we had a being in the world we had a being in His heart. When we were enemies to Him, He knew us, our misery, our madness, and our wickedness. When we wept bitterly in despairing repentance, and viewed Him only as a judge and a ruler, He viewed us as His brethren well beloved, and His heart yearned toward us. He never mistook His chosen but always beheld them as objects of His infinite affection. "The Lord knows those who are his"[2] is as true of the prodigals who are feeding pigs as of the children who sit at the table.

But, sadly *we did not know our royal Brother*, and out of this ignorance grew a host of sins. We withheld our hearts from Him and allowed Him no entrance to our love. We mistrusted Him and gave no credit to His words. We rebelled against Him and paid Him no loving homage. The Sun of Righteousness shone forth, and we could not see Him. Heaven came down to earth, and earth perceived it not. Let God be praised, those days are over with us; yet even now what we know of Jesus is small compared with what He knows of us. We have only begun to study Him, but He knows us altogether. It is a blessed circumstance that the ignorance is not on His side, for then it would be a hopeless case for us. He will not say to us, "I never knew you," but He will confess our names in the day of His appearing, and meanwhile will show Himself to us as He does not to the world.

[1]Psalm 139:16  [2]2 Timothy 2:19

12

### *And God saw that the light was good.*

GENESIS 1:4

This morning we noticed the goodness of the light, and the Lord's dividing it from the darkness. We now note the special eye that the Lord had for the light. "God saw the light"—He looked at it with complacency, gazed upon it with pleasure, saw that it good." If the Lord has given you light, dear reader, He looks on that light with peculiar interest; for not only is it dear to Him as His own handiwork, but it is like Himself, for "God is light." It is pleasant for the believer to know that God's eye tenderly observes that work of grace that He has begun. He never loses sight of the treasure that He has placed in our earthen vessels. Sometimes we cannot see the light, but God always sees the light, and that is much better than our seeing it. Better for the judge to see my innocence than for me to think I see it. It is very comfortable for me to know that I am one of God's people—but whether I know it or not, if the Lord knows it, I am still safe. This is the foundation, "The Lord knows those who are his."[1] You may be sighing and groaning because of inbred sin, and mourning over your darkness; yet the Lord sees "light" in your heart, for He has put it there, and all the cloudiness and gloom of your soul cannot conceal your light from His gracious eye. You may have sunk low in despondency, and even despair; but if your soul has any longing toward Christ, and if you are seeking to rest in His finished work, God sees the "light." He not only sees it, but He also preserves it in you. "I, the Lord, do keep it." This is a precious thought to those who, after anxious watching and guarding of themselves, feel their own powerlessness to do so. The light thus preserved by His grace, He will one day develop into the splendor of noonday, and the fullness of glory. The light within is the dawn of the eternal day.

[1] 2 Timothy 2:19

## *Now the hand of the LORD had been upon me the evening before . . .*

EZEKIEL 33:22

In the matter of *judgment* this may be the case, and if so, let me consider the reason for such a visitation and accept it as from His hand. I am not the only one who is chastened in the night season; let me cheerfully submit to the affliction and carefully endeavor to profit by it. But the hand of the Lord may also be felt in another manner, strengthening the soul and lifting the spirit upward toward eternal things. O that I may in this sense feel the Lord dealing with me! A sense of the divine presence and indwelling bears the soul toward heaven as upon the wings of eagles. At such times we are full to the brim with spiritual joy, and forget the cares and sorrows of earth; the invisible is near, and the visible loses its power over us. Servant-body waits at the foot of the hill, and the master-spirit worships upon the summit in the presence of the Lord. O that a hallowed season of divine communion may be granted to me this evening! The Lord knows that I need it very greatly. My graces languish, my corruptions rage, my faith is weak, my devotion is cold; all these are reasons why His healing hand should be laid upon me. His hand can cool the heat of my burning brow and calm the turmoil of my palpitating heart. That glorious right hand that molded the world can renew my mind; the unwearied hand that bears the earth's huge pillars can sustain my spirit; the loving hand that encloses all the saints can cherish me; and the mighty hand that breaks in pieces the enemy can subdue my sins. Why should I not feel that hand touching me this evening? Come, my soul, address God with the potent plea that Jesus' hands were pierced for your redemption, and you shall surely feel that same hand upon you that once touched Daniel and set him upon his knees that he might see visions of God.

## *My sister, my bride.*

SONG OF SOLOMON 4:12

Observe the sweet titles with which the heavenly Solomon with intense affection addresses His bride, the church. "*My sister*, one near to Me by ties of nature, partaker of the same sympathies. *My bride*, nearest and dearest, united to Me by the tenderest bands of love; My sweet companion, part of My own self. *My sister*, by My Incarnation, which makes Me bone of your bone and flesh of your flesh; *my bride*, by heavenly betrothal, in which I have married you to Myself in righteousness. *My sister*, whom I knew of old, and over whom I watched from her earliest infancy; *My bride*, taken from among the daughters, embraced by arms of love and joined to me forever." See how true it is that our royal Kinsman is not ashamed of us, for He dwells with manifest delight upon this twofold relationship. We have the word "my" twice in our version; as if Christ dwelt with rapture on His possession of His Church. His delights were with the sons of men because those sons of men were His own chosen ones. He, the Shepherd, sought the sheep because they were His sheep; He has gone about "to seek and to save that which was lost," because that which was lost was His long before it was lost to itself or lost to Him. The church is the exclusive portion of her Lord; none else may claim a partnership or pretend to share her love. Jesus, Your church delights to have it so! Let every believing soul drink solace out of these wells. Soul, Christ is near to you in ties of relationship. Christ is dear to you in bonds of marriage union, and you are dear to Him; behold, He grasps both of your hands with both His own, saying, "*My* sister, *my* bride." Consider how the Lord gets such a double hold of you that He neither can nor will ever let you go. Be not, O beloved, slow to return the hallowed flame of His love.

### *For your love is better than wine.*

SONG OF SOLOMON 1:2

*N*othing gives the believer so much joy as fellowship with Christ. He has enjoyment as others have in the common mercies of life—he can be glad both in God's gifts and God's works; but in all these separately, yes, and in all of them added together, he does not find such substantial delight as in the matchless person of his Lord Jesus. He has wine that no vineyard on earth ever yielded; he has bread that all the cornfields of Egypt could never bring forth. Where can such sweetness be found as we have tasted in communion with our Beloved? In our esteem, the joys of earth are little better than husks for pigs compared with Jesus, the heavenly manna. We would rather have one mouthful of Christ's love and a sip of his fellowship than a whole world full of carnal delights. What is the chaff to the wheat? What is the sparkling paste to the true diamond? What is a dream to the glorious reality? What is life's merriment compared to our Lord Jesus in His most despised estate? If you know anything of the inner life, you will confess that our highest, purest, and most enduring joys must be the fruit of the tree of life, which is in the midst of the Paradise of God. No spring yields such sweet water as that well of God, which was dug with the soldier's spear. All earthly bliss is of the earth earthy, but the comforts of Christ's presence are like Himself, heavenly. We can review our communion with Jesus and find in it no empty regrets; there are no dregs in this wine, no dead flies in this ointment. The joy of the Lord is solid and enduring. Vanity has not looked upon it, but discretion and prudence testify that it abides the test of years and is in time and in eternity worthy to be called "the only true delight." For nourishment, consolation, exhilaration, and refreshment, no wine can rival the love of Jesus. Let us drink to the full this evening.

## *Serve the LORD with gladness.*

PSALM 100:2

Delight in divine service is a token of acceptance. Those who serve God with a sad countenance, because they do what is unpleasant to them, are not serving Him at all; they bring the *form* of loyalty, but the *life* is absent. Our God requires no slaves to grace His throne; He is the Lord of the empire of love, and would have His servants dressed in the uniform of joy. The angels of God serve Him with songs, not with groans; a murmur or a sigh would be a mutiny in their ranks. That obedience that is not voluntary is disobedience, for the Lord looks at the heart, and if He sees that we serve Him from force, and not because we love Him, He will reject our offering. Service coupled with cheerfulness is heart-service and therefore true. Take away joyful willingness from the Christian, and you have removed *the test of his sincerity*. If a man be driven to battle, he is no patriot; but he who marches into the fray with flashing eye and beaming face, singing, "It is sweet for one's country to die," proves himself to be sincere in his patriotism. Cheerfulness is *the support of our strength*; in the joy of the Lord are we strong. It acts as *the remover of difficulties*. It is to our service what oil is to the wheels of a railway carriage. Without oil the axle soon grows hot, and accidents occur; and if there be not a holy cheerfulness to oil our wheels, our spirits will be clogged with weariness. The man who is cheerful in his service of God proves that obedience is his element; he can sing,

*Make me to walk in your commands,*
*It's a delightful road.*

Reader, let us put this question—do you serve the Lord with gladness? Let us show to the people of the world, who think our religion to be slavery, that it is to us a delight and a joy! Let our gladness proclaim that we serve a good Master.

## *In my flesh I shall see God.*

JOB 19:26

Consider the subject of Job's devout anticipation: "I shall see God." He does not say, "I shall see the saints"—though doubtless that will be untold happiness—but "I shall see God." It is not "I shall see the pearly gates, I shall behold the walls of jasper, I shall gaze upon the crowns of gold," but "I shall see God." This is the sum and substance of heaven; this is the joyful hope of all believers. It is their delight to see Him now in the ordinances by faith. They love to behold Him in communion and in prayer; but there in heaven they shall have an open and unclouded vision, and thus seeing "him as he is,"[1] shall be made completely like Him. *Likeness to God*—what more can we wish for? And *a sight of God*—what can we desire better? Some read the passage, "Yet I shall see God in my flesh" and find here an allusion to Christ as the Word made flesh, and that glorious beholding of Him that shall be the splendor of the latter days. Whether so or not, it is certain that Christ shall be the object of our eternal vision; nor shall we ever want any joy beyond that of seeing Him. Do not think that this will be a narrow sphere for the mind to dwell in. It is but one source of delight, but that source is infinite. All His attributes shall be subjects for contemplation, and as He is infinite under each aspect, there is no fear of exhaustion. His works, His gifts, His love to us, and His glory in all His purposes and in all His actions, these shall make a theme that will be ever new. The patriarch looked forward to this sight of God as a personal enjoyment. "Whom I shall see for myself, and my eyes shall behold, and not another."[2] Take realizing views of heaven's bliss; think what it will be to you. "Your eyes will behold the king in his beauty."[3] All earthly brightness fades and darkens as we gaze upon it, but here is a brightness that can never dim, a glory that can never fade—*"I shall see God."*

[1] 1 John 3:2  [2] Job 19:27  [3] Isaiah 33:17

## *I have prayed for you.*

LUKE 22:32

How encouraging is the thought of the Redeemer's never-ceasing intercession for us. When we pray, He pleads for us; and when we are not praying, He is advocating our cause, and by His supplications shielding us from unseen dangers. Notice the word of comfort addressed to Peter—"Simon, Simon, behold, Satan demanded to have you, that he might sift you like wheat, but"[1]—what? "But go and pray for yourself"? That would be good advice, but it is not so written. Neither does He say, "But I will keep you watchful, and so you shall be preserved." That would be a great blessing. No, it is, *"But I have prayed for you* that your faith may not fail."[2] We little know what we owe to our Savior's prayers. When we reach the hilltops of heaven and look back upon all the way whereby the Lord our God has led us, how we shall praise Him who, before the eternal throne, undid the mischief that Satan was doing upon earth. How we shall thank Him because He never held His peace but day and night pointed to the wounds upon His hands and carried our names upon His breastplate! Even before Satan had begun to tempt, Jesus had forestalled him and entered a plea in heaven. Mercy outruns malice. Consider, He does not say, "Satan hath desired to have you." He checks Satan even in his very desire and nips it in the bud. He does not say, "But I have desired to pray for you." No, but "I have prayed for you—I have done it already; I have gone to court and entered a counterplea even before an accusation is made." O Jesus, what a comfort it is that You have pleaded our cause against our unseen enemies; You have unmasked their ambushes. Here is a matter for joy, gratitude, hope, and confidence.

[1]Luke 22:31  [2]Luke 22:32

## *I have yet something to say on God's behalf.*

JOB 36:2

We ought not to court publicity for our virtue or notoriety for our zeal; but at the same time it is a sin to be always seeking to hide what God has bestowed upon us for the good of others. A Christian is not to be a village in a valley, but "a city set on a hill";[1] he is not to be a candle under a bushel, but a candle in a candlestick, giving light to all. Retirement may be lovely in its season, and to hide one's self is doubtless modest, but the hiding of *Christ* in us can never be justified, and the keeping back of truth, which is precious to ourselves, is a sin against others and an offense against God. If you have a nervous temperament and a retiring disposition, take care that you do not indulge this trembling propensity, lest you should be useless to the church. Seek in the name of Him who was not ashamed of you to do some little violence to your feelings and tell others what Christ has told to you. If you cannot speak with trumpet tongue, use the still small voice. If the pulpit must not be your tribune, if the press may not carry on its wings your words, yet say with Peter and John, "I have no silver and gold, but what I do have I give to you."[2] By Sychar's well talk to the Samaritan woman, if you cannot preach a sermon on the mountain; utter the praises of Jesus in the house, if not in the temple; in the field, if not in the public square; in your own household, if you cannot in the great family of man. From the hidden springs within, let sweetly flowing streams of testimony flow forth, giving drink to every passerby. Hide not your talent; trade with it, and you shall bring in good interest to your Lord and Master. To speak for God will be refreshing to ourselves, cheering to saints, useful to sinners, and honoring to the Savior.

[1]Matthew 5:14  [2]Acts 3:6

## *. . . made the iron float.*

2 KINGS 6:6

The axe head seemed hopelessly lost, and as it was borrowed, the honor of the prophetic band was likely to be imperiled, and so the name of their God to be compromised. Contrary to all expectation, the iron was made to mount from the depth of the stream and to swim; for things impossible with man are possible with God. I knew a man in Christ but a few years ago who was called to undertake a work far exceeding his strength. It appeared so difficult as to involve absurdity in the bare idea of attempting it. Yet he was called to it, and his faith rose with the occasion. God honored his faith, unlooked-for aid was sent, and the iron did swim. Another of the Lord's family was in dreadful financial straits. He would have been able to meet all claims and much more if he could have realized a certain portion of his estate, but he was overtaken with a sudden pressure. He sought for friends in vain, but faith led him to the unfailing Helper, and lo, the trouble was averted, his footsteps were enlarged, and the iron did swim. A third had a sorrowful case of depravity to deal with. He had taught, reproved, warned, invited, and interceded, but all in vain. Old Adam was too strong for young Melanchthon; the stubborn spirit would not relent. Then came an agony of prayer, and before long a blessed answer was sent from heaven. The hard heart was broken; the iron did swim.

Beloved reader, what is your desperate case? What heavy matter have you to deal with this evening? Bring it here. The God of the prophets lives, and lives to help His saints. He will not suffer you to lack any good thing. Believe in the Lord of hosts! Approach Him pleading the name of Jesus, and the iron shall swim; you too shall see the finger of God working marvels for His people. According to your faith be it unto you, and yet again the iron shall swim.

## *Beginning to sink he cried out, "Lord, save me."*

MATTHEW 14:30

*Sinking times are praying times* with the Lord's servants. Peter neglected prayer at starting upon his venturous journey, but when he began to sink, his danger made him a suppliant, and his cry, though late, was not too late. In our hours of bodily pain and mental anguish, we find ourselves as naturally driven to prayer as the wreck is driven upon the shore by the waves. The fox runs to its hole for protection; the bird flies to the wood for shelter; and even so the tried believer hastens to the mercy-seat for safety. Heaven's great harbor of refuge is All-prayer; thousands of weather-beaten vessels have found a haven there, and the moment a storm comes on, it is wise for us to make for it with full sail.

*Short prayers are long enough.* There were but three words in the petition that Peter gasped out, but they were sufficient for his purpose. Not length but strength is desirable. A sense of need is a mighty teacher of brevity. If our prayers had less of the tail feathers of pride and more wing, they would be all the better. Verbiage is to devotion as chaff to the wheat. Precious things lie in small compass, and all that is real prayer in many a long address might have been uttered in a petition as short as that of Peter.

*Our extremities are the Lord's opportunities.* Immediately a keen sense of danger forces an anxious cry from us, the ear of Jesus hears, and with Him ear and heart go together, and the hand does not long linger. At the last moment we appeal to our Master, but His swift hand makes up for our delays by instant and effectual action. Are we nearly engulfed by the boisterous waters of affliction? Let us then lift up our souls unto our Savior, and we may rest assured that He will not suffer us to perish. When we can do nothing, Jesus can do everything; let us enlist His powerful aid upon our side, and all will be well.

## *But I give myself to prayer.*

PSALM 109:4

Lying tongues were busy against the reputation of David, but he did not defend himself; he moved the case into a higher court and pleaded before the great King Himself. Prayer is the safest method of replying to words of hatred. The psalmist prayed in no coldhearted manner; he gave himself to the exercise—threw his whole soul and heart into it—straining every sinew and muscle, as Jacob did when wrestling with the angel. Thus, and thus only, shall any of us speed at the throne of grace. As a shadow has no power because there is no substance in it, even so that supplication in which a man's proper self is not thoroughly present in agonizing earnestness and vehement desire is utterly ineffectual, for it lacks that which would give it force. "Fervent prayer," says an old divine, "like a cannon planted at the gates of heaven, makes them fly open." The common fault with most of us is our readiness to yield to distractions. Our thoughts go roving here and there, and we make little progress toward our desired end. Like quicksilver our mind will not hold together but rolls off this way and that. How great an evil this is! It injures us, and what is worse, it insults our God. What should we think of a petitioner if, while having an audience with a prince, he should be playing with a feather or catching a fly?

Continuance and perseverance are intended in the expression of our text. David did not cry once and then relapse into silence; his holy clamor was continued till it brought down the blessing. Prayer must not be our intermittent work but our daily business, our habit and vocation. As artists give themselves to their models, and poets to their classical pursuits, so must we addict ourselves to prayer. We must be immersed in prayer as in our element, and so pray without ceasing. Lord, teach us so to pray, that we may be more and more efficacious in supplication.

## *An anointed one shall be cut off and shall have nothing.*

DANIEL 9:26

Blessed be His name, there was no cause of death in Him. Neither original nor actual sin had defiled Him, and therefore death had no claim upon Him. No man could have taken His life from Him justly, for He had done no man wrong, and no man could even have taken Him by force unless He had been pleased to yield Himself to die. But lo, one sins, and another suffers. Justice was offended by us but found its satisfaction in Him. Rivers of tears, mountains of offerings, seas of the blood of bulls, and hills of frankincense could not have availed for the removal of sin; but Jesus was cut off for us, and the cause of wrath was cut off at once, for sin was put away forever. Herein is wisdom, whereby substitution, the sure and speedy way of atonement, was devised! Herein is condescension, which brought the Messiah, the Prince, to wear a crown of thorns and die upon the cross! Herein is love, which led the Redeemer to lay down His life for His enemies!

It is not enough, however, to admire the spectacle of the innocent bleeding for the guilty—we must make sure of our personal interest. The special object of the Messiah's death was the salvation of His Church. Do we have a part and a place among those for whom He gave His life as a ransom? Did the Lord Jesus stand as our representative? Are we healed by His stripes? It will be a terrible thing indeed if we should come short of a portion in His sacrifice; it were better for us that we had never been born. Solemn as the question is, it is a joyful circumstance that it is one that may be answered clearly and without mistake. To all who believe on Him the Lord Jesus is a present Savior, and upon them all the blood of reconciliation has been sprinkled. Let all who trust in the merit of Messiah's death be joyful at every remembrance of Him, and let their holy gratitude lead them to the fullest consecration to His cause.

### *It happened, late one afternoon,*
### *when David arose from his couch and*
### *was walking on the roof of the king's house . . .*

2 SAMUEL 11:2

At that hour David saw Bathsheba. We are never out of the reach of temptation. Both at home and away we are liable to meet with allurements to evil. The morning opens with peril, and the shades of evening find us still in jeopardy. They are well kept whom God keeps, but woe to those who go out into the world, or even dare to walk their own house unarmed. Those who think themselves secure are more exposed to danger than any others. The armor-bearer of Sin is Self-confidence.

David should have been engaged in fighting the Lord's battles, instead of which he rested in Jerusalem, giving himself up to luxurious repose, for he arose from his bed at eventide. Idleness and luxury are the devil's jackals and find him abundant prey. In stagnant waters noxious creatures swarm, and neglected soil soon yields a dense tangle of weeds and briars. Oh, for the constraining love of Jesus to keep us active and useful! When I see the King of Israel sluggishly leaving his couch at the close of the day and falling at once into temptation, let me take warning and set holy watchfulness to guard the door.

Is it possible that the king had mounted his housetop for retirement and devotion? If so, what a caution is given us to count no place, however secret, a sanctuary from sin! While our hearts are so like a tinderbox, and sparks so plentiful, we need to use all diligence in all places to prevent a blaze. Satan can climb housetops and enter closets, and even if we could shut out that foul fiend, our own corruptions are enough to work our ruin unless grace prevents it. Reader, beware of evening temptations. Be not secure. The sun is down, but sin is up. We need a watchman for the night as well as a guardian for the day. O blessed Spirit, keep us from all evil this night. Amen.

### He interpreted to them in all the Scriptures the things concerning himself.

LUKE 24:27

The two disciples on the road to Emmaus had a most profitable journey. Their companion and teacher was *the best of tutors*, the interpreter one of a thousand, in whom are hid all the treasures of wisdom and knowledge. The Lord Jesus condescended to become a preacher of the Gospel, and He was not ashamed to exercise His calling before an audience of two persons. Neither does He now refuse to become the teacher of even one. Let us court the company of so excellent an Instructor, for till He is made unto us wisdom we shall never be wise unto salvation.

This unrivaled tutor used as His class-book *the best of books*. Although able to reveal fresh truth, He preferred to expound the old. He knew by His omniscience what was the most instructive way of teaching, and by turning at once to Moses and the prophets, He showed us that the surest road to wisdom is not speculation, reasoning, or reading human books, but meditation upon the Word of God. The readiest way to be spiritually rich in heavenly knowledge is to dig in this mine of diamonds, to gather pearls from this heavenly sea. When Jesus Himself sought to enrich others, He mined in the quarry of Holy Scripture.

The favored pair were led to consider *the best of subjects*, for Jesus spoke of Jesus and expounded the things concerning Himself. Here the diamond cut the diamond, and what could be more admirable? The Master of the House unlocked His own doors, conducted the guests to His table, and placed His own choice foods upon it. He who hid the treasure in the field Himself guided the searchers to it. Our Lord would naturally discourse upon the sweetest of topics, and He could find none sweeter than His own person and work. With an eye to these we should always search the Word. O for grace to study the Bible with Jesus as both our teacher and our lesson!

## *Then he opened their minds to understand the Scriptures.*

LUKE 24:45

He whom we viewed last evening as opening Scripture, we here perceive opening the understanding. In the first work He has many fellow-laborers, but in the second He stands alone; many can bring the Scriptures to the mind, but the Lord alone can prepare the mind to receive the Scriptures. Our Lord Jesus differs from all other teachers. They reach the ear, but He instructs the heart; they deal with the outward letter, but He imparts an inward taste for the truth, by which we perceive its savor and spirit. The most unlearned of men become ripe scholars in the school of grace when the Lord Jesus by His Holy Spirit unfolds the mysteries of the kingdom to them and grants the divine anointing by which they are enabled to behold the invisible. Happy are we if we have had our understandings cleared and strengthened by the Master! How many men of profound learning are ignorant of eternal things! They know the killing letter of revelation, but its killing spirit they cannot discern; they have a veil upon their hearts that the eyes of carnal reason cannot penetrate. Such was our case a little time ago. We who now see were once utterly blind; truth was to us as beauty in the dark, a thing unnoticed and neglected. Had it not been for the love of Jesus we should have remained to this moment in utter ignorance, for without His gracious opening of our understanding, we could no more have attained to spiritual knowledge than an infant can climb the Pyramids or an ostrich fly up to the stars. Jesus' College is the only one in which God's truth can be really learned; other schools may teach us what is to be believed, but Christ's alone can show us how to believe it. Let us sit at the feet of Jesus and by earnest prayer call upon His blessed help, that our dull wits may grow brighter, and our feeble understandings may receive heavenly things.

> ### *Turn my eyes from looking at worthless things; and give me life in your ways.*
>
> PSALM 119:37

There are various kinds of vanity. The cap and bells of the fool, the merriment of the world, the dance, and the cup of the dissolute—all these men know to be vanities; they wear upon their chest their proper name and title. Far more treacherous are those equally vain things—the cares of this world and the deceitfulness of riches. A man may follow vanity as truly in a portfolio as in a theater. If he is spending his life in amassing wealth, he passes his days in a vain show. Unless we follow Christ and make our God the great object of life, we only differ in appearance from the most frivolous. It is clear that there is much need of the prayer of our text: "Give me life in your ways." The psalmist confesses that he is dull, heavy, all but dead. Perhaps, dear reader, you feel the same. We are so sluggish that the best motives cannot quicken us, apart from the Lord Himself. What! Will not hell quicken me? Shall I think of sinners perishing, and yet not be awakened? Will not heaven quicken me? Can I think of the reward that awaits the righteous and yet be cold? Will not death quicken me? Can I think of dying and standing before my God, and yet be slothful in my Master's service? Will not Christ's love constrain me? Can I think of His dear wounds, can I sit at the foot of His cross, and not be stirred with fervency and zeal? It seems so! No mere consideration can quicken us to zeal, but God Himself must do it; hence the cry, "Give me life in *your* ways." The psalmist breathes out his whole soul in vehement pleadings; his body and his soul unite in prayer. "Turn my eyes," says the body. "Give me life," cries the soul. This is a fit prayer for every day. O Lord, hear it in my case this night.

*And he was very thirsty, and he called upon
the LORD and said, "You have granted this great
salvation by the hand of your servant, and
shall I now die of thirst . . . ?"*

JUDGES 15:18

Samson was thirsty and ready to die. The difficulty was totally different from any that the hero had met before. Merely to get thirst quenched is nothing like so great a matter as to be delivered from a thousand Philistines! But when the thirst was upon him, Samson felt that particular difficulty to be more weighty than the great past difficulty out of which he had so specially been delivered. It is very usual for God's people, when they have enjoyed a great deliverance, to find a little trouble too much for them. Samson slays a thousand Philistines and piles them up in heaps, and then faints for a little water! Jacob wrestles with God at Peniel and overcomes Omnipotence itself, and then goes "limping because of his hip!"[1] Strange that there must be a shrinking of the sinew whenever we win the day. As if the Lord must teach us our littleness, our nothingness, in order to keep us within bounds. Samson boasted right loudly when he said, "I have slain a thousand men." His boastful throat soon grew hoarse with thirst, and he betook himself to prayer. God has many ways of humbling His people. Dear child of God, if after great mercy you are laid very low, your case is not an unusual one. When David had mounted the throne of Israel, he said, "I am this day weak, though anointed king." You must expect to feel weakest when you are enjoying your greatest triumph. If God has wrought for you great deliverances in the past, your present difficulty is only like Samson's thirst, and the Lord will not let you faint, nor allow your enemy to triumph over you. The road of sorrow is the road to heaven, but there are wells of refreshing water all along the route. So, tested and tired pilgrim, cheer your heart with Samson's words, and rest assured that God will deliver you before long.

[1]Genesis 32:31

## *"Does Job fear God for no reason?"*

JOB 1:9

This was the wicked question of Satan concerning that upright man of old, but there are many in the present day concerning whom it might be asked with justice, for they love God after a fashion because He prospers them; but if things went ill with them, they would give up all their boasted faith in God. If they can clearly see that since the time of their supposed conversion the world has gone prosperously with them, then they will love God in their poor, carnal way; but if they endure adversity, they rebel against the Lord. Their love is the love of the table, not of the host; a love of the cupboard, not of the master of the house. As for the true Christian, he expects to have his reward in the next life and to endure hardness in this. The promise of the old covenant is adversity. Remember Christ's words—"Every branch of mine that does not bear fruit"—what?—"*he takes away, and every branch that does bear fruit he prunes, that it may bear more fruit.*"[1] If you bring forth fruit, you will have to endure affliction. "Alas," you say, "that is a terrible prospect." But this affliction works out such precious results, for the Christian who is the subject of it must learn to rejoice in tribulations because as his tribulations abound, so his consolations abound by Christ Jesus. Rest assured, if you are a child of God, you will be no stranger to the rod. Sooner or later every bar of gold must pass through the fire. Fear not, but rather rejoice that such fruitful times are in store for you, for in them you will be weaned from earth and made meet for heaven; you will be delivered from clinging to the present and made to long for those eternal things that are so soon to be revealed to you. When you feel that as regards the present you do serve God for nothing, you will then rejoice in the infinite reward of the future.

[1]John 15:2

## *We will extol your love more than wine.*

SONG OF SOLOMON 1:4

Jesus will not let His people forget His love. If all the love they have enjoyed should be forgotten, He will visit them with fresh love. "Do you forget my cross?" says He. "I will cause you to remember it; for at My table I will manifest Myself anew to you. Do you forget what I did for you in the council-chamber of eternity? I will remind you of it, for you shall need a counselor and shall find Me ready at your call." Mothers do not let their children forget them. If the boy has gone to Australia and does not write home, his mother writes, "Has John forgotten his mother?" Then there comes back a sweet epistle, which proves that the gentle reminder was not in vain. So is it with Jesus. He says to us, "Remember Me," and our response is, "We will remember Your love." We *will* remember Your love and its matchless history. It is as ancient as the glory that You had with the Father before the world was. We remember, O Jesus, Your eternal love when You became our Surety and chose us as Your bride. We remember the love that suggested the sacrifice of Yourself, the love that, until the fullness of time, mused over that sacrifice until what was written of You ("Lo, I come") was fulfilled. We remember Your love, O Jesus, as it was manifest to us in Your holy life, from the manger of Bethlehem to the Garden of Gethsemane. We track You from the cradle to the grave—for Your every word and deed was love—and we rejoice in Your love, which death did not exhaust—Your love that shone resplendent in Your resurrection. We remember that burning fire of love that will never let You hold Your peace until Your chosen ones be all safely housed, until Zion be glorified and Jerusalem settled on her everlasting foundations of light and love in heaven.

## But Martha was distracted with much serving.

LUKE 10:40

Her fault was not that she *served*: The condition of a servant is commendable in the Christian. "I serve" should be the motto of all the princes of the royal family of heaven. Nor was it her fault that she had "*much* serving." We cannot do too much. Let us do all that we possibly can; let head and heart and hands be engaged in the Master's service. It was no fault of hers that she was busy preparing a feast for the Master. Happy Martha, to have an opportunity of entertaining so blessed a guest; and happy, too, to have the spirit to throw her whole soul so heartily into the engagement. Her fault was that she grew "*distracted* with much serving," so that she forgot *Him* and only remembered the service. She allowed service to override communion, and so presented one duty stained with the blood of another. We ought to be Martha and Mary in one: We should do much service and have much communion at the same time. For this we need great grace. It is easier to serve than to commune. Joshua never grew weary in fighting with the Amalekites; but Moses, on the top of the mountain in prayer, needed two helpers to sustain his hands. The more spiritual the exercise, the sooner we tire in it. The choicest fruits are the hardest to rear; the most heavenly graces are the most difficult to cultivate. Beloved, while we do not neglect external things, which are good enough in themselves, we ought also to see to it that we enjoy living, personal fellowship with Jesus. See to it that sitting at the Savior's feet is not neglected, even though it be under the specious pretext of doing Him service. The first thing for our soul's health, the first thing for His glory, and the first thing for our own usefulness is to keep ourselves in perpetual communion with the Lord Jesus and to see that the vital spirituality of our faith is maintained over and above everything else in the world.

### *Do we then overthrow the law by this faith?*
### *By no means! On the contrary,*
### *we uphold the law.*

ROMANS 3:31

When the believer is adopted into the Lord's family, his relationship to old Adam and the law ceases at once; but then he is under a new rule and a new covenant. Believer, you are God's child; it is your first duty to obey your heavenly Father. A servile spirit you have nothing to do with: You are not a slave but a child. And now, inasmuch as you are a beloved child, you are bound to obey your Father's faintest wish, the least intimation of His will. Does He bid you fulfill a sacred ordinance? It is at your peril that you neglect it, for you will be disobeying your Father. Does He command you to seek the image of Jesus? Is it not your joy to do so? Does Jesus tell you, "You therefore must be perfect, as your heavenly Father is perfect"?[1] Then not because the law commands, but because your Savior enjoins, you will labor to be perfect in holiness. Does He bid his saints to love one another? Do it, not because the law says, "Love your neighbor," but because Jesus says, "If you love me, you will keep my commandments."[2] And this is the commandment that He has given unto you, "that you love one another." Are you told to distribute to the poor? Do it, not because charity is a burden that you dare not shirk, but because Jesus teaches, "Give to him that asks of you." Does the Word say, "Love God with all your heart"? Look at the commandment and reply, "Ah, commandment, Christ has fulfilled you already. I have no need, therefore, to fulfill you for my salvation, but I rejoice to yield obedience to you because God is my Father now, and He has a claim upon me, which I would not dispute." May the Holy Ghost make your heart obedient to the constraining power of Christ's love, that your prayer may be, "I will run in the way of your commandments when you enlarge my heart!"[3] Grace is the mother and nurse of holiness, and not the apologist of sin.

[1]Matthew 5:48　[2]John 14:15　[3]Psalm 119:32

### And all who heard it wondered at what the shepherds told them.

LUKE 2:18

We must not cease to wonder at the great marvels of our God. It would be very difficult to draw a line between holy wonder and *real worship*; for when the soul is overwhelmed with the majesty of God's glory, though it may not express itself in song or even utter its voice with bowed head in humble prayer, yet it silently adores. Our incarnate God is to be worshiped as "the Wonderful." That God should consider His fallen creature, man, and instead of sweeping him away with the broom of destruction should Himself undertake to be man's Redeemer and to pay his ransom price is indeed marvelous! But to each believer redemption is most marvelous as he views it in relation to himself. It is a miracle of grace indeed that Jesus should forsake the thrones and royalties above to suffer ignominiously below *for you*. Let your soul lose itself in wonder, for wonder is in this way a very practical emotion. Holy wonder will lead you to *grateful worship* and *heartfelt thanksgiving*. It will cause within you *godly watchfulness*; you will be afraid to sin against such a love as this. Feeling the presence of the mighty God in the gift of His dear Son, you will put your shoes from off your feet, because the place whereon you stand is holy ground. You will be moved at the same time to *glorious hope*. If Jesus has done such marvelous things on your behalf, you will feel that heaven itself is not too great for your expectation. Who can be astonished at anything when he has once been astonished at the manger and the cross? What is there wonderful left after one has seen the Savior? Dear reader, it may be that from the quietness and solitariness of your life you are scarcely able to imitate the shepherds of Bethlehem, who told what they had seen and heard, but you can at least fill up the circle of the worshipers before the throne by wondering at what God has done.

## *But Mary treasured up all these things, pondering them in her heart.*

LUKE 2:19

There was an exercise, on the part of this blessed woman, of three powers of her being: her *memory*—she kept all these things; her *affections*—she kept them in her heart; her *intellect*—she pondered them; so memory, affection, and understanding were all exercised about the things that she had heard. Beloved, remember what you have heard of your Lord Jesus and what He has done for you; make your heart the golden pot of manna to preserve the memorial of the heavenly bread whereon you have fed in days gone by. Let your memory treasure up everything about Christ that you have either felt or known or believed, and then let your fond affections hold Him fast forevermore. Love the person of your Lord! Bring forth the alabaster box of your heart, even though it be broken, and let all the precious ointment of your affection come streaming onto His pierced feet. Let your intellect be exercised concerning the Lord Jesus. Meditate upon what you read. Stop not at the surface; dive into the depths. Be not as the swallow, which touches the brook with her wing, but as the fish, which penetrates the lowest wave. Abide with your Lord: Let Him not be to you as a wayfaring man who tarries for a night, but constrain Him, saying, "Stay with us . . . the day is now far spent."[1] Hold Him, and do not let Him go. The word *ponder* means to weigh. Make ready the balances of judgment. Oh, but where are the scales that can weigh the Lord Christ? "He takes up the coastlands like fine dust"—who shall take *Him* up? He weighs "the mountains in scales"—in what scales shall we weigh *Him*?[2] If your understanding cannot comprehend, let your affections apprehend; and if your spirit cannot compass the Lord Jesus in the grasp of understanding, let it embrace Him in the arms of affection.

[1]Luke 24:29  [2]Isaiah 40:15, 12

> ### *And the shepherds returned, glorifying and praising God for all they had heard and seen, as it had been told them.*
>
> LUKE 2:20

What was the subject of their praise? They *praised God for what they had heard*—for the good tidings of great joy that a Savior was born unto them. Let us copy them; let us also raise a song of thanksgiving that we have heard of Jesus and His salvation. They also *praised God for what they had seen*. There is the sweetest music—what we have experienced, what we have felt within, what we have made our own. It is not enough to hear about Jesus: Mere hearing may tune the harp, but the fingers of living faith must create the music. If you have seen Jesus with the God-giving sight of faith, suffer no cobwebs to linger among the harp-strings, but loud with the praise of sovereign grace, awake your psaltery and harp. One point for which they praised God was *the agreement between what they had heard and what they had seen*. Observe the last sentence—"as it had been told them." Have you not found the Gospel to be in yourselves just what the Bible said it would be? Jesus said He would give you rest—have you not enjoyed the sweetest peace in Him? He said you would have joy and comfort and life through believing in Him—have you not received all these? Are not His ways ways of pleasantness, and His paths paths of peace? Surely you can say with the queen of Sheba, "The half was not told me."[1] I have found Christ more sweet than His servants ever said He was. I looked upon His likeness as they painted it, but it was a mere daub compared with Himself; for the King in His beauty outshines all imaginable loveliness. Surely what we have "*seen*" keeps pace with, no, far exceeds what we have "*heard*." Let us, then, glorify and praise God for a Savior so precious and so satisfying.

[1] 1 Kings 10:7

## *The dove came back to him in the evening.*

GENESIS 8:11

Blessed be the Lord for another day of mercy, even though I am now weary with its toils. Unto the preserver of men lift I my song of gratitude. The dove found no rest out of the ark and therefore returned to it; and my soul has learned yet more fully than ever, this day, that there is no satisfaction to be found in earthly things—God alone can give rest to my spirit. As to my business, my possessions, my family, my attainments, these are all well enough in their way, but they cannot fulfill the desires of my immortal nature. "Return, O my soul, to your rest; for the LORD has dealt bountifully with you."[1] It was at the still hour, when the gates of the day were closing, that with weary wing the dove came back to the master. O Lord, enable me this evening thus to return to Jesus. She could not endure to spend a night hovering over the restless waste, not can I bear to be even for another hour away from Jesus, the rest of my heart, the home of my spirit. She did not merely alight upon the roof of the ark—she "came back to him." Even so would my longing spirit look into the secret of the Lord, pierce to the interior of truth, enter into that which is within the veil, and reach to my Beloved in very deed. To Jesus must I come: Short of the nearest and dearest communion with Him my panting spirit cannot stay. Blessed Lord Jesus, be with me, reveal Yourself, and abide with me all night, so that when I awake I may be still with You. I note that the dove brought in her mouth an olive branch plucked off, the memorial of the past day and a prophecy of the future. Have I no pleasing record to bring home? No pledge and earnest of loving-kindness yet to come? Yes, my Lord, I present You my grateful acknowledgments for tender mercies that have been new every morning and fresh every evening; and now, I pray, put forth Your hand and take Your dove into Your bosom.

[1]Psalm 116:7

### *In him we have obtained an inheritance.*

EPHESIANS 1:11

When Jesus gave Himself for us, He gave us all the rights and privileges that went with Himself; so now, although as eternal God He has essential rights to which no creature may venture to pretend, yet as Jesus, the Mediator, the federal Head of the covenant of grace, He has no heritage apart from us. All the glorious consequences of His obedience unto death are the joint riches of all who are in Him, and on whose behalf He accomplished the divine will. See, He enters into glory, but not for Himself alone, for it is written, "Jesus has gone as a forerunner *on our* behalf."[1] Does He stand in the presence of God? Christ appears "in the presence of God on our behalf."[2] Consider this, believer: You have no right to heaven in yourself; your right lies in Christ. If you are pardoned, it is through *His* blood; if you are justified, it is through *His* righteousness; if you are sanctified, it is because *He* is made of God unto you sanctification; if you shall be kept from falling, it will be because you are preserved in Christ Jesus; and if you are perfected at the last, it will be because you are complete in *Him*. Thus Jesus is magnified—for all is in Him and by Him; thus the inheritance is made certain to us—for it is obtained in Him; thus each blessing is the sweeter, and even heaven itself the brighter, because it is Jesus our Beloved in whom we have obtained all. Where is the man who shall estimate our divine portion? Weigh the riches of Christ in scales and His treasure in balances, and then think to count the treasures that belong to the saints. Reach the bottom of Christ's sea of joy, and then hope to understand the bliss that God has prepared for them that love Him. Overleap the boundaries of Christ's possessions, and then dream of a limit to the fair inheritance of the elect. "All are yours, and you are Christ's, and Christ is God's."[3]

[1]Hebrews 6:20  [2]Hebrews 9:24  [3]1 Corinthians 3:22-23

## *Then Ahimaaz ran by the way of the plain, and outran the Cushite.*

2 SAMUEL 18:23

Running is not everything. There is much in the way that we select: A swift foot over hill and down dale will not keep pace with a slower traveler upon level ground. How is it with my spiritual journey? Am I laboring up the hill of my own works and down into the ravines of my own humiliations and resolutions, or do I run by the plain way of "Believe and live"? How blessed is it to wait upon the Lord by faith! The soul runs without weariness and walks without fainting in the way of believing. Christ Jesus is the way of life, and He is a plain way, a pleasant way, a way suitable for the tottering feet and feeble knees of trembling sinners. Am I found in this way, or am I hunting after another track such as priestcraft or metaphysics may promise me? I read of the way of holiness, that the wayfaring man, though a fool, shall not err therein. Have I been delivered from proud reason and been brought as a little child to rest in Jesus' love and blood? If so, by God's grace I shall outrun the strongest runner who chooses any other path. This truth I may remember to my profit in my daily cares and needs. It will be my wisest course to go at once to my God, and not to wander in a roundabout manner to this friend and that. He knows my wants and can relieve them. To whom should I repair but to Himself by the direct appeal of prayer and the plain argument of the promise? "Straightforward makes the best runner." I will not parley with the servants but hasten to their master.

In reading this passage, it strikes me that if men vie with each other in common matters, and one outruns the other, I ought to be in solemn earnestness so to run that I may obtain. Lord, help me to gird up the loins of my mind, and may I press forward toward the mark for the prize of my high calling of God in Christ Jesus.

## *Your love to me was extraordinary.*

2 SAMUEL 1:26

Come, dear readers, let each one of us speak for himself of the wonderful love, not of Jonathan, but of Jesus. We will not relate what we have been told, but the things that we have tasted and handled—of the love of Christ. Your love to me, O Jesus, was wonderful when I was a stranger wandering far from You, fulfilling the desires of the flesh and of the mind. Your love restrained me from committing the sin that is unto death and withheld me from self-destruction. Your love held back the axe when Justice said, "Cut it down! Why does it clutter the ground?" Your love drew me into the wilderness, stripped me there, and made me feel the guilt of my sin and the burden of my iniquity. Your love spoke comfortably to me when I was deeply troubled—"Come to Me, and I will give you rest." Oh, how matchless Your love when, in a moment, You washed my sins away and made my polluted soul, which was crimson with the blood of my nativity and black with the grime of my transgressions, to be white as the driven snow and pure as the finest wool. How You commended Your love when You whispered in my ears, "I am yours, and you are Mine." Those were kind words when you declared, "The Father Himself loves you." And sweet were the moments when You commended to me the love of the Spirit. My soul shall never forget those chambers of fellowship where You unveiled Yourself to me. Moses had his cleft in the rock, where he saw the train, the back parts, of his God. We, too, have had our clefts in the rock, where we have seen the full splendors of the Godhead in the person of Christ. Did David remember the tracks of the wild goat, the land of Jordan and the Hermonites? We, too, can remember spots dear to our memory, equal to these in blessedness. Precious Lord Jesus, give us a fresh taste of Your wondrous love with which to begin the month. Amen.

## *Now the records are ancient.*

### 1 CHRONICLES 4:22

But not so ancient as those precious things that are the delight of our souls. Let us for a moment recount them, repeating them as misers count their gold. *The sovereign choice* of the Father, by which He elected us unto eternal life, before creation, is a matter of vast antiquity, since no date can be conceived for it by the mind of man. We were chosen from before the foundations of the world. *Everlasting love* went with the choice, for it was not a bare act of divine will by which we were set apart, but the divine affections were concerned. The Father loved us in and from the beginning. Here is a theme for daily contemplation. *The eternal purpose* to redeem us from our foreseen ruin, to cleanse and sanctify us and at last to glorify us, was of infinite antiquity and runs side by side with immutable love and absolute sovereignty. *The covenant* is always described as being everlasting, and Jesus, the second party in it, is from eternity. He struck hands in sacred covenant long before the first stars began to shine, and it was in Him that the elect were ordained unto eternal life. In this way a most blessed covenant union was established between the Son of God and His elect people, which will remain as the foundation of their safety when time shall be no more. Is it not profitable to be conversant with these ancient things? Is it not shameful that they should be so readily neglected and even rejected by the majority of professing Christians? If they knew more of their own sin, would they not be more ready to adore distinguishing grace? Let us both admire and adore tonight, as we sing—

> *A monument of grace,*
> *A sinner saved by blood;*
> *The streams of love I trace*
> *Up to the Fountain, God;*
> *And in His sacred bosom see*
> *Eternal thoughts of Love to me.*

## Tell me . . . where you pasture your flock, where you make it lie down at noon.

SONG OF SOLOMON 1:7

These words may be taken as expressions of the believer's desire for Christ's fellowship and his longing for present communion with Him. Where do You feed Your flock? In *Your house*? I will go, if I may find You there. In private *prayer*? Then I will pray without ceasing. In *the Word*? Then I will read it diligently. In *Your ordinances*? Then I will pursue them with all my heart. Tell me where this happens, for wherever You stand as the Shepherd, there will I lie down as a sheep; for no one but Yourself can supply my need. I cannot be satisfied to be apart from You. My soul hungers and thirsts for the refreshment of Your presence. "Where you make it lie down at noon." Whether at dawn or at noon, my only rest must be where You are and Your beloved flock. My soul's rest must be a grace-given rest and can only be found in You. Where is the shadow of that rock? Why should I not rest beneath it? "Why should I be as one that turns aside by the flocks of your companions?" (see v. 76). You have companions—why should I not be one? Satan tells me I am unworthy; but I always was unworthy, and yet You have long loved me; and therefore my unworthiness cannot be a barrier to having fellowship with You now. It is true I am weak in faith and prone to fall, but my very feebleness is the reason why I should always be where You feed Your flock, that I may be strengthened and preserved in safety beside the still waters. Why should I turn aside? There is no reason why I should, but there are a thousand reasons why I should not, for Jesus beckons me to come. If He withdrew Himself a little, it is but to make me value His presence more. Now that I am grieved and distressed at being away from Him, He will lead me again to that sheltered nook where the lambs of His fold are sheltered from the burning sun.

## . . . *a refuge from the avenger of blood.*

JOSHUA 20:3

It is said that in the land of Canaan, cities of refuge were so arranged that any man might reach one of them within half a day at the most. In the same way the word of our salvation is near to us; Jesus is a present Savior, and the way to Him is short. It is but a simple renunciation of our own merit and a laying hold of Jesus to be our all in all. With regard to the roads to the city of refuge, we are told that they were strictly preserved, every river was bridged, and every obstruction removed, so that the man who fled might find an easy passage to the city. Once a year the elders went along the roads to check on their condition, so that nothing might impede the flight of anyone and cause them, through delay, to be overtaken and slain. How graciously do the promises of the Gospel remove stumbling blocks from the way! Wherever there were junctions and turnings, there were signposts clearly stating, "To the city of refuge!" This is a picture of the road to Christ Jesus. It is no roundabout road of the law; it is no obeying this, that, and the other; it is a straight road: "Believe, and live." It is a road so hard that no self-righteous man can ever tread it, but so easy that every sinner who knows himself to be a sinner may by it find his way to heaven. As soon as the man seeking refuge reached the outskirts of the city, he was safe; it was not necessary for him to be beyond the walls—the suburbs themselves were sufficient protection. Learn from this that if you merely touch the hem of Christ's garment, you shall be made whole; if you can only lay hold upon him with "faith as a grain of mustard seed," you are safe.

> *A little genuine grace ensures*
> *The death of all our sins.*

So waste no time; do not dillydally, for the avenger of blood moves quickly; and it could be that he is at your heels even this evening.

44

## *At that time Jesus declared . . .*

MATTHEW 11:25

This is a pointed way in which to begin a verse—"At that time Jesus declared." If you look at the context you will realize that no one had asked Him a question and that He was not in conversation with any human being. Yet it is written, "Jesus declared, I thank you, Father." When a man answers, he answers a person who has been speaking to him. Who, then, had been speaking to Christ? His Father. Yet there is no record of it; and this should teach us that Jesus had constant fellowship with His Father, and that God spoke into His heart so often, so continually, that it was not a circumstance peculiar enough to be recorded. It was the habit and life of Jesus to talk with God. Let us then learn the lesson that this simple statement concerning Him teaches us. May we also enjoy silent fellowship with the Father, so that often we answer Him, and although our friends don't know to whom we speak, we will be responding to that secret voice that they do not hear but that our own ear, opened by the Spirit of God, recognizes with joy. God has spoken to us; let us speak to God—either to affirm that God is true and faithful to His promise, or to confess the sin of which the Spirit of God has convinced us, or to acknowledge the mercy that God's providence has given, or to express agreement with the great truths that God the Holy Spirit has revealed to us. Intimate communion with the Father of our spirit is a great privilege! It is a secret hidden from the world, a joy with which even the nearest friend does not interfere. If we desire to hear the whispers of God's love, our ear must be purged and fit to listen to His voice. This very evening may our hearts be in such a condition, so that when God speaks to us, we, like Jesus, may be prepared at once to answer Him.

### *Pray for one another.*

JAMES 5:16

Be encouraged to cheerfully offer intercessory prayer, by remembering that *such prayer is the sweetest God ever hears.* The prayer of Christ is of this character. In all the incense that our Great High Priest now puts into the golden censer, there is not a single grain for Himself. His intercession must be the most acceptable of all supplications—and the more our prayer like Christ's, the sweeter it will be. Thus while petitions for ourselves will be accepted, our pleadings for others, having in them more of the fruits of the Spirit—more love, more faith, more brotherly kindness—will be, through the precious merits of Jesus, the sweetest sacrifice that we can offer to God. Remember, again, that *intercessory prayer is exceedingly prevalent* [powerful]. What wonders it has accomplished! The Word of God teems with its marvelous deeds. Believer, you have a mighty engine in your hand; use it well, use it constantly, use it with faith, and you will surely be a blessing to others. When you have the King's ear, speak to Him for the suffering members of His body. When you are favored to draw very near to His throne, and the King says to you, "Ask, and it will be given to you," let your petitions be, not for yourself alone, but for the many who need His aid. If you have any grace at all and are not an intercessor, that grace must be as small as a grain of mustard seed. You have just enough grace to float your soul clear from the quicksand, but you have no depth of grace or else you would carry in your vessel a heavy cargo of the wants of others, and you would bring back from your Lord rich blessings for them that apart from you they might not have obtained.

> *Oh, let my hands forget their skill,*
> *My tongue be silent, cold, and still,*
> *This bounding heart forget to beat,*
> *If I forget the mercy-seat!*

### *Then they heard a loud voice from heaven saying to them, "Come up here."*

REVELATION 11:12

Without considering these words in their prophetic connection, let us regard them as the invitation of our great
Forerunner to His sanctified people. In due time there shall
be heard "a loud voice from heaven" to every believer, saying,
"Come up here." This should be to the saints *the subject of joyful
anticipation*. Instead of dreading the time when we will leave this
world to go to the Father, we should be longing for the hour of
our emancipation. Our song should be—

> *My heart is with Him on His throne,*
> *And ill can brook delay;*
> *Each moment listening for the voice,*
> *"Rise up and come away."*

We are not called down to the grave but up to the skies.
Our heaven-born spirits should long for their native air. Yet the
heavenly summons should be *the object of patient waiting*. Our
God knows best when to bid us, "Come up here." We must not
wish to antedate the period of our departure. I know that strong
love will make us cry,

> *O Lord of Hosts, the waves divide,*
> *And land us all in heaven.*

But patience must have her perfect work. God ordains with
accurate wisdom the most fitting time for the redeemed to live
below. Surely, if there could be regrets in heaven, the saints might
mourn that they did not live longer here to do more good. Oh, for
more sheaves for my Lord's harvest, more jewels for His crown!
But how unless there be more work? True, there is the other side
of it, that, living so briefly, our sins are the fewer; but oh, when
we are fully serving God, and He is asking us to scatter precious
seed and reap a hundredfold, we would even say it is well for
us to stay where we are. Whether our Master shall say, "Go" or
"Stay," let us be equally well pleased as long as He indulges us
with His presence.

## *He will save his people from their sins.*

MATTHEW 1:21

Many people, if they are asked what they understand by salvation, will reply, "Being saved from hell and taken to heaven." This is one result of salvation, but it is not one tenth of what is contained in that blessing. It is true our Lord Jesus Christ does redeem all His people from the wrath to come; He saves them from the fearful condemnation that their sins had brought upon them; but His triumph is far more complete than this. He saves His people "from their sins"—a complete deliverance from our worst foes. Where Christ works a saving work, He casts Satan from his throne and will not let him be master any longer. No man is a true Christian if sin reigns in his mortal body. Sin will be in us—it will never be utterly expelled till the spirit enters glory; but it will never have *dominion*. There will be a striving for dominion—a lusting against the new law and the new spirit that God has implanted—but sin will never get the upper hand so as to be absolute monarch of our nature. Christ will be Master of the heart, and sin must be mortified. The Lion of the tribe of Judah shall prevail, and the dragon shall be cast out. Professing Christian, is sin subdued in you? If your *life* is unholy, your *heart* is unchanged; and if your heart is unchanged, you are an unsaved person. If the Savior has not sanctified you, renewed you, given you a hatred of sin and a love of holiness, He has done nothing in you of a saving character. The grace that does not make a man better than others is a worthless counterfeit. Christ saves His people not in their sins but *from* them. ". . . for the holiness without which no one will see the Lord."[1] "Let everyone who names the name of the Lord depart from iniquity."[2] If not saved from sin, how shall we hope to be counted among His people? Lord, save me now from all evil, and enable me to honor my Savior.

[1]Hebrews 12:14   [2]2 Timothy 2:19

## *Lead us not into temptation;*
## *but deliver us from evil.*

LUKE 11:4 [KJV]

The things we are taught to seek or avoid in prayer, we should equally pursue or avoid in action. We should with sincerity avoid temptation, seeking to walk so guardedly in the path of obedience that we may never tempt the devil to tempt us. We are not to enter the jungle in search of the lion. We might pay dearly for such presumption. This lion may cross our path or leap upon us from the jungle, but we have nothing to do with hunting him. He that meets with him, even though he wins the day, will find it a tough struggle. Let the Christian pray that he may be spared the encounter. Our Savior, who had experience of what temptation meant, thus earnestly admonished His disciples, "Pray that you do not enter into temptation."

But let us do as we will, we shall be tempted; hence the prayer, "deliver us from evil." God had one Son without sin; but He has no son without temptation. The natural man is born to trouble as the sparks fly upward, and just as certain the Christian man is born to temptation. We must be always on our watch against Satan because, like a thief, he gives no intimation of his approach. Believers who have had experience of the ways of Satan know that there are certain seasons when he will most probably make an attack, just as at certain seasons bleak winds may be expected; thus the Christian is put on a double guard by fear of danger, and the danger is averted by preparing to meet it. Prevention is better than cure: It is better to be so well armed that the devil will not attack you than to endure the perils of the fight even though you come off a conqueror. Pray this evening first that you may not be tempted, and then if temptation be permitted, pray that you may be delivered from the evil one.

> ### *I have blotted out your transgressions like a cloud and your sins like mist; return to me, for I have redeemed you.*
>
> ISAIAH 44:22

Pay attention to THE INSTRUCTIVE PICTURE: Our sins are like a *cloud*. As clouds appear in many shapes and shades, so do our transgressions. As clouds obscure the light of the sun and darken the landscape below, so do our sins hide from us the light of Jehovah's face and cause us to sit in the shadow of death. They are earthborn things and arise from the miry places of our lives; and when they collect and their measure is full, they threaten us with storm and tempest. Sadly, unlike clouds, our sins yield us no genial showers but rather threaten to deluge us with a fiery flood of destruction. How can it be fair weather when the dark clouds of sin remain within our souls?

Let our happy gaze ponder THE NOTABLE ACT of divine mercy—"blotted out." God Himself appears upon the scene and in divine generosity, instead of manifesting His anger, reveals His grace. He at once and forever effectually removes the mischief, not by blowing away the cloud, but by blotting it out from existence once and for all. Against the justified man no sin remains; the great transaction of the cross has eternally removed his transgressions from him. On Calvary's summit the great deed, by which the sin of all the chosen was forever put away, was completely and effectually performed.

Practically let us obey THE GRACIOUS COMMAND: "Return to me." Why should pardoned sinners live at a distance from their God? If all of our sins have been forgiven, let no legal fear hold us back from the boldest access to our Lord. Let backslidings be bemoaned, but let us not persevere in them. Let us, in the power of the Holy Spirit, work strenuously to return to intimate communion with the Lord. O Lord, restore us now, tonight!

## *You have abandoned the love you had at first.*

REVELATION 2:4

We will always remember that best and brightest of hours when we first saw the Lord, lost our burden, received the gift of grace, rejoiced in full salvation, and went on our way in peace. It was springtime in the soul; the winter was past; the mutterings of Sinai's thunders were hushed; the flashings of its lightnings were no more perceived; God was beheld as reconciled; the law threatened no vengeance, and justice demanded no punishment. Then the flowers appeared in our heart. Hope, love, peace, and patience sprang from the ground; the hyacinth of repentance, the snowdrop of pure holiness, the crocus of golden faith, the daffodil of early love—all decked the garden of the soul. The time of the singing of birds had arrived, and we rejoiced with thanksgiving; we magnified the holy name of our forgiving God, and our resolve was, "Lord, I am Yours, Yours alone. All I am, and all I have, I devote to You. You have bought me with Your blood—let me spend myself and be spent in Your service. In life and in death let me be consecrated to You." *How well have we kept this resolve?* Our first love burned with a holy flame of devotion to Jesus—is it the same now? Is it possible that Jesus may say to us, "I have something against you, because you have left your first love"? Sadly we have done little for our Master's glory. Our winter has lasted all too long. We are as cold as ice when we should feel a summer's glow and bloom with sacred flowers. We give God pennies when He deserves much more, deserves our heart's blood to be coined in the service of His church and of His truth. But shall we continue in this way? O Lord, after You have blessed us so richly, shall we be ungrateful and become indifferent to Your good cause and work? Quicken us that we may return to our first love and do our first works! Send us a joyful spring, O Sun of Righteousness.

### He will give you another Helper,
### to be with you forever.

JOHN 14:16

God the Father revealed Himself to Old Testament believers before the coming of His Son and was known to Abraham, Isaac, and Jacob as God Almighty. Then Jesus came, and the ever-blessed Son in His own proper person was the delight of His people's eyes. At the time of the Redeemer's ascension, the Holy Spirit became the head of the present era, and His power was gloriously displayed in and after Pentecost. He remains at this hour the present Immanuel—God with us, dwelling in and with His people, quickening, guiding, and ruling in our lives. Is His presence recognized as it ought to be? We cannot control His working; He is sovereign in all His operations, but are we sufficiently anxious to obtain His help or sufficiently watchful lest we grieve Him and He withdraws His help? Without Him we can do nothing, but by His almighty energy the most extraordinary results can be produced: Everything depends upon His revealing or concealing His power. Do we always look up to Him for our inner life and our outward service with the respectful dependence that is appropriate? Do we not too often run before His call and act independently of His aid? Let us humble ourselves this evening for past neglect, and now entreat the heavenly dew to rest upon us, the sacred oil to anoint us, the celestial flame to burn within us. The Holy Spirit is not a temporary gift—He remains with the church. When we seek Him as we should, we will find Him. He is jealous, but He is full of pity; if He leaves in anger, He returns in mercy. Condescending and tender, He does not grow tired of us but constantly displays His grace.

> *Sin has been hammering my heart*
> *Unto a hardness, void of love.*
> *Let supplying grace to cross his art*
> *Drop from above.*

## *There is therefore now no condemnation.*

ROMANS 8:1

Come, my soul, think about this. Believing in Jesus, you are actually and effectually cleared from guilt; you are led out of prison. You are no longer in chains as a slave; you are delivered now from the bondage of the law; you are freed from sin and can walk around as a free man—the Savior's blood has procured your full acquittal. You now have a right to approach your Father's throne. No flames of vengeance are there to scare you now—no fiery sword; justice cannot strike the innocent. Your disabilities are removed. Once you were unable to see your Father's face; now you can. You could not speak with Him; but now you can approach Him with boldness. Once there was a fear of hell upon you; but now you have no fear of it, for how can there be punishment for the guiltless? He who believes is not condemned and cannot be punished. And more than all, the privileges you might have enjoyed, if you had never sinned, are yours now that you are justified. All the blessings that you would have had if you had kept the law are yours, because Christ has kept it for you. All the love and acceptance that perfect obedience could have obtained belong to you, because Christ was perfectly obedient on your behalf and has imputed all His merits to your account, that you might be exceedingly rich through Him who for your sake became exceedingly poor. How great the debt of love and gratitude you owe to your Savior!

*A debtor to mercy alone,*
*Of covenant mercy I sing;*
*Nor fear with Your righteousness on,*
*My person and offerings to bring:*

*The terrors of law and of God,*
*With me can have nothing to do;*
*My Savior's obedience and blood*
*Hide all my transgressions from view.*

### *She had been immediately healed.*

LUKE 8:47

One of the most touching and instructive of the Savior's miracles is before us tonight. The woman was very ignorant. She imagined that virtue came out of Christ by a law of necessity, without His knowledge or direct will. Moreover, she was a stranger to the generosity of Jesus' character, or she would not have gone behind to steal the cure that He was so ready to provide. Misery should always place itself right in the face of mercy. Had she known the love of Jesus' heart, she would have said, "I need only to put myself where He can see me—His omniscience will teach Him my case, and His love will immediately work my cure." We admire her faith, but we marvel at her ignorance. After she had obtained the cure, she rejoiced with trembling: She was glad that the divine virtue had worked a marvel in her; but she feared in case Christ should retract the blessing and negate the grant of His grace. Little did she comprehend the fullness of His love! We do not have as clear a view of Him as we could wish; we do not know the heights and depths of His love. But we know of a certainty that He is too good to withdraw from a trembling soul the gift that it has been able to obtain. But here is the marvel of it: Although her knowledge was small, her faith, because it was real faith, saved her, and saved her at once. There was no tedious delay—faith's miracle was instantaneous. If we have faith as a grain of mustard seed, salvation is our present and eternal possession. If in the list of the Lord's children we are described as the feeblest of the family, yet, being heirs through faith, no power, human or devil, can eject us from salvation. If we dare not lean our heads upon His bosom with John, yet if we can venture in the crowd behind Him and touch the hem of his garment, we are made whole. Take courage, timid one! Your faith has saved you; go in peace. "Since we *have been* justified by faith, we *have* peace with God."[1]

[1] Romans 5:1

### From ivory palaces stringed instruments make you glad.

PSALM 45:8

And who are those who enjoy the privilege of making the Savior glad? His church—His people. But is it possible? He makes *us* glad, but *how can we make Him glad?* By our love. We think it so cold, so faint; and so, indeed, we must sorrowfully confess it to be, but it is very sweet to Christ. Listen to such love expressed in Solomon's song: "How beautiful is your love, my sister, my bride! How much better is your love than wine!" See, loving heart, this is how He delights in you. When you rest in Him you do not only receive, but you also give Him joy; when you gaze with love upon His beauty, you not only obtain comfort but impart delight. Our *praise* also gives Him joy—not the song of the lips alone, but the melody of the heart's deep gratitude. Our *gifts* are also very pleasant to Him; He loves to see us lay our time, our talents, our substance upon the altar, not for the value of what we give, but for the sake of the motive from which the gift springs. To Him the lowly offerings of His saints are more acceptable than the thousands of gold and silver. *Holiness* is like frankincense and myrrh to Him. Forgive your enemy, and you make Christ glad; distribute of your substance to the poor, and He rejoices; be the means of saving souls, and you give Him to see of the travail of His soul; proclaim His Gospel, and you are a sweet savor unto Him; go among the ignorant and lift up the cross, and you have given Him honor. It is in your power even now to break the alabaster box and pour the precious oil of joy upon His head, like the woman in the Bible, whose testimony is still remembered wherever the Gospel is preached. Will you not join her in expressing your love and devotion for the Lord Jesus? And even in ivory palaces the songs of the saints will be heard.

### *. . . your good Spirit.*

NEHEMIAH 9:20

Common, too common, is the sin of forgetting the Holy Spirit. This is folly and ingratitude. He deserves better from us, for He is good, supremely good. As God, He is good essentially. He shares in the threefold ascription of "Holy, holy, holy" that ascends to the Triune God. He is unmixed purity, truth, and grace. He is good benevolently, tenderly bearing with our waywardness, striving with our rebellious wills, quickening us from our death in sin, and then training us for heaven as a loving father trains his children. How generous, forgiving, and tender is this patient Spirit of God. He is good operatively. All His works are good in the most eminent degree: He suggests good thoughts, prompts good actions, reveals good truths, applies good promises, assists in good attainments, and leads to good results. There is no spiritual good in all the world of which He is not the author and sustainer, and heaven itself will owe the perfect character of its redeemed inhabitants to His work. He is good officially: Whether as Comforter, Instructor, Guide, Sanctifier, Quickener, or Intercessor, He fulfills His office well, and each work is filled with the highest good to the church of God. Those who yield to His influences become good; those who obey His impulses do good; those who live under His power receive good. Let us then act toward Him according to the dictates of gratitude. Let us revere His person and adore Him as God over all, blessed forever; let us own His power and our need of Him by waiting upon Him in all our holy enterprises; let us hourly seek His help and never grieve Him; and let us speak His praise whenever occasion occurs. The church will never prosper until it more reverently believes in the Holy Spirit. He is so good and kind that it is sad indeed that He should be grieved by slights and negligences.

## ... *although the* Lord *was there* ...

EZEKIEL 35:10

Edom's princes saw the whole country left desolate and counted upon its easy conquest; but there was one great difficulty in their way—quite unknown to them—"*The* Lord *was there*"; and in His presence lay the special security of the chosen land. Whatever may be the machinations and devices of the enemies of God's people, there is still the same effectual barrier to thwart their plan. The saints are God's heritage, and He is among them and will protect His own. This assurance grants us comfort in our troubles and spiritual conflicts! We are constantly opposed and yet perpetually preserved! How often Satan shoots his arrows against our *faith*, but our faith defies the power of hell's fiery darts; they are not only turned aside, but they are quenched upon its shield, for "the Lord was there." *Our good works* are the subjects of Satan's attacks. A believer never yet had a virtue or a grace that was not the target for hellish bullets: whether it was bright and sparkling hope, or warm and fervent love, or all-enduring patience, or zeal flaming like coals of fire, the old enemy of everything that is good has tried to destroy it. The only reason why anything virtuous or lovely survives in us is this: "the Lord was there."

If the Lord is with us through life, we do not need to fear death; for *when we come to die*, we will find that "the Lord is there." Where the billows are most tempestuous, and the water is most chill, we shall feel the bottom and know that it is good; our feet shall stand upon the Rock of Ages when time is passing away. Dear friend, from the beginning of a Christian's life to the end, the only reason he does not perish is because "*the* Lord *was there.*" When the God of everlasting love shall change and leave His elect to perish, then may the church of God be destroyed; but not until then, because it is written, JEHOVAH SHAMMAH, "*The* Lord *was there.*"

## *Father, I have sinned.*

LUKE 15:18

It is quite certain that those whom Christ has washed in His precious blood need not make a confession of sin as culprits or criminals before God the Judge, because Christ has forever taken away all their sins in a legal sense, so that they no longer stand where they can be condemned, but are once for all accepted in the Beloved. But having become children, and offending as children, should they not every day go before their heavenly Father and confess their sin and acknowledge their iniquity in that character? Nature teaches that it is the duty of erring children to make a confession to their earthly father, and the grace of God in the heart teaches us that we, as Christians, owe the same duty to our heavenly Father. We daily offend and ought not to rest without daily pardon. Suppose that my trespasses against my Father are not at once taken to Him to be washed away by the cleansing power of the Lord Jesus—what will be the consequence? If I have not sought forgiveness and been washed from these offenses against my Father, I shall feel at a distance from Him; I shall doubt His love to me; I shall tremble before Him; I shall be afraid to pray to Him: I shall grow like the prodigal who, although still a child, was yet far away from his father. But if with a child's sorrow at offending so gracious and loving a Parent, I go to Him and tell Him everything, and do not rest until I realize that I am forgiven, then I shall feel a holy love to my Father and shall go through my Christian career not only as saved, but as one enjoying present peace in God through Jesus Christ my Lord. There is a wide distinction between confessing sin *as a culprit* and confessing sin *as a child*. The Father's bosom is the place for penitent confessions. We have been cleansed once for all, but our feet still need to be washed from the defilement of our daily walk as children of God.

## He first found his own brother Simon.

JOHN 1:41

This case is an excellent pattern of all cases where spiritual life is vigorous. *As soon as a man has found Christ, he begins to find others.* I will not believe that you have tasted of the honey of the Gospel if you can eat it all yourself. True grace puts an end to all spiritual monopoly. Andrew first found his own brother Simon, and then others. *Relationship has a very strong demand upon our first individual efforts.* Andrew, you did well to begin with Simon. I doubt whether there are not some Christians giving away tracts at other people's houses who would do well to give away a tract at their own—whether there are not some engaged in works of usefulness abroad who are neglecting their special sphere of usefulness at home. You may or may not be called to evangelize the people in any particular locality, but certainly you are called to witness to your own servants, your own family and acquaintances. Let your faith begin at home. Many tradesmen export their best commodities—the Christian should not. He should have all his conversation everywhere be the best; but let him take care to display and share the sweetest fruit of spiritual life and testimony in his own family. When Andrew went to find his brother, he little imagined how eminent Simon would become. *Simon Peter was worth ten Andrews* so far as we can gather from sacred history, and yet Andrew was instrumental in bringing him to Jesus. You may be very deficient in talent yourself, and yet you may be the means of drawing to Christ one who shall become eminent in grace and service. Dear friend, you hardly know the possibilities that are in you. You may simply speak a word to a child, and in that child there may be slumbering a noble heart that shall stir the Christian church in years to come. Andrew has only two talents, but he finds Peter. Go out and do the same.

### Then Jesus was led up by the Spirit into the wilderness to be tempted by the devil.

MATTHEW 4:1

A holy character does not prevent temptation—Jesus was tempted. When Satan tempts us, his sparks fall upon tinder; but in Christ's case, it was like striking sparks on water; yet the enemy continued his evil work. Now, if the devil goes on striking when there is no result, how much more will he do it when he knows what inflammable stuff our hearts are made of. Though you become greatly sanctified by the Holy Spirit, expect that the great dog of hell will bark at you still. In the haunts of men we expect to be tempted, but even seclusion will not guard us from the same trial. Jesus Christ was led away from human society into the wilderness and was tempted by the devil. Solitude has its charms and its benefits and may be useful in checking the lust of the eye and the pride of life; but the devil will follow us into the most lovely retreats. Do not suppose that it is only the worldly-minded who have dreadful thoughts and blasphemous temptations, for even spiritually minded persons endure the same; and in the holiest position we may suffer the darkest temptation. The utmost consecration of spirit will not insure you against satanic temptation. Christ was consecrated through and through. It was His meat and drink to do the will of Him that sent Him—and yet He was tempted! Your hearts may glow with an angelic flame of love for Jesus, and yet the devil will try to bring you down to lukewarm uselessness. If you will tell me when God permits a Christian to lay aside his armor, I will tell you when Satan has left off temptation. Like the old knights in wartime, we must sleep with helmet and breastplate buckled on, for the arch-deceiver will seize our first unguarded moment to make us his prey. May the Lord keep us watchful in all seasons and grant us a final escape from the jaw of the lion and the paw of the bear.

## *Do you understand what you are reading?*

ACTS 8:30

We would be more able teachers, and not so easily carried away by every wind of doctrine, if we sought to have a more intelligent understanding of the Word of God. As the Holy Spirit, the Author of the Scriptures, is the only one who can enlighten us rightly to understand them, we should constantly ask His help to lead us into truth. When the prophet Daniel was called upon to interpret Nebuchadnezzar's dream, what did he do? He set himself to earnest prayer that God would open up the vision. The apostle John, in his vision at Patmos, saw a book sealed with seven seals that none was found worthy to open or so much as to look upon. The book was afterward opened by the Lion of the tribe of Judah, who had prevailed to open it; but it is written first, "I wept much." The tears of John, which were his liquid prayers, were, so far as he was concerned, the sacred keys by which the folded book was opened. Therefore, if, for your own and others' profiting, you desire to be "filled with the knowledge of his will in all spiritual wisdom and understanding,"[1] remember that prayer is your best means of study. Like Daniel, you shall understand the dream and its interpretation when you have sought it from God; and like John you shall see the seven seals of precious truth unloosed after you have wept much. Stones are not broken except by a constant, diligent use of the hammer; and the stone-breaker must go down on his knees. Use the hammer of diligence, and let the knee of prayer be exercised, and there is not a stony doctrine in revelation that is useful for you to understand that will not fly into shivers under the exercise of prayer and faith. You may force your way through anything with the leverage of prayer. Thoughts and reasoning are like the steel wedges that give a hold upon truth; but prayer is the lever that pries open the iron chest of sacred mystery, that we may get the treasure hidden inside.

[1]Colossians 1:9

## The LORD is slow to anger and great in power.

NAHUM 1:3

Jehovah "is *slow to anger*." When mercy comes into the world, she drives winged horses; the axles of her chariot-wheels are red-hot with speed. But when wrath goes forth, it toils on with tardy footsteps, for God takes no pleasure in the sinner's death. God's rod of mercy is always in His hands outstretched; His sword of justice is in its scabbard, held down by that pierced hand of love that bled for the sins of men. "The LORD is slow to anger" because He is *"great in power."* He is truly great in power who has power over himself. When God's power restrains Himself, then it is power indeed: The power that binds omnipotence is omnipotence surpassed. A man who has a strong mind can bear to be insulted and only resents the wrong when a sense of right demands his action. The weak mind is irritated at a little; the strong mind bears it like a rock that doesn't move though a thousand breakers dash upon it and cast their pitiful malice in spray upon its summit. God marks His enemies, and yet He bestirs not Himself but holds in His anger. If He were less divine than He is, He would long have since sent forth the whole of His thunders and emptied the cannons of heaven; He would have long ago blasted the earth with the wondrous fires of its lower regions, and man would have been utterly destroyed. But the greatness of His power brings us mercy. Dear reader, what is your condition this evening? Can you by humble faith look to Jesus and say, "My substitute, You are my rock, my trust"? Then, beloved, do not be afraid of God's power; for if by faith you have fled to Christ for refuge, the power of God need no more terrify you than the shield and sword of the warrior need terrify those whom he loves. Rather rejoice that He who is "great in power" is your Father and Friend.

## . . . *take up his cross daily and follow me.*

LUKE 9:23

You do not make your own cross, although unbelief is a master carpenter at cross-making; neither are you permitted to choose your own cross, although self-will wants to be lord and master. But your cross is prepared and appointed for you by divine love, and you must cheerfully accept it; you are to take up the cross as your chosen badge and burden, and not to stand complaining. This night Jesus bids you submit your shoulder to His easy yoke. Do not kick at it in petulance, or trample on it in pride, or fall under it in despair, or run away from it in fear, but take it up like a true follower of Jesus. Jesus was a cross-bearer; He leads the way in the path of sorrow. Surely you could not desire a better guide! And if He carried a cross, what nobler burden would you desire? The *Via Crucis* is the way of safety; fear not to tread its thorny paths.

Beloved, the cross is not made of feathers or lined with velvet; it is heavy and galling to disobedient shoulders; but it is not an iron cross, though your fears have painted it with iron colors; it is a wooden cross, and a man can carry it, for the Man of Sorrows tried the load. Take up your cross, and by the power of the Spirit of God you will soon be so in love with it that like Moses you would not exchange the reproach of Christ for all the treasures of Egypt. Remember that Jesus carried it; remember that it will soon be followed by the crown, and the thought of the coming weight of glory will greatly lighten the present heaviness of trouble. May the Lord help you bow your spirit in submission to the divine will before you fall asleep tonight, so that waking with tomorrow's sun, you may go forth to the day's cross with the holy and submissive spirit that is fitting for a follower of the Crucified.

### *O LORD of hosts, how long will you have no mercy on Jerusalem? . . . And the LORD answered gracious and comforting words to the angel.*

ZECHARIAH 1:12-13

What a sweet answer to an anxious inquiry! This night let us rejoice in it. O Zion, there are good things in store for you; your time of travail will soon be over; your children shall come forth; your captivity shall end. Bear patiently the rod for a season, and under the darkness still trust in God, for His love burns toward you. God loves the church with a love too deep for human imagination: He loves her with all His infinite heart. Therefore let her sons be of good courage; she cannot be far from prosperity to whom God speaks "gracious and comforting words." The prophet goes on to tell us: "I am exceedingly jealous for Jerusalem and for Zion." The Lord loves His church so much that He cannot bear that she should go astray to others; and when she has done so, He cannot endure that she should suffer too much or too heavily. He will not have his enemies afflict her: He is displeased with them because they increase her misery. When God seems most to leave His church, His heart is warm toward her. History shows that whenever God uses a rod to chasten His servants, He always breaks it afterwards, as if He loathed the rod that gave his children pain. "As a father shows compassion to his children, so the LORD shows compassion to those who fear him."[1] God has not forgotten us because He strikes—His blows are no evidences of absence of love. If this is true of His church *collectively*, it is also necessarily true of *each individual member*. You may fear that the Lord has passed you by, but it is not so: He who counts the stars and calls them by their names is in no danger of forgetting His own children. He knows your case as thoroughly as if you were the only creature He ever made or the only saint He ever loved. Approach Him and be at peace.

[1]Psalm 103:13

### But Jonah rose to flee to Tarshish from the presence of the LORD. He went down to Joppa.

JONAH 1:3

Instead of going to Nineveh to preach the Word, as God told him, Jonah disliked the work and went down to Joppa to escape from it. There are occasions when God's servants shrink from duty. But what is the consequence? What did Jonah lose by his conduct? *He lost the presence and comfortable enjoyment of God's love.* When we serve our Lord Jesus as believers should do, God is with us; and though we have the whole world against us, if we have God with us, what does it matter? But the moment we retreat and seek to establish our own agenda, we are at sea without a pilot. Then we will bitterly lament and groan out, "O my God, where have You gone? How could I have been so foolish as to shun Your service, and in this way lose all the bright shinings of Your face? This is a price too high. Let me return to my allegiance, that I may rejoice in Your presence." In the next place, *Jonah lost all peace of mind.* Sin soon destroys a believer's comfort. It is the poisonous tree whose leaves distill deadly drops that destroy the life of joy and peace. *Jonah lost everything upon which he might have drawn for comfort in any other case.* He could not plead the promise of divine protection, for he was not in God's ways; he could not say, "Lord, I meet with these difficulties in the discharge of my duty; therefore help me through them." He was reaping his own deeds; he was filled with his own ways. Christian, do not play the Jonah unless you wish to have all the waves and the billows rolling over your head. You will find in the long run that it is far harder to shun the work and will of God than to at once yield yourself to it. *Jonah lost his time*, for he had to go to Tarshish after all. It is hard to contend with God; let us yield ourselves to Him immediately.

### If the leprous disease has covered all his body, he shall pronounce him clean of the disease.

LEVITICUS 13:13

Although this regulation appears to be strange, yet there was wisdom in it, for the removal of the disease proved that the character was healthy. This evening it may be well for us to discover this principle to our profit. We, too, are in a sense lepers and may read the law of the leper as applicable to ourselves. When a man sees himself to be completely lost and ruined, covered with the defilement of sin, with no part free from pollution; when he disclaims all righteousness of his own and pleads guilty before the Lord, then he is clean through the blood of Jesus and the grace of God. Hidden, unfelt, unconfessed iniquity is the true leprosy of the soul; but when sin is seen and felt, it has received its deathblow, and the Lord looks with eyes of mercy upon the afflicted soul. Nothing is more deadly than self-righteousness or more hopeful than contrition. We must confess that we are "nothing else but sin," for no confession short of this will be the whole truth; and if the Holy Spirit is at work in us, convincing us of sin, there will be no difficulty about making such an acknowledgment—it will spring spontaneously from our lips. This text affords great comfort to truly awakened sinners: The very circumstance that so grievously discouraged them is here turned into a sign and symptom of a hopeful state! Digging out the foundation is the first thing in building—and a thorough sense of sin is one of the earliest works of grace in the heart. Spiritual lepers, aware of their condition, should take heart from the text and come as they are to Jesus.

> For let our debts be what they may, however great or small,
> As soon as we have naught to pay, our Lord forgives us all.
> 'Tis perfect poverty alone that sets the soul at large:
> While we can call one mite our own, we have no full discharge.

### ... whose origin is from of old,
### from ancient days.

MICAH 5:2

The Lord Jesus had purposes for His people *as their representative before the throne, long before they appeared upon the stage of time.* It was "from ancient days" that He signed the contract with His Father that He would pay blood for blood, suffering for suffering, agony for agony, and death for death on behalf of His people; it was "from ancient days" that He gave Himself up without a murmuring word. From the crown of His head to the sole of His foot He sweat great drops of blood; He was spat upon, pierced, mocked, torn, and crushed beneath the pains of death. All of this was "from ancient days." Let our souls pause in wonder at God's purposes from of old. Not only when you were born into the world did Christ love you, but His delights were with the sons of men before there were any sons of men! He often thought of them; from everlasting to everlasting He had set His affection upon them. Since He has been so long about your salvation, will not He accomplish it? Has He from everlasting been going forth to save me, and will He lose me now? It is inconceivable that having carried me in His hand, as His precious jewel, He would let me now slip from between His fingers. Did He choose me before the mountains were brought forth or the channels of the ocean were formed, and will He reject me now? Impossible! I am sure He would not have loved me for so long if He had not been a faithful Lover. If He could grow weary of me, He would have been tired of me long before now. If He had not loved me with a love as deep as hell and as strong as death, He would have turned from me long ago. What joy above all joys to know that I am His everlasting and inalienable inheritance, given to Him by His Father before the earth was formed! Everlasting love shall be the pillow on which I rest my head tonight.

### The jar of flour was not spent, neither did the jug of oil become empty, according to the word of the LORD that he spoke by Elijah.

1 KINGS 17:16

Consider the faithfulness of divine love. It is clear that this woman had daily necessities. She had to feed her son and herself in a time of famine; and now, in addition, the prophet Elijah was also to be fed. But though the need was threefold, the supply was not spent, for it was *constant*. Each day she made withdrawals from the jar, but each day it remained the same. You, dear reader, have daily necessities, and because they come so frequently, you are apt to fear that the jar of flour will one day be empty, and the jug of oil will fail you. Rest assured that, according to the Word of God, this shall not be the case. Each day, though it bring its trouble, it shall also bring its help; and though you should live longer than Methuselah, and your needs should be as many as the sands of the seashore, yet God's grace and mercy will last through all your necessities, and you will never know a real lack. For three long years, in this widow's days, the heavens never saw a cloud, and the stars never wept a holy tear of dew upon the wicked earth: famine and desolation and death made the land a howling wilderness, but this woman was never hungry but always joyful in abundance. So it will be with you. You will see the sinner's hope perish, for he trusts in himself; you will see the proud Pharisee's confidence crumble, for he builds his hope upon the sand; you will even see your own plans blown apart, but you will discover that your daily needs are amply supplied. Better to have God for your guardian than the Bank of England for your possession. You might spend the wealth of the nations, but you can never exhaust the infinite mercies of God.

## Now we have received . . . the Spirit who is from God, that we might understand the things freely given us by God.

1 CORINTHIANS 2:12

Dear reader, have you received the Spirit who is from God? The necessity of the work of the Holy Spirit in the heart may be clearly seen from this fact, that *all which has been done by God the Father and by God the Son will be ineffectual to us unless the Spirit reveals these things to our souls.* What effect does the doctrine of election have upon any man until the Spirit of God enters into him? Election is a dead letter in my consciousness until the Spirit of God calls me out of darkness into marvelous light. Then through my calling, I see my election, and knowing myself to be called of God, I know myself to have been chosen in the eternal purpose. A covenant was made with the Lord Jesus Christ by His Father; but what good is that covenant to us until the Holy Spirit brings us its blessings and opens our hearts to receive them? These blessings in Christ Jesus are beyond our reach, but the Spirit of God takes them down and hands them to us, and so they actually become ours. Covenant blessings in themselves are like bread in heaven, far out of mortal reach, but the Spirit of God opens the windows of heaven and scatters the living bread around the camp of the redeemed. Christ's finished work is like wine stored in the wine-vat; through unbelief we can neither draw nor drink. The Holy Spirit dips our vessel into this precious wine, and then we drink; but without the Spirit we are as truly dead in sin as though the Father never had elected, and though the Son had never bought us with His blood. The Holy Spirit is absolutely necessary to our well-being. Let us walk lovingly toward Him and tremble at the thought of grieving Him.

### Behold, I am laying in Zion a stone, a cornerstone chosen and precious.

1 PETER 2:6

As all the rivers run into the sea, so all delights center in the Lord Jesus. The glances of His eyes outshine the sun: the beauties of His face are fairer than the choicest flowers; no fragrance is like the breath of His mouth. Gems of the mine and pearls from the sea are worthless things when measured by His preciousness. Peter tells us that Jesus is precious, but he did not and could not tell us how precious, nor could any of us compute the value of God's unspeakable gift. Words cannot convey the preciousness of the Lord Jesus to His people, nor fully tell how essential He is to their satisfaction and happiness. Believer, have you not found in the occasion of plenty a sore famine if your Lord has been absent? The sun was shining, but Christ had hidden Himself, and all the world was dark to you; or it was night, and since the bright and morning star was gone, no other star could yield you so much as a ray of light. What a howling wilderness is this world without our Lord! If once He hides Himself from us, withered are the flowers of our garden; our pleasant fruits decay; the birds suspend their songs, and a tempest overturns our hopes. All earth's candles cannot make daylight if the Sun of Righteousness be eclipsed. He is the soul of our soul, the light of our light, the life of our life. Dear reader, what would you do in the world without Him when you wake up and look ahead to the day's battle? What would you do at night when you come home jaded and weary if there were no door of fellowship between you and Christ? Blessed be His name, He will not leave us to face the struggle without Him, for Jesus never forsakes His own. Yet, let the thought of what life would be without Him enhance His preciousness.

## To me, though I am the very least of all the saints, this grace was given, to preach to the Gentiles the unsearchable riches of Christ.

EPHESIANS 3:8

The apostle Paul felt it a great privilege to be allowed to preach the Gospel. He did not look upon his calling as a drudgery, but he entered upon it with intense delight. Although Paul was thankful for his calling, his success in it greatly humbled him. The fuller a ship becomes, the deeper it sinks in the water. Idlers may indulge a fond conceit of their abilities, because they are untried; but the earnest worker soon learns his own weakness. If you seek humility, try hard work; if you would know your nothingness, attempt some great thing for Jesus. If you want to feel how utterly powerless you are apart from the living God, attempt especially the great work of proclaiming the unsearchable riches of Christ, and you will know, as you never knew before, what a weak, unworthy thing you are. Although the apostle thus knew and confessed his weakness, he was never perplexed as to the *subject* of his ministry. From his first sermon to his last, Paul preached Christ, and nothing but Christ. He lifted up the cross and extolled the Son of God who bled on it. Follow his example in all your personal efforts to spread the glad tidings of salvation, and let "Christ and him crucified" be your ever-recurring theme. The Christian should be like those lovely spring flowers that, when the sun is shining, open their golden cups, as if saying, "Fill us with your beams!" But when the sun is hidden behind a cloud, they close their cups and droop their heads. So should the Christian feel the sweet influence of Jesus. Jesus must be his sun, and He must be the flower that yields itself to the Sun of Righteousness. Oh, to speak of Christ alone—this is the subject that is both "seed to the sower and bread to the eater."[1] This is the live coal for the lip of the speaker, and the master-key to the heart of the hearer.

[1]Isaiah 55:10

## *He saw the Spirit of God descending like a dove.*

MATTHEW 3:16

As the Spirit of God descended upon the Lord Jesus, the head, so He also, in measure, descends upon the members of the mystical body. His descent is to us after the same fashion as that in which it fell upon our Lord. There is often a sudden *swiftness* about it; before we are even aware of it, we are impelled onward and heavenward beyond all expectation. Yet there is none of the hurry of earthly haste, for the wings of the dove are as soft as they are swift. *Quietness* seems essential to many spiritual operations; the Lord is in the still small voice, and like the dew, His grace is distilled in silence. The dove has always been the chosen type of *purity*, and the Holy Spirit is holiness itself. Where He comes, everything that is pure and lovely and of good report is made to abound, and sin and uncleanness depart. Peace reigns also where the Holy Dove comes with power; He bears the olive branch, which shows that the waters of divine wrath are assuaged. *Gentleness* is a sure result of the Sacred Dove's transforming power: Hearts touched by His benign influence are meek and lowly from that point and forever. *Harmlessness* follows as a matter of course; eagles and ravens may hunt their prey—the turtledove can endure wrong but cannot inflict it. We must be harmless as doves. The dove is an apt picture of *love*; the voice of the turtle is full of affection. And so the soul visited by the blessed Spirit abounds in love to God, in love to the brethren, and in love to sinners, and above all, in love to Jesus. The brooding of the Spirit of God upon the face of the deep first produced *order and life*, and in our hearts He causes and fosters new life and light. Blessed Spirit, as You did rest upon our dear Redeemer, even so rest upon us from this time forward and forever.

## They feast on the abundance of your house.

PSALM 36:8

Sheba's queen was amazed at the sumptuousness of Solomon's table. She lost all heart when she saw the provision of a single day; and she marveled equally at the company of servants who enjoyed the king's feast. But what is this in comparison to the abundance of the God of grace? Ten thousand thousand of His people are daily fed; hungry and thirsty, they bring large appetites with them to the banquet, but not one of them returns unsatisfied; there is enough for each, enough for all, enough forevermore. Although the company that eats at Jehovah's table is as countless as the stars of heaven, yet each one has his own portion. Think how much grace one saint requires, so much that nothing but the Infinite could supply him for one day; and yet the Lord spreads His table not for one, but for many saints; not for one day, but for many years; not for many years only, but for generation after generation. Consider the full feasting spoken of in the text; the guests at mercy's banquet are satisfied—more, abundantly satisfied, and not with ordinary fare, but with the peculiar abundance of God's own house; and such feasting is guaranteed by a faithful promise to all those children of men who put their trust under the shadow of Jehovah's wings. I once thought that if I could just get the leftovers at God's back door of grace I would be satisfied, like the woman who said, "The dogs eat the crumbs that fall from their masters' table." But no child of God is ever served with scraps and leftovers; like Mephibosheth, they all eat from the King's own table. In matters of grace, we all have Benjamin's portion—we all have ten times more than we could have expected; and though our necessities are great, yet are we often amazed at the marvelous fullness of grace that God gives us richly to enjoy.

## *Say to my soul, "I am your salvation!"*

PSALM 35:3

What does this sweet prayer teach me? It shall be my evening's petition; but first let it grant me an instructive meditation. The text informs me first of all that *David had his doubts*; for why should he pray, "Say to my soul, 'I am your salvation'" if he were not sometimes exercised with doubts and fears? Let me, then, be encouraged that I am not the only saint who has to face such faltering faith. If David doubted, I need not conclude that I am not a Christian because I have doubts. The text reminds me that *David was not content while he had doubts and fears*, but he proceeded directly to the mercy-seat to pray for assurance, for he valued it as much as gold. I too must work to foster a continual sense of being accepted in the Beloved and must have no joy when His love is not shed abroad in my soul. When my Bridegroom is gone, my soul must long for Him. I learn also that *David knew where to obtain full assurance.* He went to his God in prayer, crying, "Say to my soul, 'I am your salvation.'" I need to be often alone with God if I am to enjoy a clear sense of Jesus' love. When my prayers cease, my eye of faith will grow dim. Much in prayer, much in heaven; slow in prayer, slow in progress. I notice that *David would not be satisfied unless his assurance had a divine source.* "Say to my soul . . . " Lord, speak to me! Nothing less than a divine testimony in the soul will ever content the true Christian. Moreover, David could not rest unless his assurance had *a vivid personality* about it. "Say to my soul, 'I am your salvation.'" Lord, if You said this to all the saints, it means little unless You should say it to me. Lord, I have sinned; I do not deserve Your smile; I scarcely dare to ask for it. But oh, say to *my* soul, even to *my* soul, "I am your salvation." Let me have a present, personal, infallible, indisputable sense that I am Yours and that You are mine.

## *Before destruction a man's heart is haughty.*

PROVERBS 18:12

It is an old and common saying that "coming events cast their shadows before them." The wise man teaches us that a haughty heart is the precursor of evil. Pride is as clearly the sign of destruction as the change of mercury in the barometer is the sign of rain, and far more infallibly so than that. When men have ridden the high horse, destruction has always overtaken them. Let David's aching heart show that there is an eclipse of a man's glory when he dotes upon his own greatness (2 Samuel 24:10). Observe Nebuchadnezzar, the mighty builder of Babylon, creeping on the earth, devouring grass like a beast, his nails grown like the bird's claws, and his hair like eagle's feathers (Daniel 4:33). Pride made the boaster a beast, as once before it made an angel a devil. God hates high looks and never fails to bring them down. All the arrows of God are aimed at proud hearts. O Christian, is your heart haughty this evening? For pride can get into the Christian's heart as well as into the sinner's; it can delude him into dreaming that he is "rich, I have prospered, and I need nothing."[1] Are you glorying in your graces or your talents? Are you proud of yourself and your spiritual experiences? Be careful, reader—there is a destruction coming to you also. Your flaunting poppies of self-conceit will be pulled up by the roots, your mushrooming graces will wither in the burning heat, and your self-sufficiency will become as straw for the dunghill. If we forget to live at the foot of the cross in deepest lowliness of spirit, God will not forget to discipline us for our good. A destruction will come to you, O unduly exalted believer, the destruction of your joys and of your comforts, although there can be no destruction of your soul. Therefore, "Let the one who boasts, boast *in the Lord*."[2]

[1] Revelation 3:17　[2] 1 Corinthians 1:31

### *It is better to take refuge in the LORD than to trust in man.*

PSALM 118:8

No doubt the reader has been tempted to rely upon the things that are seen instead of resting alone upon the invisible God. Christians often look to man for help and advice, and so spoil the noble simplicity of their reliance upon God. Does this evening's passage meet the eye of a child of God who is filled with anxiety? Then let us reason with you. You trust in Jesus, and only in Jesus, for your salvation; then why are you troubled? *"Because of my great care."* Is it not written, "Cast your burden upon the Lord"? "Do not be anxious about anything, but in everything by prayer and supplication with thanksgiving let your requests be made known to God."[1] Can you trust God for your physical needs? *"Ah! I wish I could."* If you cannot trust God with the physical, how dare you trust Him with the spiritual? Can you trust Him for your soul's redemption, and yet not rely upon Him for a few lesser mercies? Is God not enough for your need, or is His all-sufficiency too narrow for your wants? Do you need another to watch for you when you have Him who sees every secret thing? Is His heart faint? Is His arm weary? If so, seek another God; but if He is infinite, omnipotent, faithful, true, and all-wise, why do you run around seeking another confidence? Why do you scour the earth to find another foundation when this is strong enough to bear all the weight that you can ever build on it? Christian, do not mix your wine with water; do not tarnish the gold of faith with the dross of human confidence. Wait only upon God, and let your expectation be from Him. Do not covet Jonah's gourd but rest in Jonah's God. Let the sandy, shaky foundations be the choice of fools; but you, like one who sees the approaching storm, build for yourself an abiding place upon the Rock of Ages.

[1] Philippians 4:6

### *She called his name Ben-oni [son of sorrow]; but his father called him Benjamin [son of my right hand].*

GENESIS 35:18

To every matter there is a bright as well as a dark side. Rachel was overwhelmed with the sorrow of her own travail and death; Jacob, while mourning the loss of his wife, could see the mercy of the child's birth. It is good for us if, while the flesh mourns over trials, our faith triumphs in divine faithfulness. Samson's lion yielded honey, and so will our adversities, if rightly considered. The stormy sea feeds multitudes with its fish; the wild wood blooms with beautiful flowers; the stormy wind sweeps away disease, and the biting frost loosens the soil. Dark clouds distill bright drops, and black earth grows lovely flowers. A vein of good is to be found in every mine of evil. Sad hearts have peculiar skill in discovering the most disadvantageous point of view from which to gaze upon a trial; if there were only one swamp in the world, they would soon be up to their necks in it, and if there were only one lion in the desert they would hear it roar. About us all there is a tinge of this wretched folly, and we are apt, at times, like Jacob, to cry, "All these things are against me." Faith's way of walking is to cast all care upon the Lord, and then to anticipate good results from the worst calamities. Like Gideon's men, she does not fret over the broken pitcher but rejoices that the lamp shines with even more brilliance. Out of the rough oyster-shell of difficulty she extracts the rare pearl of honor, and from the deep ocean-caves of distress she discovers the priceless coral of experience. When her flood of prosperity ebbs, she finds treasures hidden in the sands; and when her sun of delight goes down, she turns her telescope of hope to the starry promises of heaven. When death itself appears, faith points to the light of resurrection beyond the grave, thus making our dying Ben-oni to be our living Benjamin.

## *Abide in me.*

JOHN 15:4

Communion with Christ is a certain cure for every ill. Whether it be the woodworm of sadness or the smothering impact of earthly treasure, close fellowship with the Lord Jesus will take bitterness from the one and excess from the other. Live near to Jesus, Christian, and it is a matter of secondary importance whether you live on the mountain of honor or in the valley of humiliation. Living near to Jesus, you are covered with the wings of God, and underneath you are the everlasting arms. Let nothing keep you from that hallowed communion that is the unique privilege of a life hidden in Christ. Do not be content with the occasional meeting, but always seek to retain His company, for only in His presence will you find either comfort or safety. Jesus should not be for us a friend who calls us now and then, but one with whom we are in constant touch. You have a difficult road before you: Make sure, pilgrim, that you do not go without your guide. You have to pass through the fiery furnace; do not enter unless, like Shadrach, Meshach, and Abednego, you have the Son of God to be your companion. You have to storm the walls of your corrupt heart: Do not attempt it until, like Joshua, you have seen the Captain of the Lord's host, with His sword drawn in His hand. When you meet with many temptations, do not rest upon the arm of flesh. In every case, in every condition, you will need Jesus, but most of all when the iron gates of death shall open to you. Keep close to the Captain of your salvation, lean upon His strength, ask Him to refresh you by His Spirit, and you will stand before Him at the end, without spot or blemish and at peace. Seeing you have lived with Him, and lived in Him here, you will abide with Him forever.

## *Man . . . is few of days and full of trouble.*

JOB 14:1

It may be of great service to us, before we fall asleep, to remember this mournful fact, for it may lead us to hold lightly to earthly things. There is nothing very pleasant in the recollection that we are not above the arrows of adversity, but it may humble us and prevent us from boasting like the psalmist that out mountain stands firm, that we shall never be moved. It may prevent us from making our roots too deep in this soil from which we are so soon to be transplanted into the heavenly garden. Let us keep in mind the frail tenure upon which we hold our *temporal mercies*. If we remember that all the trees of earth are marked for the woodman's axe, we will not be so ready to build our nests in them. We should love, but we should love with the love that expects death, and that reckons upon separations. Our *dear relations* are simply loaned to us, and the hour when we must return them to the lender's hand may be sooner than we think. This is also true of our *worldly goods*. Do not riches take to themselves wings and fly away? Our *health* is equally precarious. Frail flowers of the field, we must not reckon upon blooming forever. There is a time appointed for weakness and sickness, when we will have to glorify God by suffering and not by earnest activity. There is no single point in which we can hope to escape from the sharp arrows of affliction; out of our few days there is not one secure from sorrow. Man's life is a cask full of bitter wine; he who looks for joy in it would be better looking for honey in a salty ocean. Beloved reader, do not set your affections upon things of earth, but seek those things that are above, for *here* the moth devours, and the thief steals, but *there* all joys are perpetual and eternal. The path of trouble is the way home. Lord, make this thought a pillow for many a weary head!

## *You shall be called Sought Out.*

ISAIAH 62:12

The surpassing grace of God is seen very clearly in that we were not only sought, but sought *out*. Men *seek* for a thing that is lost upon the floor of the house, but in such a case there is only seeking, not seeking out. The loss is more perplexing and the search more persevering when a thing is sought *out*. We were mingled with the mire: We were as when some precious piece of gold falls into the sewer, and men gather out and carefully inspect a mass of abominable filth, and continue to stir and rake, and search among the heap until the treasure is found. Or, to use another figure, we were lost in a maze; we wandered here and there, and when mercy came after us with the Gospel, it did not find us at the first coming—it had to search for us and seek us out; for we as lost sheep were so desperately lost and had wandered into such a strange country that it did not seem possible that even the Good Shepherd could track our devious roamings. Glory be to unconquerable grace, we were *sought out*! No darkness could hide us, no filthiness could conceal us; we were found and brought home. Glory be to infinite love—God the Holy Spirit restored us!

If the lives of some of God's people could be written, they would fill us with holy astonishment. Strange and marvelous are the ways that God used in their case to find His own. Blessed be His name, He never relinquishes the search until the chosen are sought out effectually. They are not a people sought today and cast away tomorrow. Almightiness and wisdom combined will make no failures; they shall be called, "*Sought Out*!" That any should be sought out is matchless grace, but that we should be sought out is grace beyond degree! We can find no reason for it but God's own sovereign love and can only lift up our heart in wonder and praise the Lord that this night we wear the name of "*Sought Out*."

## *To whom do you belong?*

### 1 SAMUEL 30:13

In the life of faith, neutrality is not an option. We are either ranked under the banner of the Lord Jesus, to serve and fight His battles, or we are slaves of the dark prince, Satan. "To whom do you belong?"

Reader, let me assist you in your response. *Have you been "born again"?* If you have, you belong to Christ; but without the new birth you cannot be His. *In whom do you trust?* For those who believe in Jesus are the sons of God. *Whose work are you doing?* You are sure to serve your master, for he whom you serve is thereby owned to be your lord. What company do you keep? If you belong to Jesus, you will keep company with those who wear the uniform of the cross. "Birds of a feather flock together." *What is your conversation?* Is it heavenly or is it earthly? *What have you learned from your Master?* For servants learn a great deal from the masters to whom they are apprenticed. If you have served your time with Jesus, it will be said of you, as it was of Peter and John, "they recognized that they had been with Jesus."[1]

We press the question, "To whom do you belong?" Answer honestly before you fall asleep for the night. If you are not Christ's, you are in a hard service—*run away from your cruel master!* Enter into the service of the Lord of Love, and you will enjoy a life of blessedness. If you are Christ's, let me advise you to do four things. You belong to Jesus—obey *Him*; let His word be your law; let His wish be your will. You belong to the Beloved; then *love Him*; let your heart embrace Him; let your whole soul be filled with Him. You belong to the Son of God; then *trust Him*; rest on nothing or no one but on Him. You belong to the King of kings; then *be decided for Him*. Thus even without being marked with a sign everyone will know to whom you belong.

[1]Acts 4:14

## *So he put out his hand and took her and brought her into the ark with him.*

GENESIS 8:9

Tired out by her wanderings, the dove finally returns to the ark as her only resting place. How heavily she flies—she will drop—she will never reach the ark! But she struggles on. Noah has been looking out for his dove all day long and is ready to receive her. She has just enough strength to reach the edge of the ark; she can hardly alight upon it and is ready to drop when Noah puts forth his hand and pulls her in unto him. Note that: *"brought her into the ark with him."* She did not fly right in herself, because she was too fearful or too weary to do so. She flew as far as she could, and then he put out his hand and pulled her in with him. This act of mercy was shown to the wandering dove, and she was not scolded for her wanderings. Just as she was, she was pulled into the ark. So you, seeking sinner, with all your sin, will be received. "Only return"—those are God's two gracious words— "only return." What! Nothing else? No; "only return." She had no olive branch in her mouth this time, nothing at all but just herself and her wanderings; but it is "only return," and she does return, and Noah pulls her in. Wanderer, fly, fainting one; fly, dove, as you are. Though you imagine yourself to be as black as the raven with the filth of sin, come back to the Savior. Every moment you delay increases your misery; your attempts to plume yourself and make yourself fit for Jesus are all vanity. Come to Him just as you are. If you are running and hiding from God, then return as a backslider with all your backslidings about you. Return, return, return! Jesus is waiting for you! He will stretch forth His hand and pull you in—in to Himself, your heart's true home.

## I will guard my ways.

PSALM 39:1

Fellow-pilgrim, do not say in your heart, "I will go here and there, and I will not sin," for you are never so out of danger of sinning as to boast of security. The road is very muddy; it will be hard to pick your path so as not to soil your garments. This is a dirty world, and you will need to stay alert if you are to keep your hands clean. There is a robber at every turn of the road to rob you of your jewels; there is a temptation in every mercy; there is a snare in every joy; and if you ever reach heaven, it will be a miracle of divine grace to be ascribed entirely to your Father's power. Be on your guard. When a man carries fireworks in his hand, he should be careful that he does not go near a candle; and you too must take care that you do not succumb to temptation. Even your everyday activities are sharp-edged tools; you must mind how you handle them. There is nothing in this world to foster a Christian's piety, but everything to destroy it. How concerned you should be to look up to God, that He may keep you! Your prayer should be, "Hold me up, and I shall be safe." Having prayed, you must also watch, guarding every thought, word, and action, with holy jealousy. Do not expose yourselves unnecessarily; but if called to exposure, if you are called to go where the darts are flying, never venture forth without your shield; for if once the devil finds you without your armor, he will rejoice that his hour of triumph is come and will soon make you fall down wounded by his arrows. Although you cannot be killed, you may be wounded. Be sober-minded; be watchful—danger may befall you at a time when everything seems to be secure. Therefore, pay attention, stay alert, watch and pray. No man ever fell into error through being too watchful. May the Holy Spirit guide us in all our ways, so they shall always please the Lord.

## . . . *he did with all his heart,*
## *and prospered.*

2 CHRONICLES 31:21

This is no unusual occurrence; it is the general rule of the moral universe that the prosperous are those who do their work with all their hearts, while others are almost certain to fail when they go about their business halfheartedly. God does not give harvests to lazy men except harvests of thistles, nor is He pleased to send wealth to those who will not dig in the field to find its hidden treasure. It is universally confessed that if a man would prosper, he must be diligent in business. It is the same in the matter of faith as it is in other things. If you would prosper in your work for Jesus, let it be *heart* work, and let it be done with all your heart. Put as much force, energy, heartiness, and earnestness into faith as ever you do into business, for it deserves far more. The Holy Spirit helps our weaknesses, but He does not encourage our laziness; He loves active believers. Who are the most useful men in the Christian church? The men who do what they undertake for God *with all their hearts*. Who are the most successful Sunday school teachers? The most talented? No. The most zealous; those whose hearts are on fire—they are the ones who see their Lord riding forth prosperously in the majesty of His salvation. Wholeheartedness shows itself in perseverance; there may be failure at first, but the earnest worker will say, "It is the Lord's work, and it must be done; my Lord has called me to do it, and in His strength I will accomplish it." Christian, are you serving your Master with all your heart? Remember the earnestness of Jesus! Think what heart-work was His! He could say, "*Zeal for Your house has consumed me.*" When He sweat great drops of blood, it was no light burden He had to carry upon those blessed shoulders; and when He poured out His heart, it was no weak effort He was making for the salvation of His people. Was Jesus in earnest, and we are lukewarm?

## *Keep back your servant also from presumptuous sins.*

PSALM 19:13

Such was the prayer of the *"man after God's own heart."* Did holy David need to pray like this? How needful, then, such a prayer must be for us babes in grace! It is as if he said, "Keep me back, or I shall rush headlong over the precipice of sin." Our evil nature, like an ill-tempered horse, is apt to run away. May the grace of God put the bridle upon it and hold it in, that it rush not into mischief. What would the best of us do if it were not for the checks that the Lord sets upon us both in providence and in grace! The psalmist's prayer is directed against the worst form of sin—that which is done with deliberation and willfulness. Even the holiest need to be "kept back" from the vilest transgressions. It is a solemn thing to find the apostle Paul warning saints against the most loathsome sins: "Put to death therefore what is earthly in you: sexual immorality, impurity, passion, evil desire, and covetousness, which is idolatry."[1] What! Do saints really need to be warned against such sins as these? Yes, they do. The whitest robes, unless their purity be preserved by divine grace, will be defiled by the blackest spots. Experienced Christian, do not boast in your experience; you will trip if you look away from Him who is able to keep you from falling. You whose love is fervent, whose faith is constant, whose hopes are bright, do not say, "We shall never sin," but rather cry, "Lead us not into temptation." There is enough kindling in the heart of the best of men to light a fire that shall burn to the lowest hell, unless God shall quench the sparks as they fall. Who would have dreamed that righteous Lot could be found drunk and committing immorality? Hazael said, "Is Your servant a dog, that he should do this thing?" and we are very apt to use the same self-righteous question. May infinite wisdom cure us of the madness of self-confidence.

[1]Colossians 3:5

## *Blessed are the peacemakers,*
## *for they shall be called sons of God.*

MATTHEW 5:9

This is the seventh of the beatitudes: and seven was the number of perfection among the Hebrews. It may be that the Savior placed the peacemaker seventh on the list because he most nearly approaches the perfect man in Christ Jesus. He who would have perfect blessedness, so far as it can be enjoyed on earth, must attain to this seventh benediction and become a peacemaker. There is a significance also in the position of the text. The verse that precedes it speaks of the blessedness of "the pure in heart, for they shall see God." It is important to understand that we are to be "first pure, then peaceable."[1] Our peaceableness is never to be a contract with sin or toleration of evil. We must set our faces like flint against everything that is contrary to God and His holiness: When purity in our souls is a settled matter, we can go on to peaceableness. In the same way, the verse that follows seems to have been put there on purpose. However peaceable we may be in this world, yet we shall be misrepresented and misunderstood; and we should not be surprised, for even the Prince of Peace, by His very peacefulness, brought fire upon the earth. He Himself, though He loved mankind and did no ill, was "despised and rejected by men; a man of sorrows, and acquainted with grief."[2] Just in case the peaceable in heart should be surprised when they meet with enemies, the following verse reads, "Blessed are those who are persecuted for righteousness' sake, for theirs is the kingdom of heaven." So, the peacemakers are not only pronounced to be blessed, but they are surrounded with blessings. Lord, give us grace to climb to this seventh beatitude! Purify our minds that we may be "first pure, then peaceable" and fortify our souls, that our peaceableness may not lead us into cowardice and despair when we are persecuted for Your sake.

[1]James 3:17  [2]Isaiah 53:3

## *As the Father has loved me,*
## *so have I loved you.*

JOHN 15:9

As the Father loves the Son, in the same manner Jesus loves His people. What is that divine method? He loved Him *without beginning*, and thus Jesus loves His members. *"I have loved you with an everlasting love."*[1] You can trace the beginning of human affection; you can easily find the beginning of your love to Christ. But His love to us is a stream whose source is hidden in eternity. God the Father loves Jesus *without any change*. Christian, take this for your comfort, that there is no change in Jesus Christ's love to those who rest in Him. Yesterday you were on the mountain, and you said, "He loves me." Today you are in the valley of humiliation, but He loves you still the same. On the hills and among the peaks, you heard His voice, which spoke so sweetly of His love; and now on the sea, or even in the sea, when all His waves and billows go over you, His heart is still faithful to His ancient choice. The Father loves the Son *without any end*, and this is how the Son loves His people. Saint, you need not fear the prospect of death, for His love for you will never cease. Rest confident that even down to the grave Christ will go with you, and that up again from it He will be your guide to the celestial hills. Moreover, the Father loves the Son *without any measure*, and the same immeasurable love the Son bestows upon His chosen ones. The whole heart of Christ is dedicated to His people. He "loved us and gave himself for us." His is a love that passes knowledge. We have indeed an immutable Savior, a precious Savior, one who loves without measure, without change, without beginning, and without end, even as the Father loves Him! There is rich food here for those who know how to digest it. May the Holy Spirit lead us into its marrow and fatness!

[1]Jeremiah 31:3

## *And she ate until she was satisfied,*
## *and she had some left over.*

RUTH 2:14

Whenever we are privileged to eat the bread that Jesus gives, we are, like Ruth, satisfied with a full and sweet provision. When Jesus is the host, no guest goes empty from the table. Our head is satisfied with the precious truth that Christ reveals; our *heart* is content with Jesus as the altogether lovely object of affection; our *hope* is satisfied, for who do we have in heaven but Jesus? And our desire is fulfilled, for what more can we wish for than to "gain Christ and be found in him"?[1] Jesus fills our *conscience* until it is at perfect peace, our *judgment* with persuasion of the certainty of His teachings, our *memory* with recollections of what He has done, and our *imagination* with the prospects of what He is still to do. As Ruth was "satisfied," so is it with us. We have drunk deeply; we have thought that we could take in all of Christ; but when we have done our best, we have had to leave a vast remainder. We have sat at the table of the Lord's love and said, "Nothing but the infinite can ever satisfy me; I am such a great sinner that I must have infinite merit to wash my sin away." But we have had our sin removed and found that there was merit to spare; we have had our hunger relieved at the feast of sacred love and found that there was an abundance of spiritual food remaining. There are certain sweet things in the Word of God that we have not enjoyed yet, and that we are obliged to leave for a while; for we are like the disciples to whom Jesus said, "I still have many things to say to you, but you cannot bear them now."[2] Yes, there are graces to which we have not attained, places of fellowship nearer to Christ that we have not reached, and heights of communion that our feet have not climbed. At every banquet of love there are many baskets left over. Let us magnify the generosity of kindly Boaz.

[1]Philippians 3:9 [2]John 16:12

## Husbands, love your wives, as Christ loved the church.

EPHESIANS 5:25

What a golden example Christ gives to His disciples! Few masters could venture to say, "If you would practice my teaching, imitate my life." But as the life of Jesus is the exact transcript of perfect virtue, He can point to Himself as the paragon of holiness, as well as the teacher of it. The Christian should take nothing less than Christ for his model. Under no circumstances should we be content unless we reflect the grace that was in Him. As a husband, the Christian is to look upon the portrait of Christ Jesus, and he is to paint according to that copy. The true Christian is to be such a husband as Christ was to His church. The love of a husband is *special*. The Lord Jesus cherishes for the church a peculiar affection, which is set upon her above the rest of mankind: "I am praying for them. I am not praying for the world."[1] The elect church is the favorite of heaven, the treasure of Christ, the crown of His head, the bracelet of His arm, the breastplate of His heart, the very center and core of His love. A husband should love his wife with a *constant* love, for in this way Jesus loves His church. He does not vary in His affection. He may change in His display of affection, but the affection itself is still the same. A husband should love his wife with an *enduring* love, for nothing shall "separate us from the love of . . . Christ."[2] A true husband loves his wife with a *hearty* love, fervent and intense. It is not mere lip service. What more could Christ have done in proof of His love than He has done? Jesus has a *delighted love* toward His spouse: He prizes her affection and delights in her with sweet satisfaction. Believer, you wonder at Jesus' love; you admire it—*are you imitating it?* In your domestic relationships, is the rule and measure of your love *"even as Christ loved the church"*?

[1]John 17:9   [2]Romans 8:39

### *Can you bind the chains of the Pleiades or loose the cords of Orion?*

JOB 38:31

If we are inclined to boast of our abilities, the grandeur of nature will quickly show us how puny we are. We cannot move the least of all the twinkling stars or quench so much as one of the sunbeams of the morning. We speak of power, but the heavens laugh us to scorn. When the stars shine forth in spring-like joy, we cannot restrain their influences; and when Orion reigns above, and the year is bound in winter's chains, we cannot relax the icy grip. The seasons arrive by divine appointment, and it is impossible for men to change the cycle. Lord, what is man?

In the spiritual, as in the natural, world, man's power is limited on all hands. When the Holy Spirit sheds abroad His delights in the soul, none can disturb; all the cunning and malice of men are unable to prevent the genial, quickening power of the Comforter. When He deigns to visit a church and revive it, the most inveterate enemies cannot resist the good work; they may ridicule it, but they can no more restrain it than they can push back the spring when the Pleiades rule the hour. God wills it, and so it must be. On the other hand, if the Lord in sovereignty, or in justice, binds up a man so that his soul is in bondage, who can give him liberty? He alone can remove the winter of spiritual death from an individual or a people. He looses the bands of Orion, and none but He. What a blessing it is that He can do it. O that He would perform the wonder tonight. Lord, end my winter, and let my spring begin. I cannot with all my longings raise my soul out of her death and dullness, but all things are possible with You. I need heavenly influences, the clear shinings of Your love, the beams of Your grace, the light of Your countenance—these are as summer suns to me. I suffer greatly from sin and temptation; these are my terrible wintry signs. Lord, work wonders in me, and for me.

### *Father, I desire that they also,*
### *whom you have given me,*
### *may be with me where I am.*

JOHN 17:24

O death! Why do you touch the tree beneath whose spreading branches weariness finds rest? Why do you snatch away the excellent of the earth, in whom is all our delight? If you must use your axe, use it upon the trees that yield no fruit; then you may be thanked. But why will you chop down the best trees? Hold your axe, and spare the righteous. But no, it must not be; death strikes the best of our friends; the most generous, the most prayerful, the most holy, the most devoted must die. And why? It is through Jesus' prevailing prayer—"Father, I desire that they also, whom you have given me, may be with me where I am." It is *that* which bears them on eagle's wings to heaven. Every time a believer moves from this earth to paradise, it is an answer to Christ's prayer. A good old divine remarks, "Many times Jesus and His people pull against one another in prayer. You bend your knee in prayer and say 'Father, I desire that Your saints be with me where I am'; Christ says, 'Father, I desire that they also, whom you have given me, may be with me where I am.'" In this way the disciple is at cross-purposes with his Lord. The soul cannot be in both places: The beloved one cannot be with Christ and with you too. Now, which of the two who plead shall win the day? If you had your choice, if the King should step from His throne and say, "Here are two supplicants praying in opposition to one another," which shall be answered? Oh, I am sure, though it were agony, you would jump to your feet and say, "Jesus, not my will, but Yours be done." You would give up your prayer for your loved one's life, if you could realize the thoughts that Christ is praying in the opposite direction—"Father, I desire that they also, whom you have given me, may be with me where I am." Lord, You shall have them. By faith we let them go.

# *I tell you, if these were silent, the very stones would cry out.*

LUKE 19:40

But could the stones cry out? Assuredly they could if He who opens the mouth of the dumb should bid them lift up their voice. Certainly if they were to speak, they would have much to declare in praise of Him who created them by the word of His power; they could extol the wisdom and power of their *Maker* who called them into being. Shall *we* not speak well of Him who made us new and out of stones raised up children unto Abraham? The old rocks could tell of chaos and order and the handiwork of God in successive stages of creation's drama; are we not also able to talk of God's decrees, of God's great work in ancient times, in all that He did for His church in the days of old? If the stones were to speak, they could tell of their *breaker*, how he took them from the quarry and made them fit for the temple. And aren't we also able to tell of our glorious Breaker, who broke our hearts with the hammer of His Word, that He might build us into His temple? If the stones should cry out, they would magnify their *builder*, who polished them and fashioned them into a beautiful palace; and shall not we talk of our Architect and Builder, who has put us in our place in the temple of the living God? If the stones could cry out, they might have a long, long story to tell by way of memorial, for many a time a great stone has been rolled as a memorial before the Lord; and we too can testify, stones of help and pillars of remembrance. The broken stones of the law cry out against us, but Christ Himself, who has rolled away the stone from the door of the tomb, speaks for us. Stones might well cry out, but we will not let them: We will silence their noise as we break into sacred song and bless the majesty of the Most High; we will spend all our days glorifying Him whom Jacob calls the Shepherd and Stone of Israel.

## In that same hour he rejoiced in the Holy Spirit.

LUKE 10:21

The Savior was "a man of sorrows,"[1] but every thoughtful mind has discovered the fact that down deep in His innermost soul He carried an inexhaustible treasury of refined and heavenly joy. Of all the human race, there was never a man who had a deeper, purer, or more abiding peace than our Lord Jesus Christ. "He was anointed with the oil of gladness beyond your companions."[2] His vast benevolence must, from the very nature of things, have afforded Him the deepest possible delight, for benevolence is joy. There were a few remarkable seasons when this joy manifested itself. "In that same hour Jesus rejoiced in the Holy Spirit, and said, I thank you, Father, Lord of heaven and earth. . . ."[3] Christ had His songs, even in the darkness; even though His face was marred, and His countenance had lost the luster of earthly happiness, yet sometimes it was illumined with a matchless splendor of unparalleled satisfaction as He thought upon the recompense of the reward and in the midst of the congregation sang His praise unto God. In this, the Lord Jesus is a blessed picture of His church on earth. At this hour the church expects to walk in sympathy with her Lord along a thorny road; through much tribulation she is making her way to the crown. To bear the cross is her office, and to be scorned and counted an alien by her mother's children is her lot; and yet the church has a deep well of joy, of which none can drink but her own children. There are stores of wine and oil and corn hidden in the midst of our Jerusalem, upon which the saints of God are continuously sustained and nurtured. And sometimes, as in our Savior's case, we have our seasons of intense delight, for "There is a river whose streams make glad the city of God."[4] Even though we are exiles, we rejoice in our King; yes, in Him we exceedingly rejoice, while in His name we set up our banners.

[1]Isaiah 53:3  [2]Psalm 45:7  [3]Luke 10:21  [4]Psalm 46:4

## *The Son of Man.*

JOHN 3:13

How constantly our Master used the title, "the Son of man!" If He had chosen, He might always have spoken of Himself as the Son of God, the Everlasting Father, the Wonderful Counselor, the Prince of Peace; but behold the lowliness of Jesus! He prefers to call Himself the Son of man. Let us learn a lesson of humility from our Savior; let us never court great titles nor proud degrees. There is here, however, a far sweeter thought. Jesus loved manhood so much that He delighted to honor it; and since it is a high honor, and indeed the greatest dignity of manhood, that Jesus is the Son of man, He is willing to display this name, that He may as it were hang royal stars upon the breast of manhood and display the love of God to Abraham's seed. *Son of man*—whenever He said this, He shed a halo around the head of Adam's children. Yet there is perhaps a more precious thought still. Jesus Christ called Himself the Son of man to express His oneness and sympathy with His people. In this way He reminds us that He is the one whom we may approach without fear. As a man, we may take to Him all our griefs and troubles, for He knows them by experience. In that He Himself has suffered as "the Son of Man," He is able to rescue and comfort us. We bless You, Lord Jesus, for using such a title to remind us and assure us that You are a brother. This is for us a token of Your grace, Your humility, Your love.

*Oh see how Jesus trusts Himself*
*Unto our childish love,*
*As though by His free ways with us*
*Our earnestness to prove!*

*His sacred name a common word*
*On earth He loves to hear;*
*There is no majesty in Him*
*Which love may not come near.*

> ### . . . when He comes in the glory of his Father
> ### with the holy angels.

MARK 8:38

If we have been partakers with Jesus in His shame, we shall also share with Him the luster that surrounds Him when He appears again in glory. Are you in communion with Christ Jesus? Does a vital union bind you to Him? Then you are today with Him in His shame; you have taken up His cross and have gone with Him outside the camp bearing His reproach; you will doubtless be with Him when the cross is exchanged for the crown. But examine yourself this evening; for if you are not with Him in regeneration, you will not be with Him when He comes in His glory. If you run from the dark side of fellowship, you will not understand its bright, happy chapter when the King comes *with all His holy angels*. What! *Are angels with Him?* And yet He did not take up angels—He took up the seed of Abraham. Are the holy angels *with Him?* Come, my soul; if you are indeed His own beloved, you cannot be far from Him. If His friends and His neighbors are called together to see His glory, shall you be distant? Though it be a day of judgment, yet you cannot be far from that heart that, having admitted angels into intimacy, has admitted you into union with Himself. Has He not said to you, O my soul, "I will betroth you to me in righteousness and in justice, in steadfast love and in mercy"? Has He not declared us to be in union with Him? If the angels, who are but friends and neighbors, shall be with Him, it is abundantly certain that His own beloved in whom is all His delight shall be near to Him and sit at His right hand. Here is a morning star of hope for you, of such exceeding brilliance that it may well light up your darkest and most desolate experience.

### She said, "Yes, Lord, yet even the dogs eat the crumbs that fall from their masters' table."

MATTHEW 15:27

This woman gained comfort in her misery by thinking *great thoughts of Christ*. The Master had talked about the children's bread. "Now," she argued, "since You are the Master of the table of grace, I know that You are a generous housekeeper, and there is sure to be plenty of bread on Your table. There will be such an abundance for the children that there will be crumbs to throw on the floor for the dogs, and the children will fare none the worse because the dogs are fed." She thought Him one who kept so fine a table that all that she needed would only be a crumb in comparison; yet remember, what she wanted was to have the devil cast out of her daughter. It was a very great thing to her, but she had such a high esteem of Christ that she said, "It is nothing to Him; it is but a crumb for Christ to give." This is the royal road to comfort. Great thoughts of your sin alone will drive you to despair; but great thoughts of Christ will guide you into the haven of peace. "My sins are many, but oh, it is nothing to Jesus to take them all away. The weight of my guilt presses me down as a giant's foot would crush a worm, but it is no more than a grain of dust to Him, because He has already borne its curse in His own body on the tree. It will be only a small thing for Him to give me full remission, although it will be an infinite blessing for me to receive it." The woman opens her needy soul very wide, expecting great things of Jesus, and He fills it with His love. Dear reader, do the same. *She won the victory by believing in Him.* Her case is an instance of prevailing faith; and if we would conquer like her, we must imitate her tactics.

## *As a pleasing aroma I will accept you.*

EZEKIEL 20:41

The merits of our great Redeemer are as a pleasing aroma to the Most High. Whether we speak of the active or passive righteousness of Christ, there is an equal fragrance. There was a pleasing aroma in His active life by which He honored the law of God and made every precept to glitter like a precious jewel in the pure setting of His own person. Such, too, was His passive obedience, when He endured with unmurmuring submission hunger and thirst, cold and nakedness, and at the end sweat as it were great drops of blood in Gethsemane. He gave His back to the smiters and His cheeks to them that plucked out the hair and was fastened to the cruel wood, that He might suffer the wrath of God in our behalf. These two things are sweet before the Most High; and for the sake of His doing and His dying, His substitutionary sufferings and His vicarious obedience, the Lord our God accepts us. What a preciousness there must be in Him to overcome our lack of preciousness! What a pleasing aroma to put away our nasty odor! What a cleansing power in His blood to take away sin such as ours! And what glory in His righteousness to make such unacceptable creatures to be accepted in the Beloved! Consider, believer, how sure and unchanging is our acceptance, since it is *in Him*! Take care that you never doubt your acceptance in Jesus. You cannot be accepted without Christ; but when you have received His merit, you cannot be unaccepted. Despite all your doubts and fears and sins, Jehovah's gracious eye never looks upon you in anger; though He sees sin in you, in yourself, yet when He looks at you through Christ, He sees no sin. You are always accepted in Christ, are always blessed and dear to the Father's heart. Therefore lift up a song, and as you see the smoking incense of the Savior's merit coming up this evening before the sapphire throne, let the incense of your praise go up also.

## *I called him, but he gave no answer.*

SONG OF SOLOMON 5:6

Prayer sometimes lingers, like a petitioner at the gate, until the King comes with the blessings that she seeks. The Lord, when He has given great faith, has been known to test it by long delays. He has allowed His servants' voices to echo in their ears as if the heavens were brass. They have knocked at the golden gate, but it has remained immovable, as though it were rusted upon its hinges. Like Jeremiah, they have cried, "You have wrapped yourself with a cloud so that no prayer can pass through."[1] In this manner true saints have continued to wait patiently without a reply, not because their prayers were not strong, nor because they were unaccepted, but because it so pleased Him who is a Sovereign and who gives according to His own pleasure. If it pleases Him to test our patience, shall He not do as He wishes with His children? Beggars must not be choosers either as to time, place, or form. But we must be careful not to take delays in prayer for denials. God's postdated checks will be punctually honored; we must not allow Satan to shake our confidence in the God of truth by pointing to our unanswered prayers. Unanswered petitions are not unheard. God keeps a file for our prayers—they are not blown away by the wind; they are treasured in the King's archives. This is a registry in the court of heaven in which every prayer is recorded. Struggling believer, your Lord has as it were a tear-bottle in which the costly drops of your sacred grief are put away, and a book in which your holy groanings are numbered. By-and-by your case shall prevail. Can you not be content to wait a little? Will the Lord's time not be better than yours? By-and-by He will comfortably appear, to your soul's joy, and will cause you to put away the sackcloth and ashes of long waiting and put on the scarlet and fine linen of full fruition.

[1]Lamentations 3:44

### Let us test and examine our ways,
### and return to the LORD!

LAMENTATIONS 3:40

The wife who fondly loves her absent husband longs for his return; a long protracted separation from him is a semi-death to her spirit. And so it is with souls who love the Savior much; they need to see His face; they cannot bear that He should be away, thus depriving them of communion with Him. A reproaching glance, an uplifted finger will be grievous to loving children who fear to offend their tender father and are only happy in his smile. Beloved, it was so once this way with you. A text of Scripture, a threatening, a touch of the rod of affliction, and you went to your Father's feet, crying, "Let me know why you contend against me." Is that still the case? Or are you content to follow Jesus from a distance? Can you contemplate broken communion with Christ without being alarmed? Can you bear to have your Beloved walking contrary to you, because you walk contrary to Him? Have your sins separated between you and your God, and is your heart at rest? Let me affectionately warn you, for it is a grievous thing when we can live contentedly without the present enjoyment of the Savior's face. *Let us work to feel what an evil thing this is*—little love to our own dying Savior, little joy in His company, little time with the Beloved! Hold a true Lent in your souls, while you sorrow over your hardness of heart. Do not stop at sorrow! Remember where you first received salvation. *Go at once to the cross*. There, and there only, can you get your spirit quickened. No matter how hard, how insensible, how dead we may have become, let us go again in all the rags and poverty and defilement of our natural condition. Let us clasp that cross, let us look into those languid eyes, let us bathe in that fountain filled with blood—this will bring back to us our first love; this will restore the simplicity of our faith and the tenderness of our heart.

**Then Rizpah the daughter of Aiah took sackcloth
and spread it for herself on the rock,
from the beginning of harvest until rain fell upon
them from the heavens. And she did not allow
the birds of the air to come upon them by day,
or the beasts of the field by night.**

2 SAMUEL 21:10

If the love of a woman to her slain sons could make her prolong her mournful vigil for so long a period, shall we grow tired of considering the sufferings of our blessed Lord? She drove away the birds of prey, and shall not we chase from our meditations those worldly and sinful thoughts that defile both our minds and the sacred themes upon which we are occupied? Be gone, you birds of evil wing! Leave the sacrifice alone! She bore the heat of summer, the night dews and the rains, unsheltered and alone. Sleep was chased from her weeping eyes: her heart was too full for slumber. Consider how she loved her children! Shall Rizpah endure while we quit at the first little inconvenience or trial? Are we such cowards that we cannot bear to suffer with our Lord? She chased away even the wild beasts with unusual courage, and will we not be ready to encounter every foe for Jesus' sake? Her children were slain by other hands than hers, and yet she wept and watched. What ought we to do who have by our sins cruci-fied our Lord? Our obligations are boundless; our love should be fervent and our repentance thorough. To watch with Jesus should be our business, to protect His honor our occupation, to abide by His cross our solace. Those ghastly corpses might well have frightened Rizpah, especially by night, but in our Lord, at whose cross we are sitting, there is nothing revolting but every-thing attractive. Never was living beauty so enchanting as a dying Savior. Jesus, we will watch with You still, and may You graciously unveil Yourself to us; then shall we not sit beneath sackcloth but in a royal pavilion.

### It is the time to seek the LORD.

HOSEA 10:12

The month of April is said to derive its name from the Latin verb *aperio*, which means to open, because all the buds and blossoms are now opening, and we have arrived at the gates of the flowery season. Reader, if you are not yet saved, may your heart, in keeping with the universal awakening of nature, be opened to receive the Lord. Every blossoming flower warns you that *it is time to seek the Lord*; do not be out of tune with nature, but let your heart bud and bloom with holy desires. If you tell me that the warm blood of youth leaps in your veins, then I entreat you, give your vigor to the Lord. It was my unspeakable happiness to be called in early youth, and I am thankful to the Lord every day for that. Salvation is priceless, let it come when it may, but oh, an early salvation has a double value in it. Young men and women, since you may die before you reach your prime, *"It is the time to seek the LORD."* You who feel the first signs of decay, quicken your pace: That chest pain, that biopsy report, are warnings that you must not trifle with; with you it is definitely time to seek the Lord. Did I observe a little gray, a little thinning in your hair? Years are flying by, and death is drawing nearer by the day; let each return of spring arouse you to set your house in order. Dear reader, if you are now advanced in years, let me entreat and implore you to delay no longer. There is a day of grace for you now—be thankful for that—but it is a limited season and grows shorter every time the clock ticks. Here in the silence of your room, on this first night of another month, I speak to you as best I can by paper and ink, and from my inmost soul, as God's servant, I lay before you this warning, *"It is the time to seek the LORD."* Do not make light of this; it may be your last call from destruction, the final syllable from the lip of grace.

### He shall see his offspring; he shall prolong his days; the will of the LORD shall prosper in his hand.

ISAIAH 53:10

Ask God to fulfill this promise quickly, all you who love the Lord. It is easy work to pray when our desires are fixed and established on God's own promise. How can He who gave the word refuse to keep it? Immutable truth cannot demean itself by a lie, and eternal faithfulness cannot degrade itself by neglect. God must bless His Son—His covenant binds Him to it. The Spirit prompts us to ask for Jesus what God the Father decrees to give Him. Whenever you are praying for the kingdom of Christ, let your eyes behold the dawning of the blessed day that draws near, when the Crucified will receive His coronation in the place where men rejected Him. Take courage, you who prayerfully work for Christ with only scant success—it will not always be this way; better times are ahead. Your eyes cannot see the wonderful future: borrow the telescope of faith; wipe the misty breath of your doubts from the viewfinder; look through it and behold the coming glory. Reader, let us ask, *do you* make this your constant prayer? Remember that the same Christ who tells us to say, "Give us each day our daily bread," first gave us this petition, "Hallowed be your name; your kingdom come; your will be done in earth as it is in heaven." Do not let your prayers be all about your own sins, your own desires, your own imperfections, your own trials, but let them climb the starry ladder and get up to Christ Himself, and then as you draw near to the blood-sprinkled mercy-seat, offer this prayer continually: "Lord, extend the kingdom of Your dear Son." When you fervently present such a petition, it will elevate the spirit of all your devotions. Make sure that you prove the sincerity of your prayer by working to promote the Lord's glory.

### All we like sheep have gone astray;
### we have turned every one to his own way; and
### the LORD has laid on him the iniquity of us all.

ISAIAH 53:6

Here a confession of sin is shared by all the elect people of God. They have all fallen, and therefore, in one voice, from the first who entered heaven to the last who shall arrive they all say, "All we like sheep have gone astray." This confession is not only unanimous, it is also special and particular: "We have turned every one to his own way." All are sinful, but each individual faces his or her own peculiar sinfulness, which is not found in someone else. It is the mark of genuine repentance that while it naturally associates itself with other penitents, it also takes up a position of loneliness. "We have turned every one to his own way" is a confession that each individual had sinned against light peculiar to himself or sinned with an aggravation that he could not perceive in others. This confession is *unreserved*; there is not a word to detract from its force, nor a syllable by way of excuse. This confession bids farewell to every plea of self-justification. It is the declaration of those who are consciously guilty—guilty with aggravations, guilty without excuse: they stand with their weapons of rebellion broken in pieces and cry, "All we like sheep have gone astray; we have turned every one to his own way." Yet we hear no mournful wailings attending this confession of sin; for the next sentence makes it almost a song. "The LORD has laid on him the iniquity of us all." It is the most grievous sentence of the three, but it overflows with comfort. How strange that where misery was concentrated, mercy reigned; where sorrow reached her climax, weary souls find rest. The Savior bruised is the healing of bruised hearts. Consider how the humble confession gives way to assured confidence by simply gazing at Christ on the cross!

## Come, let us go up to the mountain of the LORD.

ISAIAH 2:3

It is exceedingly beneficial to our souls to rise above this present evil world to something nobler and better. The cares of this world and the deceitfulness of riches are apt to choke everything good within us, and we grow fretful, desponding, perhaps proud and carnal. It is good for us to cut down these thorns and briers, because heavenly seed sown among them is not likely to yield a harvest. Where will we find a better scythe with which to cut them down than communion with God and the things of the kingdom? There are places in the world where the lowlands are a breeding ground for sickness. Doctors will often suggest that their patients head for the mountains where they can breathe the clear, fresh air. Heeding such advice, the valley dwellers leave their homes among the marshes and the fever mists to inhale the bracing elements upon the hills. It is to such an exploit of climbing that I invite you this evening. May the Spirit of God assist us to leave the mists of fear and the fevers of anxiety and all the ills that gather in this valley of earth, and to ascend the mountains of anticipated joy and blessedness. May God the Holy Spirit cut the cords that keep us here below and enable us to climb! We are too often like chained eagles fastened to the perch, and even worse, unlike the eagle, we begin to love our chain and might even, if it came to the test, be loath to have it snapped. May God now grant us grace, if we cannot escape from the chain as to our flesh, yet to do so as to our spirits; and leaving the body, like a servant, at the foot of the hill, may our soul, like Abraham, reach the top of the mountain, so that we can enjoy communion with the Most High.

## *Humility comes before honor.*

PROVERBS 15:33

Humiliation of soul always brings *a positive blessing with it*. If we empty our hearts of self, God will fill them with His love. If we desire close communion with Christ, we should remember the word of the Lord: "This is the one to whom I will look: he who is humble and contrite in spirit and trembles at my word."[1] Stoop if you want to climb to heaven. Is it not said of Jesus, "He who descended is the one who also ascended"?[2] So must you. You must grow downwards, that you may grow upwards; for the sweetest fellowship with heaven will be enjoyed by humble souls and by them alone. God will deny no blessing to a thoroughly humbled spirit. "Blessed are the poor in spirit, for theirs is the kingdom of heaven,"[3] with all its riches and treasures. All of God's resources will be made available to the soul that is humble enough to be able to receive them without growing proud because of it. God blesses each of us up to the level and extent of what it is safe for Him to do. If you do not get a blessing, it is because it is not safe for you to have one. If our heavenly Father were to let your unhumbled spirit win a victory in His holy war, you would snatch the crown for yourself, and in the next battle you would fall a victim. He keeps you low for your own safety! When a man is sincerely humble and never tries to take the credit or the praise, there is scarcely any limit to what God will do for him. Humility makes us ready to be blessed by the God of all grace and equips us to deal efficiently with our fellows. True humility is a flower that will adorn any garden. This is a sauce that will season every dish of life and improve it in every case. Whether in prayer or praise, whether in work or suffering, the genuine salt of humility cannot be used in excess.

[1]Isaiah 66:2   [2]Ephesians 4:10   [3]Matthew 5:3

### *In the name of the LORD I cut them off!*

PSALM 118:12

Our Lord Jesus, by His death, did not purchase a right to just a part of us, but to all of us. He pondered in His passion our complete sanctification—spirit, soul, and body, that in every area He Himself might reign supreme without a rival. It is the business of the newborn nature that God has given to the regenerate to assert the rights of the Lord Jesus Christ. My soul, insofar as you are a child of God, you must conquer all the rest of yourself that remains unblessed; you must subdue all your powers and passions, and you must never be satisfied until He who is King by purchase also becomes King by gracious coronation and reigns in you supreme. Seeing, then, that sin has no right to any part of us, we are involved in good and lawful warfare when we seek, in the name of God, to drive it out. Since my body is a member of Christ, shall I tolerate subjection to the prince of darkness? My soul, Christ has suffered for your sins and redeemed you with His most precious blood; do not allow your memory to store up evil thoughts or your passions to be the occasion of sin. Do not allow your judgment to be perverted by error or your will to be led in chains of iniquity. No, my soul, you are Christ's, and sin has no right to you.

Be courageous concerning this, O Christian! Be not dispirited, as though your spiritual enemies could never be destroyed. You are able to overcome them—but not in your own strength—the weakest of them would be too much for you; but you can and shall overcome them through the blood of the Lamb. If you wonder how to dispossess them since they are greater and mightier than you, go to the strong for strength, wait humbly upon God, and the mighty God of Jacob will surely come to your rescue, and you will sing of victory through His grace.

### *Deliver me from bloodguiltiness, O God, O God of my salvation, and my tongue will sing aloud of your righteousness.*

PSALM 51:14

In this *solemn confession*, it is helpful to observe that David plainly names his sin. He does not call it manslaughter or speak of it as an imprudence by which an unfortunate accident occurred to a worthy man, but he calls it by its true name, "bloodguiltiness." He did not actually kill the husband of Bathsheba; but still it was planned in David's heart that Uriah should die, and David was before the Lord responsible for his murder. Learn in confession to be honest with God. Do not give fair names to foul sins; call them what you will, they will smell no sweeter. What God sees them to be, that you should work to feel them to be; and with an honest, open heart acknowledge their real character. Observe that David was evidently oppressed with the heinousness of his sin. It is easy to use words, but it is difficult to feel their meaning. The fifty-first Psalm is the photograph of a contrite spirit. Let us seek to display the same brokenness of heart; because no matter how excellent our words may be, if our heart is not conscious of the hell-deservingness of sin, we cannot expect to find forgiveness.

Our text has in it *an earnest prayer*—it is addressed to the God of salvation. It is His prerogative to forgive; it is His very name and office to save those who seek His face. Better still, the text calls Him the God of my salvation. We bless His name, in that while we are still going to Him through Jesus' blood, we may rejoice in the God of our salvation.

The psalmist ends with *a commendable vow*: If God will deliver him he will sing—actually, he will "sing aloud." Who can mute their praise in light of such a mercy as this! But note the subject of the song—"*your righteousness.*" We must sing of the finished work of a precious Savior; and the one who knows this forgiving love the best will sing the loudest of us all.

## I will fear no evil, for you are with me.

PSALM 23:4

Consider how the Holy Spirit can make the Christian independent of outward circumstances. What a bright light may shine within us when it is really dark outside! How firm, how happy, how calm, how peaceful we may be when the world shakes, and the foundations of the earth are removed! Even death itself, with all its terrible influences, has no power to suspend the music of a Christian's heart, but instead makes that music sweeter, clearer, more heavenly, until the last kind act that death can do is allow the earthly song to melt into the heavenly chorus, the temporal joy into the eternal bliss! Let us have confidence, then, in the blessed Spirit's power to comfort us. Dear reader, are you facing poverty? Do not fear—the Holy Spirit can give you, in your need, a greater plenty than the rich have in their abundance. You never know what joys may be stored up for you in the cottage around which grace will plant the roses of contentment. Are you conscious of your physical frailty? Do you anticipate sleepless nights and painful days? Do not be sad! Your bed may become a throne to you. You cannot tell how every pain that shoots through your body may be a refining fire to consume your dross—a beam of glory to light up the secret parts of your soul. Is your eyesight failing? Jesus will be your light. Is your hearing deteriorating? Jesus' name will be your soul's best music, and His person your dear delight. Socrates used to say, "Philosophers can be happy without music," and Christians can be happier than philosophers when all outward causes of rejoicing are removed. In You, my God, my heart shall triumph, no matter my circumstances! By Your power, O blessed Spirit, my heart shall rejoice even though all things should fail me here below.

## *Your gentleness made me great.*

PSALM 18:35

These words are capable of being translated, "Your *goodness* made me great." David gratefully ascribed all his greatness not to his own goodness, but to the goodness of God. "Your *providence*" is another reading; and providence is nothing more than goodness in action. Goodness is the bud of which providence is the flower, or goodness is the seed of which providence is the harvest. Some render it, "Your *help*," which is just another word for providence, providence being the firm ally of the saints, aiding them in the service of their Lord. Or again, "Your *humility* made me great." "Your *condescension*" may perhaps serve as a comprehensive reading, combining all these ideas, including *humility*. God's making Himself little is the cause of our being made great. We are so little that if God should display His greatness without condescension, we would be trampled under His feet; but God, who must stoop to view the skies and bow to see what angels do, turns His eye yet lower and looks to the lowly and contrite and makes them great. There are still other translations. For example, the Septuagint reads, "Your *discipline*"—Your fatherly correction—"made me great," while another paraphrase reads, "Your *word* increased me." Still the idea is the same. David ascribes all his own greatness to the condescending goodness of his Father in heaven. May this attitude be echoed in our hearts this evening while we cast our crowns at Jesus' feet and cry, "Your gentleness made me great." How marvelous is our experience of God's gentleness! How gentle His corrections! How gentle His patience! How gentle His teachings! How gentle His invitations! Meditate upon this theme, believer. Let gratitude be awakened; let humility be deepened; let love be quickened before you fall asleep tonight.

### For this very night there stood before me an angel of the God to whom I belong.

ACTS 27:23

Storms and darkness, combined with imminent risk of shipwreck, had brought the crew of the vessel into a sorry predicament; only one man among them remained perfectly calm, and by his word the rest were reassured. Paul was the only man who had enough heart to say, "I urge you to take heart." There were veteran Roman soldiers on board, and brave sailors, but their poor Jewish prisoner had more spirit than all of them. He had a secret Friend who kept his courage up. The Lord Jesus sent a heavenly messenger to whisper words of comfort in Paul's ear, and as a result his face shone, and he spoke like a man at ease.

If we fear the Lord, we may look for His timely intervention when our case is at its worst. Angels are not kept from us by storms or hindered by darkness. Seraphs do not think it is beneath them to visit the poorest of the heavenly family. If angels' visits are few and far between at ordinary times, they will be frequent in our nights of tempest and storm. Friends may leave us when we are under pressure, but our awareness of the members of the angelic world will be far more apparent. Strengthened by loving words brought to us from the throne via Jacob's ladder, we will be able to do daring feats. Dear reader, are you facing an hour of distress? Then ask for particular help. Jesus is the angel of the covenant, and if you earnestly seek His presence, it will not be denied. The encouragement which that presence brings will be remembered by those who, like Paul, have had the angel of God standing by them in a night of storm, when anchors slipped and shipwreck threatened.

> O angel of my God, be near,
> Amid the darkness hush my fear;
> Loud roars the wild tempestuous sea,
> Thy presence, Lord, shall comfort me.

## *Consider my affliction and my trouble, and forgive all my sins.*

PSALM 25:18

It is good for us when prayers about our sorrows are linked with pleas concerning our sins—when, being under God's hand, we do not focus exclusively on our pain, but remember our sins against God. It is also good to take both sorrow and sin to the same place. It was to God that David carried his sorrow: It was to God that David confessed his sin. Notice, then, we must take our sorrows to God. Even your little sorrows you may cast upon God, for He counts the hairs of your head; and your great sorrows you may commit to Him, for He holds the ocean in the hollow of His hand. Go to Him, whatever your present trouble may be, and you will find Him able and willing to relieve you. *But we must take our sins to God too.* We must carry them to the cross, that the blood may fall upon them, to purge away their guilt and to destroy their defiling power.

The special lesson of the text is this:—*we are to go to the Lord with sorrows and with sins in the right spirit.* Note that all David asks concerning his sorrow is, "*Consider* my affliction and my trouble"; but the next petition is vastly more explicit, definite, decided, plain—"*Forgive* all my sins." Many sufferers would have reversed it: "Remove my affliction and my pain, and consider my sins." But David does not; he cries, "Lord, when it comes to my affliction and my pain, I will not dictate to Your wisdom. Lord, look at them—I will leave them to You. I would like to have my pain removed, but do as You will. But as for my sins, Lord, I know what needs to happen—I must have them forgiven; I cannot endure to live under their curse for a moment." A Christian counts sorrow lighter in the scale than sin; he can bear to have troubles continue, but he cannot bear the burden of his transgressions.

## . . . *the king's garden* . . .

NEHEMIAH 3:15

Mention of the king's garden by Nehemiah brings to mind the *paradise* that the King of kings prepared for Adam. Sin has utterly ruined that delightful dwelling and has driven out the children of men to till the ground, which yields thorns and thistles to them. My soul, remember the Fall, for it was your fall. Weep much because the Lord of love was so shamefully ill treated by the head of the human race, of which you are a member, as undeserving as any. Behold how dragons and demons dwell on this fair earth, which was once a garden of delights.

Look now at another King's garden, which the King waters with His bloody sweat—*Gethsemane*, whose bitter herbs are far sweeter to renewed souls than the luscious fruits of Eden. In Gethsemane the mischief of the serpent in the first garden was undone: There the curse was lifted from earth and borne by the woman's promised seed. My soul, learn to ponder Christ's agony and passion; visit the garden of the olive-press, and view your great Redeemer rescuing you from your lost condition. This is the garden of gardens; indeed, here the soul may see the guilt of sin and the power of love, two sights that surpass all others.

Is there no other King's garden? Yes, *my heart*, or should be. How do the flowers flourish? Do any choice fruits appear? Does the King walk there and rest in the arbor of my spirit? Let me ensure that the plants are trimmed and watered, and the mischievous foxes hunted out. Come, Lord, and let the heavenly wind blow at Your coming, that the spices of Your garden may cast their fragrance everywhere. I must not forget the King's garden of *the church*. O Lord, send prosperity to it. Rebuild her walls, nourish her plants, ripen her fruits, and from the huge wilderness reclaim the wasteland and make of it a King's garden.

## He shall lay his hand on the head of the burnt offering, and it shall be accepted for him to make atonement for him.

LEVITICUS 1:4

Our Lord's being "made . . . sin"[1] for us is pictured here by the very significant transfer of sin to the bullock, which was done by the elders of the people. The laying of the hand was not a mere touch of contact, for in some other places of Scripture the original word has the meaning of leaning heavily, as in the expression, "Your wrath lies heavy upon me" (Psalm 88:7). Surely this is the very essence and nature of faith, which not only brings us into contact with the great Substitute, but also teaches us to lean upon Him with all the burden of our guilt. Jehovah made all the offenses of His covenant people rest upon the Substitute, and each one of the chosen is brought personally to confirm this solemn covenant act, when by grace he is enabled by faith to lay his hand upon the head of the Lamb that was slain before the foundation of the world. Believer, do you remember that wonderful day when you first realized pardon through Jesus the sin-bearer? Can you make a glad confession and join with the writer in saying, "My soul recalls the day of deliverance with delight. Burdened with guilt and full of fears, I saw my Savior as my Substitute, and I laid my hand upon Him—timidly at first, but courage grew and confidence was confirmed until I leaned my soul entirely upon Him. And now it is my unceasing joy to know that my sins are no longer imputed to me but are laid on Him. Like the debts of the wounded traveler, Jesus, like the good Samaritan, has said of all my future sinfulness, 'Set that to My account.'" Blessed discovery! Eternal solace of a grateful heart!

*My numerous sins transferr'd to Him,*
*Shall never more be found,*
*Lost in His blood's atoning stream,*
*Where every crime is drown'd!*

[1] 2 Corinthians 5:21

## Tell the righteous that it shall be well with them.

ISAIAH 3:10

*It is well with the righteous* ALWAYS. If it had said, "Tell the righteous that it is well with them in their prosperity," we would be thankful for so great a blessing, for prosperity is an hour of peril. It is a gift from heaven to be safe from its snares. If it had read, "It is well with them when under persecution," we would be thankful for such a comforting assurance, for persecution is hard to bear; but when no time is mentioned, all time is included. God's shalls must always be understood in their largest sense. From the beginning of the year to the end of the year, from the first gathering of evening shadows until a new day dawns, in all conditions and under all circumstances, it will be well with the righteous. It is so well with him that we could not imagine it to be better, for he is *well fed*—he feeds upon the flesh and blood of Jesus; he is *well clothed*—he wears the imputed righteousness of Christ; he is *well housed*—he dwells in God; he is *well married*—his soul is knit in bonds of marriage to Christ; he is *well provided for*—for the Lord is his Shepherd; he is well endowed—for heaven is his inheritance. It is well with the righteous—*well upon divine authority*; the mouth of God speaks the comforting assurance. O beloved, if God declares that all is well, ten thousand devils may declare it to be ill, but we may laugh them all to scorn. Blessed be God for a faith that enables us to believe God when the creatures contradict Him. It is, says the Word, at all times well with you, righteous one; then, beloved, if you cannot see it, let God's Word assure you; believe it on divine authority with more confidence than if your eyes and your feelings told it to you. Those God blesses are blessed indeed, and what His lip declares is truth most sure and steadfast.

## *Be their shepherd and carry them forever.*

PSALM 28:9

*G*od's people need to be carried. They are very heavy by nature. They have no wings, or if they have, they are like the dove of old that lay among the pots; and they need divine grace to make them rise up on wings covered with silver and with feathers of yellow gold. By nature sparks fly upward, but the sinful souls of men fall downward. O Lord, "carry them forever"! David himself said, "To you, O LORD, I lift up my soul,"[1] and here he feels the necessity that other men's souls should be lifted up as well as his own. When you ask for this blessing, do not forget to seek it for others also. There are three ways in which God's people require to be carried or lifted up. *They require to be lifted up in character.* Lift them up, Lord; do not allow Your people to be like the rest of the world! The world lies in the wicked one; lift them out of it! The world's people are looking for silver and gold, seeking their own pleasures and the gratification of their lusts; but, Lord, carry Your people up beyond all this; keep them from being "muck-rakers," as John Bunyan calls the man who was always scraping for gold! Set their hearts upon their risen Lord and the heavenly heritage! Moreover, *believers need to be carried in conflict.* In the battle, if they seem to fall, Lord, be pleased to give them the victory. If the foot of the enemy is upon their necks for a moment, help them to grasp the sword of the Spirit and eventually to win the battle. Lord, lift up Your children's spirits in the day of conflict; do not let them sit in the dust, mourning forever. Do not allow the adversary to disturb their peace and make them fret; but if they have been, like Hannah, persecuted, let them sing of the mercy of a delivering God.

We may also ask our Lord to *carry them at the last*! Lift them up by taking them home; carry their bodies from the tomb, and raise their souls to Your eternal kingdom in glory.

[1]Psalm 25:1

## So his hands were steady until the going down of the sun.

EXODUS 17:12

The prayer of Moses was so mighty that everything depended upon it. The petitions of Moses disconcerted the enemy more than the fighting of Joshua. Yet both were needed. In the soul's conflict, force and fervor, decision and devotion, valor and vehemence must join their forces, and all will be well. You must wrestle with your sin, but the major part of the wrestling must be done alone in private with God. Prayer like Moses' holds up the token of the covenant before the Lord. The rod was the emblem of God's working with Moses, the symbol of God's government in Israel. Learn, praying saint, to hold up the promise and the oath of God before Him. The Lord cannot deny His own declarations. Hold up the rod of promise, and have what you seek.

Moses grew tired, and then his friends assisted him. Whenever your prayer loses vigor, let faith support one hand, and let holy hope lift up the other, and prayer seating itself upon the stone of Israel, the rock of our salvation, will persevere and prevail. Beware of growing faint in your devotion. If Moses felt it, who can escape? It is far easier to fight with sin in public than to pray against it in private. It has been observed that while Joshua never grew weary in the fighting, Moses did grow weary in the praying; the more spiritual an exercise, the more difficult it is for flesh and blood to maintain it. Let us cry, then, for special strength, and may the Spirit of God, who helps our weaknesses as He helped Moses, enable us like him to continue with our steady hands "until the going down of the sun," until the evening of life is over, until we shall come to the rising of a better sun in the land where prayer is swallowed up in praise.

## *We wish to see Jesus.*

JOHN 12:21

The constant cry of the world is, "Who will show us any good?" They seek satisfaction in earthly comforts, enjoyments, and riches. But the quickened sinner knows of only one good. "I wish I knew where I might find *Him*!" When he is truly awakened to feel his guilt, if you could lay a fortune before him he would say, "Take it away: I want to find Him." It is a blessed thing for a man when he has brought his desires into focus, so that they all center in one object. When he has fifty different desires, his heart resembles a stagnant pool spreading out into a marsh, breeding disease; but when all his desires are channeled in one direction, his heart becomes like a river of pure water, running swiftly to fertilize the fields. Happy is he who has one desire, if that one desire is set on Christ, though it may not yet have been realized. When a soul desires Jesus, it is a sure indication of divine work within. Such a man will never be content with mere externals. He will say, "I want Christ; I *must* have Him—mere ordinances are of no use to me. I want *Himself*; do not offer me these; you offer me the empty pitcher, while I am dying of thirst; give me water or I die. Jesus is my soul's desire. I wish to see Jesus!"

Is this your condition, my reader, at this moment? Have you only one desire, and is that for Christ? Then you are not far from the kingdom of heaven. Have you only one wish in your heart, and that is that you may be washed from all your sins in Jesus' blood? Can you really say, "I would give all I have to be a Christian. I would give up everything I have and hope for, in order to know that I have an interest in Christ"? Then, despite all your fears, be encouraged—the Lord loves you, and you will come out into daylight soon and rejoice in the liberty with which Christ makes you free.

*April 18*

## But you said, I will surely do you good.

GENESIS 32:12

When Jacob was on the other side of the brook Jabbok, and Esau was coming with armed men, Jacob earnestly sought God's protection, and the ground of his appeal was this: "But you said, I will surely do you good." What force is in that plea! He was holding God to His word—"You said." The attribute of God's faithfulness is a splendid horn of the altar to lay hold upon; but the promise, which contains the attribute and something more, is mightier still—"You said, I will surely do you good." Would *He* say it and then not do it? "Let God be true though everyone were a liar."[1] Will *He* not be true? Will *He* not keep His word? Will not every word that comes out of His lips stand fast and be fulfilled? Solomon, at the opening of the temple, used this same mighty plea. He pleaded with God to remember the word that He had spoken to his father David and to bless that place. When a man gives a promissory note, his honor is engaged; he signs his name, and he must honor it when the due time comes or else he loses credit. It shall never be said that God dishonors His bills. The credit of the Most High was never impeached, and never shall be. He is punctual to the second: He is never before His time, but He is never behind it. Search God's Word through, and compare it with the experience of God's people, and you will find the two tally from beginning to end. Many an ancient patriarch has said with Joshua, "Not one word has failed of all the good things that the LORD your God promised concerning you. All have come to pass."[2] If you have a divine promise, you need not plead it with an "if"; you may urge it with certainty. The Lord meant to fulfill the promise or He would not have given it. God does not give His words merely to keep us quiet and to keep us hopeful for a while with the intention of putting us off in the end; but when He speaks, it is because He means to do as He has said.

[1]Romans 3:4  [2]Joshua 23:14

### *The words of the Amen.*

REVELATION 3:14

The word *Amen* solemnly confirms what went before, and Jesus is the great Confirmer; immutable forever is "the Amen" in all *His promises. Sinner*, I would comfort you with this reflection. Jesus Christ said, "Come to me, all who labor and are heavy laden, and I will give you rest."[1] If you come to Him, He will say "Amen" in your soul; His promise shall be true to you. He said in the days of His flesh, "A bruised reed he will not break."[2] Poor, broken, bruised heart, if you come to Him, He will say "Amen" to you, and it will be true in your soul as in hundreds of cases in years gone by. *Christian*, isn't this very comforting to you also, that there is not a word that has come from the Savior's lips that He has ever retracted? The words of Jesus will stand when heaven and earth pass away. If you get ahold of but half a promise, you will find it true. Watch out for those who ignore the promises and so miss much of the comfort of God's Word.

Jesus is Yes and Amen in all *His offices*. He was a Priest to pardon and cleanse once; He is Amen as Priest still. He was a King to rule and reign for His people and to defend them with His mighty arm; He is an Amen King, the same still. He was a Prophet of old, to foretell good things to come; His words remain trustworthy and true—He is an Amen Prophet. He is Amen as to the merit of His blood; He is Amen as to His righteousness. That sacred robe will remain most fair and glorious when nature shall decay. He is Amen in every single title that He bears; your Husband, never seeking a divorce; your Friend, sticking closer than a brother; your Shepherd, with you in death's dark vale; your Help and your Deliverer; your Refuge and your Strong Tower; the Vessel of your strength, your confidence, your joy, your all in all, and your Yes and Amen in everything.

[1]Matthew 11:28  [2]Matthew 12:20

### *Fight the LORD's battles.*

1 SAMUEL 18:17

The Christian is involved in a continual war, with Jesus Christ as the Captain of their salvation. He has said, "Behold, I am with you always, to the end of the age."[1] Listen to the battle cries! Now let the people of God stand firm in their ranks, and let no man's heart fail him. We may feel in these days that we are losing the battle and unless the Lord Jesus shall lift His sword we do not know what may become of the church of God in our time; but let us be courageous and bold. Seldom has there been a time like this as biblical Christianity trembles on the brink of capitulation to pluralism and empty religious routine. We are in great need of a bold voice and a strong hand to preach and publish the Gospel for which martyrs bled and confessors died. The Savior is, by His Spirit, still on earth; let this encourage us. He is always ever in the middle of the fight, and therefore the outcome of the battle is not in doubt. And as the conflict rages, what a deep satisfaction it is to know that the Lord Jesus, in His office as our great Intercessor, is prevalently pleading for His people! Turn your anxious gaze from the battle below, where, enshrouded in smoke, the faithful fight in garments rolled in blood. And lift your eyes above where the Savior lives and pleads, for while He intercedes, the cause of God is safe. Let us fight as if it all depended upon us, but let us look up and know that it all depends upon Him.

On the basis of our Savior's atoning sacrifice and in the strength of the Holy Spirit's power, we charge you who love Jesus to fight bravely in this holy war, for truth and righteousness, for the kingdom and the crown. Onward! The battle is not yours but God's, and you will yet hear Him say, "Well done, brave warrior, well done!"

[1]Matthew 28:20

## . . . *who is at the right hand of God.*

ROMANS 8:34

He who was once despised and rejected by men now occupies the honorable position of a beloved and honored Son. The right hand of God is *the place of majesty and favor*. Our Lord Jesus is His people's representative. When He died for them, they had rest; when He rose again for them, they had liberty; when He sat down at His Father's right hand, they had favor and honor and dignity. The raising and elevation of Christ is the elevation, the acceptance, and the glorifying of all His people, for He is their head and representative. This sitting at the right hand of God, then, is to be viewed as the reception of the Representative and therefore the acceptance of our souls. Believer, this is why you are free from condemnation. "Who is he that condemneth?" [KJV]. Who will condemn those men who are in Jesus at the right hand of God?

The right hand is *the place of power*. Christ at the right hand of God has all the power in heaven and on earth. Who will fight against the people who have such power vested in their Captain? My soul, what can destroy you if Omnipotence is your helper? If the protection of the Almighty covers you, what sword can harm you? Be sure of this: If Jesus is your all-prevailing King and has trampled your enemies beneath His feet, if sin, death, and hell are all defeated by Him, and you are represented in Him, there exists no possibility of your being destroyed.

> *Jesu's tremendous name*
> *Puts all our foes to flight;*
> *Jesus, the meek, the angry Lamb,*
> *A Lion is in fight.*

> *By all hell's host withstood;*
> *We all hell's host o'erthrow;*
> *And conquering them, through Jesu's blood*
> *We still to conquer go.*

### *You will not fear the terror of the night.*

PSALM 91:5

What is this "terror"? It may be the cry of fire or the noise of thieves or intrigued appearances or the shriek of sudden sickness or death. We live in the world of death and sorrow; we may anticipate facing ills and difficulties during the night as well as in the glare of the noonday sun. This should not alarm us, for whatever the terror may be, the promise is that the believer shall not be afraid. Why should he be? Let us put this more closely— why should *we*? God our Father is here, and will be with us all through the lonely hours. He is an almighty Watcher, a sleepless Guardian, a faithful Friend. Nothing can happen without His direction, for even hell itself is under His control. Darkness is not dark to Him. He has promised to be a wall of fire around His people—and who can break through such a barrier? Unbelievers may well be afraid, for they have an angry God above them, a guilty conscience within them, and a yawning hell beneath them. But we who rest in Jesus are saved from all these by His rich mercy. If we give way to foolish fear, we will dishonor our testimony and lead others to doubt the reality of godliness. We ought to be afraid of being afraid, in case we should grieve the Holy Spirit by foolish distrust. Down, then, you dismal forebodings and groundless apprehensions—God has not forgotten to be gracious, nor held back His tender mercies. It may be night in the soul, but there need be no terror, for the God of love does not change. Children of light may walk in darkness, but they are not therefore cast away. No, they are now enabled to prove their adoption by trusting in their heavenly Father in a way that hypocrites cannot do.

> *Though the night be dark and dreary,*
> *Darkness cannot hide from Thee;*
> *You are He, who, never weary,*
> *Watchest where Your people be.*

*And between the throne and the four living creatures and among the elders I saw a Lamb standing, as though it had been slain.*

REVELATION 5:6

Why should our exalted Lord appear in glory with His wounds? The wounds of Jesus are His glories, His jewels, His sacred ornaments. To the eye of the believer, Jesus is altogether lovely. We see Him as the lily of matchless purity, and as the rose crimsoned with His own blood. We behold the beauty of Christ in all His earthly pilgrimage, but there never was such matchless beauty as when He hung upon the cross. There we saw all His beauties in perfection, all His attributes developed, all His love drawn out, all His character expressed. Beloved, the wounds of Jesus are far fairer in our eyes than all the splendor and pomp of kings. The thorny crown is more than an imperial diadem. It is true that He no longer bears the scepter of reed, but there was even in that ignominy a glory that never flashed from a scepter of gold. Jesus wears the appearance of a slain Lamb as His royal dress in which He wooed our souls and redeemed them by His complete atonement. And these are not only the ornaments of Christ: They are the trophies of His love and of His victory. He has divided the spoil with the strong. He has redeemed for Himself a great multitude that no one can count, and these scars are the memorials of the fight. If Christ loves to retain the thought of His sufferings for His people, then *how precious should his wounds be to us!*

*Behold how every wound of His*
*A precious balm distils,*
*Which heals the scars that sin had made,*
*And cures all mortal ills.*

*Those wounds are mouths that preach His grace,*
*The ensigns of His love;*
*The seals of our expected bliss*
*In paradise above.*

> ***The flowers appear on the earth, the time of
> singing has come, and the voice of the turtledove
> is heard in our land.***
>
> SONG OF SOLOMON 2:12

The season of spring is welcome in its freshness. The long and dreary winter helps us to appreciate spring's genial warmth, and its promise of summer enhances its present delights. After periods of spiritual depression, it is delightful to see again the light of the Sun of Righteousness. Our slumbering graces rise from their lethargy, like the crocus and the daffodil from their beds of earth; and our heart is made glad with delicious notes of gratitude, far more tuneful than the warbling of birds. The comforting assurance of peace, which is infinitely more delightful than the turtledove's cooing, is heard within the soul. This is the time for the soul to seek communion with her Beloved; now she must rise from her natural sordidness and come away from her old associations. If we do not hoist the sail when the breeze is favorable, we make a grave mistake: Times of refreshing should never be allowed to pass us by. When Jesus Himself visits us in tenderness and entreats us to arise, can we be so ungrateful as to refuse His request? He has risen so that He may draw us after Him. He, by His Holy Spirit, has revived us so that we may in newness of life ascend to the heavenlies and enjoy fellowship with Him. We bid farewell to the coldness and indifference of a spiritual winter when the Lord creates a spring within. Then our sap flows with vigor, and our branches blossom with high resolve. O Lord, if it is not springtime in my chilly heart, I pray You make it so, for I am tired of living at a distance from You. When will You bring this long and dreary winter to an end? Come, Holy Spirit, and renew my soul! Quicken me, restore me, and have mercy on me! This very night I earnestly implore you, Lord, to take pity upon Your servant and send me a happy revival of spiritual life!

### *If anyone hears my voice and opens the door,*
### *I will come in to him.*

REVELATION 3:20

What is your desire this evening? Is it focused on heavenly things? Do you long to enjoy the high doctrine of eternal love? Do you desire liberty in very close communion with God? Do you aspire to know the heights and depths and lengths and breadths of His love? Then you must draw near to Jesus; you must get a clear sight of Him in His preciousness and completeness: you must view Him in His work—in His role as prophet, friend, and king—and in His person. He who understands Christ, receives an anointing from the Holy One, by which He knows all things. Christ is the great master-key of all the chambers of God: There is no treasure-house of God that will not open and yield up all its wealth to the soul that lives near to Jesus. Are you saying, "I wish that He would live in my heart and make it His dwelling-place forever"? Open the door, beloved, and He will come into your soul. He has been knocking continually in order that you and He may break bread together. *He eats with you* because you provide the house or the heart, and *you with Him* because He brings the meal. He could not eat with you if it were not in your heart, you finding the house; nor could you eat with Him, for you would have an empty table if He did not bring the food with Him. Fling wide, then, the portals of your soul. He will come with that love that you long to feel; He will come with that joy into which you cannot work your poor depressed spirit; He will bring the peace that now you do not have; He will come with His flagons of wine and sweet apples of love and will cheer you until you have no other sickness but that of overpowering, divine love. Only open the door to Him, drive out His enemies, give Him the keys of your heart, and He will live there forever. What wondrous love that brings such a guest to dwell in such a heart!

## *Blessed is the one who stays awake.*

REVELATION 16:15

I die every day,"[1] said the apostle. This was the life of the early Christians; they went everywhere with their lives in their hands. We are not at this time being called to pass through the same fearful persecutions: if we were, the Lord would give us grace to bear the test. But the tests of Christian life, at the present moment, though outwardly not so terrible, are still more likely to overcome us than even those of the fiery age. We have to bear the sneer of the world—that is small; its flatteries, its soft words, its oily speeches, its fawning, its hypocrisy are far worse. Our danger is that we might grow rich and become proud; we might give ourselves up to the fashions of this present evil world and lose our faith. Or if wealth does not test us, worldly care is quite as mischievous. If we cannot be torn in pieces by the roaring lion, we may be hugged to death by the bear. The devil cares very little which it is, as long as he destroys our love for Christ and our confidence in Him. I am afraid that the Christian church is far more likely to lose her integrity in these soft and easy days than in those rougher times. We must stay awake now, for we are crossing enchanted ground and are most likely to fall asleep to our own ruin, unless our faith in Jesus is a reality and our love for Jesus an ardent flame. Many in these days of easy-believism are likely to prove to be tares, and not wheat; hypocrites with attractive masks on their faces, but not the true-born children of the living God. Christian, do not think that these are times in which you can dispense with watchfulness or with holy ardor; you need these things more than ever, and may God the eternal Spirit display His omnipotence in you, that you may be able to say, in all these softer things as well as in the rougher, "We are more than conquerors through him who loved us."[2]

[1] 1 Corinthians 15:31  [2] Romans 8:37

## The LORD is king forever and ever.

PSALM 10:16

Jesus Christ is not a tyrant claiming *divine right*, but He is really and truly the Lord's anointed! "For in him all the fullness of God was pleased to dwell."[1] God has given to Him all power and all authority. As the Son of man, He is now head over all things in His church, and He reigns over heaven and earth and hell with the keys of life and death at His belt. Certain princes have been glad to call themselves kings by the *popular will*, and certainly our Lord Jesus Christ is such in His church. If it could be put to the vote whether He should be King in the church, every believing heart would crown Him. We ought to crown Him more gloriously than we do! We would regard no expense too great if we could glorify Christ. Suffering would be pleasure, and loss would be gain, if through that we could surround His brow with brighter crowns and make Him more glorious in the eyes of men and angels. Yes, He shall reign. Long live the King! All hail to You, King Jesus! Go on, you virgin souls who love your Lord. Bow at His feet; cover His path with the lilies of your love and the roses of your gratitude: "Bring forth the royal diadem, and crown Him Lord of all." Our Lord Jesus is King in Zion by *right of conquest*: He has taken the hearts of His people by storm and has defeated their enemies who held them in cruel bondage. In the Red Sea of His own blood, our Redeemer has drowned the Pharaoh of our sins: Shall He not be Lord and King? He has delivered us from sin's dominion and from the heavy curse of the law: Shall not the Liberator be crowned? We are His portion, whom He has taken out of the hand of the enemy with His sword and with His bow: Who will snatch His conquest from His hand? All hail, King Jesus! We gladly own Your gentle sway! Rule in our hearts forever, You lovely Prince of Peace.

[1]Colossians 1:19

*April 28*

## All the house of Israel have a hard forehead and a stubborn heart.

EZEKIEL 3:7

Are there no exceptions? No, not one. Even God's chosen are described in this way. If the best are so bad, then what must the worst be like? Come, my heart, consider to what extent you share in this universal accusation; as you think, prepare to be ashamed of those things of which you are guilty. The first charge is *impudence*, or hardness of forehead, an absence of holy shame, an unholy boldness in evil. Before my conversion, I could sin and feel no regret, hear of my guilt and remain unhumbled, and even confess my iniquity without any accompanying humiliation. When a sinner goes to God's house and pretends to pray to Him and praise Him, he displays a brazen-facedness of the worst kind! Sadly, since the day of my new birth I have doubted my Lord to His face, murmured unblushingly in His presence, worshiped Him in a slovenly manner, and sinned without bewailing myself on account of it. If my forehead were not like a diamond, harder than flint, I would display more holy fear and a far deeper contrition of spirit. Woe is me, for I am one of the impudent house of Israel. The second charge is *hard-heartedness*, and I dare not attempt to plead innocent here. Once I had nothing but a heart of stone, and although through grace I now have a new and fleshy heart, much of my former stubbornness remains. I am not affected by the death of Jesus as I ought to be; neither am I moved as I should be by the lostness of my fellowmen, the wickedness of the times, the chastisement of my heavenly Father, and my own failures. O that my heart would melt at the recital of my Savior's sufferings and death. Would to God I were rid of this dreadful burden within me, this hateful body of death. Blessed be the name of the Lord, the disease is not incurable; the Savior's precious blood is the universal remedy, and it will effectually soften me, even me, until my heart melts as wax before the fire.

### *The LORD takes pleasure in his people.*

PSALM 149:4

How comprehensive is the love of Jesus! There is no part of His people's interests that He does not consider, and there is nothing that concerns their welfare that is not important to Him. He doesn't merely think of you, believer, as an immortal being, but as a mortal being too. Do not deny it or doubt it: "Even the hairs of your head are all numbered."[1] "The steps of a man are established by the LORD, when he delights in his way."[2] It would be sad for us if this covering of love did not tackle all our concerns, for what mischief might be done to us in that part of our lives that did not come under our gracious Lord's protection! Believer, rest assured that the heart of Jesus cares about your smallest concerns. The breadth of His tender love is such that you may turn to Him in every case; for in all your afflictions He is afflicted, and just like a father cares for his children, so He cares for you. The smallest interests of all His saints are all borne upon the heart of the Son of God. And what a heart He has, which does not merely understand the nature of His people but also comprehends their diverse and innumerable concerns. Do you think, Christian, that you can measure the love of Christ? Consider what His love has brought you—justification, adoption, sanctification, eternal life! The riches of His goodness are unsearchable; you will never be able to convey them or even conceive them. Oh, the breadth of the love of Christ! Shall such a love as this have only half our hearts? Shall it have a cold love in return? Shall Jesus' marvelous loving-kindness and tender care be met with only faint response and delayed acknowledgment? My soul, tune your harp to a glad song of thanksgiving! Go to your rest rejoicing, for you are not a desolate wanderer but a beloved child, watched over, cared for, supplied, and defended by your Lord.

[1]Matthew 10:30  [2]Psalm 37:23

## *How precious to me are your thoughts,*
## *O God!*

PSALM 139:17

Divine omniscience provides no comfort to the ungodly mind, but to the child of God it overflows with consolation. God is always thinking about us, never turns His mind from us, always has us before His eyes; and this is precisely how we would want it, because it would be dreadful to exist for a moment outside the observation of our heavenly Father. His thoughts are always tender, loving, wise, prudent, far-reaching, and they bring countless benefits to us: It is consequently a supreme delight to remember them. The Lord always thought about His people: hence their election and the covenant of grace by which their salvation is secured. He will always think upon them: hence their final perseverance by which they shall be brought safely to their final rest. In all our wanderings the watchful glance of the Eternal Watcher is constantly fixed upon us—we never roam beyond the Shepherd's eye. In our sorrows He observes us incessantly, and not a painful emotion escapes Him; in our toils He notices all our weariness, and He writes all the struggles of His faithful ones in His book. These thoughts of the Lord encompass us in all our paths and penetrate the innermost region of our being. Not a nerve or tissue, valve or vessel of our bodily frame is uncared for; all the details of our little world are thought upon by the great God.

Dear reader, is this precious to you? Then hold to it. Do not be led astray by those philosophical fools who preach an impersonal God and talk of self-existent, self-governing matter. The Lord lives and thinks upon us; this is a far too precious truth for us to be easily robbed of it. To be noticed by a nobleman is valued so highly that he who has it counts his fortune made; but how much greater is it to be thought of by the King of kings! If the Lord thinks upon us, all is well, and we may rejoice evermore.

## *I am a rose of Sharon.*

SONG OF SOLOMON 2:1

Whatever beauty there may be in the material world, Jesus Christ possesses all of that in the spiritual world to the nth degree. Among flowers the rose is regarded as the sweetest, but Jesus is infinitely more beautiful in the garden of the soul than a rose in the gardens of earth. He takes the first place as the fairest among ten thousand. He is the sun, and all others are the stars; the heavens and the day are dark in comparison with Him, *for the King in His beauty transcends all.* "I am a rose of *Sharon.*" This was the best and rarest of roses. Jesus simply is not "a rose"; He is "a rose of Sharon," just as He calls His righteousness "gold," and then adds, "the gold of Ophir"[1]—the best of the best. He is positively lovely, and superlatively the loveliest. *There is variety in His beauty.* The rose is delightful to the eye, and its scent is pleasant and refreshing; so each of the senses of the soul, whether it be the taste or feeling, the hearing, the sight, or the spiritual smell, finds appropriate gratification in Jesus. *Even the recollection of His love is sweet.* Take a rose of Sharon, pull it leaf from leaf, and place the leaves in the jar of memory, and you will find each leaf retains its fragrance, filling the house with perfume. Christ *satisfies the highest taste* of the most educated spirit to the full. The greatest amateur in perfumes is quite satisfied with a rose: And when the soul has arrived at her highest pitch of true taste, she will still be content with Christ; indeed, she shall be more able to appreciate Him. Heaven itself possesses nothing that excels a rose of Sharon. What emblem can fully set forth His beauty? Human speech and earthborn things fail to tell of Him. Earth's choicest beauties combine to provide ultimately a feeble picture of His glory. Blessed rose, bloom in my heart forever!

[1] 1 Chronicles 29:4

### These all died in faith.

HEBREWS 11:13

Consider the epitaph of all those blessed saints who fell asleep before the coming of our Lord! The issue is not how they died—whether of old age or by violent means—but that whatever their diverse experiences, they are united in Him: "These all died in faith." In faith they lived—it was their comfort, their guide, their motive, and their support; and in the same spiritual grace they died, ending their life-song in the sweet melody that had followed them through life. They did not die trusting in the flesh or their own attainments; they never wavered from their first way of acceptance with God but held to the way of faith to the end. Faith is as precious to die by as to live by.

Dying in faith has distinct reference to *the past*. They believed the promises that had gone before and were assured that their sins were blotted out through the mercy of God. Dying in faith has to do with *the present*. These saints were confident of their acceptance with God; they enjoyed the benefits of His love and rested in His faithfulness. Dying in faith looks into *the future*. They fell asleep, affirming that the Messiah would surely come and that when He in the last days appeared upon the earth, they would rise from their graves to behold Him. To them the pains of death were but the birth-pangs of a better state. Take courage, my soul, as you read this epitaph. Your journey, through grace, is one of faith, not sight, and this has always been the pathway of the brightest and the best. Faith was the orbit in which these stars of the first magnitude shone in their day; and happy are you to be in their company. Look again tonight to Jesus, the founder and perfecter of your faith, and thank Him for giving you like precious faith with souls now in glory.

## *A very present help.*

PSALM 46:1

Covenant blessings are not meant only to be observed but to be appropriated. Even our Lord Jesus is given to us for our present use. Believer, you do not make use of Christ as you ought to do. When you are in trouble, why do you not tell Him all your grief? Does He not have a sympathizing heart, and can He not comfort and relieve you? No, you are going to all your friends, except your best Friend, and telling your story everywhere, except into the heart of your Lord. Are you burdened with this day's sins? Here is a fountain filled with blood: Use it, saint, use it. Has a sense of guilt returned upon you? The pardoning grace of Jesus may be proved again and again. Come to Him at once for cleansing. Do you deplore your weakness? He is your strength: Why not lean upon Him? Do you feel naked? Come here, soul; put on the robe of Jesus' righteousness. Do not stand looking at it, but wear it. Strip off your own righteousness, and your own fears too: Put on the fair white linen, for it was meant to wear. Do you feel yourself sick? Call upon the Beloved Physician, and He will give the medicine that will revive you. You are poor, but remember you have a kinsman, who is incredibly wealthy. What! Will you not go to Him and ask Him to give you from His abundance when He has promised that you will be joint heir with Him and has credited all that He is and all that He has to your account? There is nothing Christ dislikes more than for His people to make a show of coming to Him and yet not to use Him. He loves to be employed by us. The more burdens we put on His shoulders, the more precious He will be to us.

> *Let us be simple with Him, then,*
> *Not backward, stiff, or cold,*
> *As though our Bethlehem could be*
> *What Sinai was of old.*

## *You have been born again, not of perishable seed but of imperishable.*

1 PETER 1:23

Peter earnestly exhorted the scattered saints to love each other "earnestly from a pure heart" (verse 22), and he did so not on the basis of the law or human nature or philosophy, but from that high and divine nature that God has implanted in His people. In the same way that a sensible tutor of princes might seek to foster in them a kingly spirit and dignified behavior, finding arguments in their position and pedigree, so, looking upon God's people as heirs of glory, princes of royal blood, descendants of the King of kings, earth's truest and oldest aristocracy, Peter said to them in essence, "See that you love one another because of your noble birth, being born of imperishable seed, because of your pedigree, being descended from God, the Creator of all things, and because of your immortal destiny, for you shall never pass away, though the glory of the flesh shall fade and even its existence shall cease." We would do well if, in the spirit of humility, we recognized the true dignity of our regenerated nature and lived up to it. What is a Christian? If you compare him with a king, he adds priestly sanctity to royal dignity. The king's royalty often lies only in his crown, but with a Christian it is infused into his inmost nature. He is as much above his fellows through his new birth as a man is above the beast that perishes. Surely he shall conduct himself in all his dealings as one who is different from the crowd, chosen out of the world, distinguished by sovereign grace, part of God's "peculiar people."[1] Such trophies of God's grace cannot grovel in the dust like some, nor live in the fashion of the world's citizens. Let the dignity of your nature and the brightness of your prospects, O believers in Christ, constrain you to hold fast to holiness and to avoid the very appearance of evil.

[1]Titus 2:14, KJV

## Whoever gives thought to the word will discover good, and blessed is he who trusts in the LORD .

PROVERBS 16:20

Wisdom is man's true strength; and under its guidance he is best able to find and fulfill his reason for living. Wisely handling the matter of life gives to man the richest enjoyment and presents the noblest occupation for his powers; and in this way he finds good in the fullest sense. Without wisdom, man is like a wild donkey running here and there, wasting strength that might have been profitably employed. Wisdom is the compass by which man is to steer across the trackless waste of life; without it he is a derelict vessel, the victim of winds and waves. A man must be prudent in such a world as this or he will find no good, but will be betrayed into unnumbered ills. The pilgrim will sorely wound his feet among the briers of the wood of life if he does not pick his steps with the utmost caution. He who is in a wilderness infested with thieves must handle matters wisely if he would journey safely. If, trained by the Great Teacher, we will follow where He leads, we will find good even in the darkness, and celestial fruits to be tasted, and songs of paradise to be sung amid the groves of earth. But where shall this wisdom be found? Many have dreamed of it without possessing it. Where will we learn it? Let us listen to the voice of the Lord, for He has declared the secret. He has revealed to the sons of men where true wisdom lies, and we have it in the text, "blessed is he who trusts in the Lord." *The true way to handle a matter wisely is to trust in the Lord.* This is the sure clue to the most intricate labyrinths of life; follow it and find eternal bliss. He who trusts in the Lord has a diploma for wisdom granted by inspiration: Happy is he now, and happier he shall be above. Lord, in this sweet evening walk with me in the garden, and teach me the wisdom of faith.

## All the days of my service I would wait.

JOB 14:14

*A* *short stay on earth will make heaven more heavenly.* Nothing makes rest so enjoyable as work; nothing renders security so pleasant as exposure to danger. The bitter cups of earth will give a relish to the new wine that sparkles in the golden bowls of heaven. Our battered armor and scarred countenances will render more glorious our victory above, when we are welcomed to the seats of those who have overcome the world. We would not have *full fellowship with Christ* if we did not sojourn for a while below, for He was baptized with a baptism of suffering among men, and we must be baptized with the same if we would share His kingdom. Fellowship with Christ is so honorable that the sorest sorrow is a light price by which to procure it. Another reason for our lingering here is for *the good of others.* We would not wish to enter heaven till our work is done, and it may be that we still have a part to play shining as light in the dark wilderness of sin. Our prolonged stay here is doubtless for *God's glory.* A tested saint, like a well-cut diamond, glitters much in the King's crown. Nothing reflects so much honor on a workman as a protracted and severe trial of his work and his triumphant endurance of the ordeal without giving in or giving up. We are God's workmanship, and He will be glorified by our afflictions. It is for the honor of Jesus that we endure the trial of our faith with sacred joy. Let each man surrender his own longings to the glory of Jesus and declare: "If my lying in the dust would elevate my Lord by so much as an inch, let me still lie among the pots of earth. If to live on earth forever would make my Lord more glorious, it should be my heaven to be shut out of heaven." Our time is fixed and settled by eternal decree. Let us not be anxious about it, but wait with patience until the gates of pearl shall open.

## *Jesus said to him,*
## *"Get up, take up your bed, and walk."*

JOHN 5:8

Like many others, this impotent man had been waiting for a wonder to be performed and a sign to be given. He grew tired watching the pool, but no angel came, or at least not for him; still considering it to be his only chance, he kept waiting, not knowing that there was One near him whose word could heal him in a moment. Many are in the same condition. They are waiting for some singular emotion, remarkable impression, or celestial vision; but they wait and watch in vain. Even supposing that, in a few cases, remarkable signs are seen, yet these are rare, and no man has a right to look for them in his own case—especially not the man who feels his inability to take advantage of the moving of the water even if it came. It is sad to think of how many tens of thousands are waiting on the use of means and ordinances and vows and resolutions and have been waiting for so long and completely in vain. Meanwhile these poor souls forget that Jesus is near, and He bids them look to Him and be saved. He could heal them at once, but they prefer to wait for an angel and a wonder. To trust Him is the sure way to every blessing, and He is worthy of the most implicit confidence; but unbelief makes them prefer to wait for the water to stir than to embrace the warm welcome of His love. May the Lord turn His eye upon the multitudes who are in that position tonight; may He forgive their lack of faith in His divine power and call them by His sweet constraining voice to rise from the bed of despair and in the energy of faith take up their bed and walk. O Lord, hear our prayer for such as these in the sunset hour, and before a new dawn may they look and live.

Thankful reader, is there anything in this portion for you?

## *Agree with God, and be at peace.*

JOB 22:21

In order to properly "agree with God, and be at peace," we must know Him as He has revealed Himself, not only in *the unity of His essence and subsistence*, but also in *the plurality of His persons*. God said, "Let us make man in our image"[1]—man must not be content until he knows something of the "us" from whom his being was derived. Endeavor to know the Father. Approach Him in deep repentance, and confess that you are not worthy to be called His son; receive the kiss of His love; let the ring that is the token of His eternal faithfulness be on your finger; sit at His table and let your heart rejoice in His grace. Then press forward and seek to know much of *the Son of God* who although He is the brightness of His Father's glory humbled Himself and became man for our sakes. Know Him in the singular complexity of His nature: eternal God, and yet suffering, finite man; follow Him as He walks the waters with the tread of deity, and as He sits down at the well tired in the weariness of humanity. Do not be satisfied unless you know much of Jesus Christ as your Friend, your Brother, your Husband, your all. Do not forget *the Holy Spirit*. Endeavor to obtain a clear view of His nature and character, His attributes, and His works. Behold the Spirit of the Lord, who first of all moved upon chaos and brought forth order, who now visits the chaos of your soul and creates the order of holiness. Behold Him as the Lord and giver of spiritual life, the Illuminator, the Instructor, the Comforter, and the Sanctifier. Behold Him as He descends upon the head of Jesus, and then as He rests upon you. Such an intelligent, scriptural, and experiential belief in the Trinity is yours if you truly know God; and such knowledge *brings peace indeed*.

[1]Genesis 1:26

### *Come, my beloved, let us go out into the fields . . .*
### *let us . . . see whether the vines have budded.*

SONG OF SOLOMON 7:11-12

The bride was about to engage in hard work and desired her beloved's company in it. She does not say, "I will go," but "let us go." In like fashion, it is a blessing to work when Jesus is at our side! It is the business of God's people to be trimmers of God's vines. Like our first parents, we are put into the garden of the Lord for usefulness; let us then go out into the fields. When God's people are thinking properly, they desire to enjoy communion with Christ. Some may imagine that they cannot serve Christ actively and still have fellowship with Him; they are mistaken. There is no doubt that we may easily neglect our inward life in outward exercises and be forced to say, "They made me keeper of the vineyards, but my own vineyard have I not kept!"[1] There is no reason why this should be the case except for our own foolishness and neglect. It is certain that a professing Christian may do nothing and end up just as lifeless in spiritual things as those who are most busy. Mary was not praised for sitting still, but for her *sitting at Jesus' feet*. Even so, Christians are not to be praised for neglecting duties under the pretense of having secret fellowship with Jesus: It is not sitting, but sitting at Jesus' feet that is commendable. Do not think that activity is in itself an evil: It is a great blessing and a means of grace to us. Paul called it a grace given to him to be allowed to preach; and every form of Christian service may become a personal blessing to those engaged in it. Those who have most fellowship with Christ are not recluses or hermits, who have time on their hands, but tireless workers who are toiling for Jesus and who, in their endeavor, have Him side by side with them, so that they are workers together with God. Let us remember then, in anything we have to do for Jesus, we *can* do it and *should* do it in close communion with Him.

[1]Song of Solomon 1:6

## *. . . the only Son from the Father, full of grace and truth.*

JOHN 1:14

Believer, you can bear your testimony that Christ is *the only Son from the Father*, as well as the firstborn from the dead. You can say, "He is divine to me, even if He is regarded as simply human by the world. He has done for me what only God could do. He has subdued my stubborn will, melted a rebellious heart, opened gates of brass, and snapped bars of iron. He has turned my mourning into laughter and my desolation into joy; He has led my captivity captive and made my heart rejoice with joy unspeakable and full of glory. Let others think of Him as they will—to me He must be the only Son from the Father: Blessed be His name. And He is *full of grace*. If He had not been, I would never have been saved. He drew me when I struggled to escape from His grace; and when at last I came trembling like a condemned culprit to His mercy-seat He said, 'Take heart, My son; your sins are forgiven.' And He is *full of truth*. His promises have been true; not one has failed. I testify that no servant ever had such a master as He; no brother ever had such a relative as He has been to me; no spouse ever had such a husband as Christ has been to my soul; no sinner ever had a better Savior, no mourner a better comforter than Christ has been to my spirit. He is all I need! In life He is my life, and in death He will be the death of death; in poverty Christ is my riches; in sickness He is my great physician; in darkness He is my star, and in brightness He is my sun; He is the manna of the camp in the wilderness, and it is He who makes the feast in the promised land. Jesus is to me all grace and no wrath, all truth and no falsehood: And of truth and grace He is *full*, infinitely full. My soul, tonight bless with all your might 'the only Son.'"

## *Only be strong and very courageous.*

JOSHUA 1:7

The tender love of God for His servants makes Him concerned for how they feel inside. He wants them to be courageous. Some people think it is okay for a believer to be vexed with doubts and fears, but God does not think so. From this text it is clear that our Master does not want us entangled with fears. He desires for us to live without fretfulness, doubt, and cowardice. Our Master does not think as lightly of our unbelief as we do. When we are despondent, we are subject to a grievous ailment that is not to be trifled with but instead taken at once to the beloved Physician. Our Lord does not like to see our faces sad. It was a law of Ahasuerus that no one should come into the king's court dressed in mourning: This is not the law of the King of kings, for we may come to Him in mourning. But He still would have us put off the spirit of heaviness and put on the garment of praise, for there are so many reasons to rejoice. The Christian ought to be of a courageous spirit, in order that the Lord may be glorified when trials are bravely endured. The fearful and faint-hearted *dishonor their God*. Besides, *what a bad example it is*. This disease of doubtfulness and discouragement is an epidemic that spreads quickly among the Lord's flock. One downcast believer makes twenty souls sad. Moreover, unless your courage is kept up, *Satan will be too much for you*. Let your spirit be joyful in God your Savior; the joy of the Lord shall be your strength, and no fiend of hell shall make headway against you. But cowardice lets the banner fall. Moreover, *work is easy* for the cheerful spirit; and *success waits upon cheerfulness*. The workers, rejoicing in their God, believing with all their heart, have success guaranteed. To sow in hope will be to reap in joy; therefore, dear reader, "be strong and very courageous."

> *Do not be afraid to go down to Egypt,*
> *for there I will make you into a great nation.*
> *I myself will go down with you to Egypt,*
> *and I will also bring you up again.*

GENESIS 46:3-4

Jacob must have shuddered at the thought of leaving the land of his fathers to live among heathen strangers. It was *a new scene, and likely to be a trying one*: Who shall venture among citizens of a foreign power without some anxiety? Yet the way was *evidently appointed* for him, and therefore he resolved to go. This is frequently the experience of believers; they are called to face perils and temptations. At such times *let them imitate Jacob's example* by offering sacrifices of prayer to God and seeking His direction. Let them not take a step until they have waited upon the Lord for His blessing: *Then they will have Jacob's companion* to be their friend and helper. How blessed to feel assured that the Lord is with us in all our ways and condescends to enter into our humiliations and banishments! Even at such times we may bask in the sunshine of our Father's love. We need not hesitate to go where He promises His presence; even the darkest valley grows bright with the radiance of this assurance. Marching onward with faith in their God, believers *shall have Jacob's promise*. They will be brought up again, whether it be from the troubles of life or the chambers of death. Jacob's offspring came out of Egypt in due time, and so shall all the faithful pass unscathed through the tribulations of life and the terror of death. Let us exercise Jacob's confidence. *"Do not be afraid"* is the Lord's command and His divine encouragement to those who at His bidding are launching upon new seas; God's presence and preservation forbid so much as one unbelieving fear. Without our God we would be afraid to move; but when He bids us to, it would be dangerous to linger. Reader, go forward, and do not be afraid.

## *The LORD is my portion.*

PSALM 119:57

Look at your possessions, believer, and compare your portion with the circumstances of your friends. Some of them have their portion in the field; they are rich, and their harvests yield them a golden increase; but what are harvests compared with your God, who is the God of harvests? What are bursting granaries compared with Him who feeds you with the bread of heaven? Some have their portion in the city; their wealth is abundant and flows to them in constant streams until they become a very reservoir of gold; but what is gold compared with your God? You could not live on it; your spiritual life could not be sustained by it. Could it grant peace to a troubled conscience? Apply it to a sad heart, and see if it could prevent a single groan or minimize one grief. But you have God, and in Him you have more than gold or riches could ever buy. Some have their portion in something most men love—applause and fame; but ask yourself, is not your God more to you than that? Do you think that human accolades or thunderous applause could prepare you to face death or encourage you in the prospect of judgment? No! There are sorrows in life that wealth cannot alleviate; and there is the deep need of a dying hour, for which no riches can provide. But when you have God for your portion, you have more than everything else put together. In Him every need is met, whether in life or in death. With God for your portion you are rich indeed, for He will supply your need, comfort your heart, relieve your grief, guide your steps, walk with you in the dark valley, and then take you home to enjoy Him as your portion forever. "I have enough," said Esau; this is the best thing a worldly man can say, but Jacob replied in essence, "I have everything," which is a note too high for carnal minds.

> *He will gather the lambs in his arms;*
> *he will carry them in his bosom.*

ISAIAH 40:11

Who is He of whom such gracious words are spoken? He is *the Good Shepherd*. Why does He carry the lambs in His bosom? Because *He has a tender heart, and any weakness at once melts His heart*. The sighs, the ignorance, the feebleness of the little ones of His flock draw forth His compassion. It is *His office*, as a faithful High Priest, to consider the weak. Besides, *He purchased them with blood; they are His property*: He must and will care for those who cost Him so dearly. Then He is *responsible for each lamb*, bound by covenant love not to lose one. Moreover, *they are all a part of His glory and reward*.

But how may we understand the expression, "he will *carry* them"? Sometimes He carries them by *not permitting them to endure much trial*. Providence deals tenderly with them. Often they are carried by being filled with *an unusual degree of love*, so that they bear up and stand fast. Though their knowledge may not be deep, they have great sweetness in what they do know. Frequently He carries them by giving them *a very simple faith*, which takes the promise just as it stands and in childlike trust runs with every trouble straight to Jesus. The simplicity of their faith gives them an unusual degree of confidence, which carries them above the world.

He carries the lambs "*in his bosom.*" Here is *boundless affection*. Would He put them in His bosom if He did not love them much? Here is *tender nearness*: They are so near that they could not possibly be nearer. Here is *a holy relationship*: There are precious love-passages between Christ and His weak ones. Here is *perfect safety*: In His bosom who can hurt them? They must hurt the Shepherd first. Here is *perfect rest and sweetest comfort*. Surely we are not sufficiently aware of the infinite tenderness of Jesus!

## . . . made perfect.

HEBREWS 12:23

Remember that there are two kinds of perfection that the Christian needs—the perfection of justification in the person of Jesus, and the perfection of sanctification accomplished in him by the Holy Spirit. At present, corruption still remains even in the hearts of the regenerate—experience soon teaches us this. Within us there still are lusts and evil imaginations. But I rejoice to know that the day is coming when God shall finish the work that He has begun; and He will present my soul not only perfect in Christ, but perfect through the Spirit, without spot or blemish or any such thing. Can it be true that this poor sinful heart of mine is to become holy even as God is holy? Can it be that this spirit, which often cries, "Wretched man that I am! Who will deliver me from this body of death?"[1] shall get rid of sin and death—that I will have no evil sounds to vex my ears, and no unholy thoughts to disturb my peace? May this happy hour come quickly! When I cross the Jordan, the work of sanctification will be finished; but not until that moment shall I ever claim perfection in myself. Then my spirit will have its last baptism in the Holy Spirit's fire. I think I long to die to receive that last and final purification that will usher me into heaven. An angel will not be any purer than I shall be, for I shall be able to say, in a double sense, "I am clean," through Jesus' blood and through the Spirit's work. We should extol the power of the Holy Spirit who makes us fit to stand before our Father in heaven! Yet we must not allow the hope of perfection there to make us content with imperfection now. If it does this, our hope cannot be genuine; for a good hope is a purifying thing, even now. Grace must be at work in us *now* or it will not be perfected in us *then*. Let us pray to "be filled with the Spirit,"[2] that we may *increasingly* bring forth the fruits of righteousness.

[1]Romans 7:24  [2]Ephesians 5:18

> *And he said, "Thus says the LORD,*
> *'I will make this dry streambed full of pools.'*
> *For thus says the LORD, 'You shall not see*
> *wind or rain, but that streambed shall be filled*
> *with water, so that you shall drink, you,*
> *your livestock, and your animals.'"*

2 KINGS 3:16-17

The armies of the three kings were famishing and in need of water. God was about to send it, and in these words the prophet announced the coming blessing. Here was a case of *human helplessness*: Not a drop of water could all the valiant men procure from the skies or find in the wells of earth. In similar fashion the people of the Lord are often at their wits' end—seeing their helplessness, and then learning where their help is to be found. Notice that people were to *prepare in faith to receive the divine blessing*. They were to dig the trenches in which the water would be held. The church must learn by her efforts and prayers to make herself ready to be blessed; she must make the pools, and the Lord will fill them. This must be done in faith, in the full assurance that the blessing is about to descend. They were soon to discover a unique provision of the water they required. The shower did not pour from the clouds, as in Elijah's case; but in a silent and mysterious manner the pools were filled. The Lord has His own sovereign modes of action: He is not tied to process and time as we are but does as He pleases among the sons of men. Our part is to humbly receive from Him, and not to dictate to Him. We must also notice *the remarkable abundance of the supply*—there was enough for the needs of all. And so it is in the gospel blessing. All the needs of the congregation and of the entire church will be met by divine power in answer to prayer; and above all this, victory shall be quickly given to the armies of the Lord.

What am I doing for Jesus? What trenches am I digging? O Lord, make me ready to receive the blessing that You are so willing to bestow.

## *You are my servant, I have chosen you.*

ISAIAH 41:9

If we have received the grace of God in our hearts, its practical effect has been to make us God's *servants*. We may be unfaithful servants, we certainly are unprofitable ones, but yet, blessed be His name, we are His servants, wearing His uniform, eating at His table, and obeying His commands. We were once the servants of sin, but He who made us free has now taken us into His family and taught us obedience to His will. We do not serve our Master perfectly, but we would if we could. As we hear God's voice saying unto us, "You are My servant," we can answer with David, "I am your servant. . . . You have loosed my bonds."[1] But the Lord calls us not only His *servants*, but His *chosen ones*—"I have chosen you." We have not chosen Him first, but He has chosen us. If we are now God's servants, it wasn't always so; the change must be ascribed to sovereign grace. The eye of sovereignty singled us out, and the voice of unchanging grace declared, "I have loved you with an everlasting love."[2] Long before time began or space was created, God had written upon His heart the names of His elect people, had predestinated them to be conformed unto the image of His Son, and ordained them heirs of all the fullness of His love, His grace, and His glory. What comfort is here! Having loved us for so long, will the Lord then reject us? He knew how stiff-necked we would be, He understood that our hearts were evil, and yet He made the choice. Our Savior is no fickle lover. He dos not feel enchanted for a while with some gleams of beauty from His church's eye and then afterwards reject her because of her unfaithfulness. No, He married her in old eternity; and He hates divorce! The eternal choice is a bond upon our gratitude and upon His faithfulness, which neither can disown.

[1]Psalm 116:16   [2]Jeremiah 31:3

### ... later ...

HEBREWS 12:11

How happy are tested Christians, later. There is no deeper calm than that which follows the storm. Who has not rejoiced in clear shinings after rain? Victorious banquets are for well-accomplished soldiers. After killing the lion we eat the honey; after climbing the Hill Difficulty,[1] we sit down in the arbor to rest; after traversing the Valley of Humiliation, after fighting with Apollyon, the shining one appears, with the healing branch from the tree of life. Our sorrows, like the passing hulls of the ships upon the sea, leave a silver line of holy light behind them "later." It is peace, sweet, deep peace, that follows the horrible turmoil that once reigned in our tormented, guilty souls. Consider, then, the happy condition of a Christian! He has his best things last, and therefore in this world he receives his worst things first. But even his worst things are "later" good things, hard plowings yielding joyful harvests. Even now he grows rich by his losses, he rises by his falls, he lives by dying, and he becomes full by being emptied; if, then, his grievous afflictions yield him so much peaceable fruit in this life, what will be the full vintage of joy "later" in heaven? If his dark nights are as bright as the world's days, what shall his days be? If even his starlight is more splendid than the sun, what must his sunlight be? If he can sing in a dungeon, how sweetly will he sing in heaven! If he can praise the Lord in the fires, how will he extol Him before the eternal throne! If evil be good to him *now*, what will the overflowing goodness of God be to him *then*? Oh, blessed "later"! Who would not be a Christian? Who would not bear the present cross for the crown that comes afterwards? But here is work for patience, for the rest is not for today, nor the triumph for the present, but "later." Wait, my soul, and let patience have her perfect work.

[1]*Pilgrim's Progress*

## *And he asked that he might die.*

1 KINGS 19:4

It was a remarkable thing that the man who was never to die, for whom God had ordained an infinitely better lot, the man who would be carried to heaven in a chariot of fire and be translated and not see death, should thus pray, "Take away my life, for I am no better than my fathers." We have here a memorable proof that God does not always answer prayer in kind, though He always does in effect. He gave Elijah something better than what he asked for, and thus really heard and answered him. It was strange that the lion-hearted Elijah should be so depressed by Jezebel's threat as to ask to die, and yet it was so kind on the part of our heavenly Father not to take His desponding servant at his word. There is a limit to the doctrine of the prayer of faith. We are not to expect that God will give us everything we choose to ask for. We know that we sometimes ask and do not receive because we ask wrongly. If we ask for that which is not promised—if we run counter to the spirit that the Lord would have us cultivate—if we ask contrary to His will or to the decrees of His providence—if we ask merely for selfish gratification and without a concern for His glory, we must not expect that we will receive. But when we ask in faith, without doubting, if we do not receive the precise thing for which we asked, we shall receive an equivalent, and more than an equivalent, for it. As one remarks, "If the Lord does not pay in silver, He will in gold; and if He does not pay in gold, He will in diamonds." If He does not give you precisely what you ask for, He will give you that which is tantamount to it, and that which you will be happy to receive in its place. So, dear reader, be much in prayer, and make this evening a time of earnest intercession, but be careful what you ask for!

## *I led them with cords of kindness,*
## *with the bands of love.*

HOSEA 11:4

Our heavenly Father often leads us with the cords of love; but how slow we are to run toward Him! How reluctantly we respond to His gentle impulses! *He leads us to exercise a more simple faith in Him*; but we have not yet learned to trust like Abraham. We do not leave our worldly cares with God, but, like Martha, we burden ourselves with much serving. Our meager faith brings leanness to our souls; we do not open our mouths wide, though God has promised to fill them. Does He not this evening lead us to trust Him? Can we not hear Him say, "Come, My child, and trust Me. The curtain is opened; enter into My presence, and come boldly to the throne of My grace. I am worthy of your complete confidence; cast your cares on Me. Shake yourself from the dust of your cares, and put on the garments of joy." But, sadly though called with tones of love to the blessed exercise of this comforting grace, we will not come. At another time *He leads us to closer communion with Himself.* We have been sitting on the doorstep of God's house, and He invites us into the banqueting hall to eat with Him, but we decline the honor. There are secret rooms not yet opened to us, which Jesus invites us to enter, but we hold back. Shame on our cold hearts! We are but poor lovers of our sweet Lord Jesus, not fit to be His servants, much less to be His brides, and yet He has exalted us to be bone of His bone and flesh of His flesh, married to Him by a glorious marriage-covenant. Herein is love! But it is a love that *takes no denial.* If we do not obey the gentle leadings of His love, He will send affliction to drive us into closer intimacy with Himself. He is determined to bring us close to Him. What foolish children we are to refuse those bands of love, and in doing so to bring upon ourselves painful discipline, which He exercises for our good!

## *There is grain for sale in Egypt.*

GENESIS 42:2

Famine pinched all the nations, and it seemed inevitable that Jacob and his family should suffer great want; but the God of providence, who never forgets the objects of electing love, had stored a granary for His people by giving the Egyptians warning of the scarcity and leading them to treasure up the grain from the years of plenty. Little did Jacob expect deliverance from Egypt, but there was grain in store for him. Believer, though all things are apparently against you, rest assured that God has made a reservation on your behalf; in the roll of your griefs there is a saving clause. Somehow He will deliver you, and somewhere He will provide for you. Your rescue may come from a very unexpected source, but help will definitely come in your extremity, and you will magnify the name of the Lord. If men do not feed you, ravens will; and if the earth does not yield wheat, heaven will drop manna. Therefore be of good courage, and rest quietly in the Lord. God can make the sun rise in the west if He pleases and can make the source of distress a channel of delight. The grain in Egypt was all in the hands of the beloved Joseph; he opened or closed the granaries at will. And so the riches of providence are all in the absolute power of our Lord Jesus, who will dispense them generously to His people. Joseph was abundantly ready to help his own family; and Jesus is unceasing in His faithful care for His brethren. Our responsibility is to go after the help that is provided for us: We must not sit still in despondency, but stir ourselves. Prayer will bring us quickly into the presence of our royal Brother. Once before His throne we have only to ask and receive. His stores are not exhausted; there is still grain: His heart is not hard; He will give the grain to us. Lord, forgive our unbelief, and this evening constrain us to draw largely from Your fullness and receive grace for grace.

### *Behold, you are beautiful, my beloved.*
SONG OF SOLOMON 1:16

From every angle our Well-beloved is most fair. Our various experiences are meant by our heavenly Father to provide new vantage points from which we may view the loveliness of Jesus. How friendly are our trials when they allow us a clearer view of Jesus than ordinary life could afford us! We have seen Him from the mountain peaks, and He has shone upon us as the sun in His strength; but we have seen Him also from the lions' dens, and even there He has lost none of His loveliness. In the experience of suffering and pain, from the borders of the grave, we have turned our eyes to our soul's spouse, and He has never been other than "beautiful." Many of His saints looked upon Him from the gloom of dungeons and from the martyr's flames; yet they never uttered an ill word of Him, but died extolling His surpassing charms. To keep our gaze on the Lord Jesus is noble and pleasant employment. Is it not unspeakably delightful to view the Savior in all His works and to perceive Him matchless in each? To shift the kaleidoscope, as it were, and to find fresh combinations of matchless grace? In the manger and in eternity, on the cross and on His throne, in the garden and in His kingdom, among thieves or in the midst of cherubim, He is everywhere glorious in His beauty. Examine carefully every little act of His life and every trait of His character, and He is as lovely in the minute as in the majestic. Judge Him as you will, you cannot censure; weigh Him as you please, and He will not be found wanting. Eternity shall not discover the shadow of a spot in our Beloved, but rather as ages revolve, His hidden glories will shine with even more inconceivable splendor, and His unutterable loveliness will continually ravish all celestial minds.

## *You have not bought me sweet cane with money.*

ISAIAH 43:24

Worshipers at the temple were keen to bring presents of sweet perfumes to be burned upon the altar of God. But Israel, in the time of her backsliding, became ungenerous and made fewer offerings to her Lord. This was an evidence of coldness of heart toward God and His house. Reader, does this never happen with you? Is it not possible that the complaint of this text may occasionally, if not frequently, be brought against you? Those who are poor in pocket, if rich in faith, will be accepted even though their gifts are small; but, poor reader, do you give in fair proportion to the Lord, or is the widow's mite kept back from the sacred treasury? The rich believer should be thankful for the wealth entrusted to him but should not forget his large responsibility, for where much is given, much will be required. But, rich reader, are you mindful of your obligations, and is your giving to the Lord proportionate to the benefit you enjoy? Jesus gave His blood for us; what shall we give to Him? We are His, and He has purchased us for Himself—can we act as if we were our own? O for more consecration! O for more love! Blessed Jesus, how good it is of You to accept our sweet cane bought with money! Nothing is too costly as a tribute to Your unrivaled love, and yet You receive with favor the smallest sincere token of affection! You receive our poor forget-me-nots and love-tokens as though they were intrinsically precious, though indeed they are but as the bunch of wild flowers that the child brings to his mother. Let us never grow stingy toward You, and from this hour may we never hear You complain of us again for withholding the gifts of our love. We will give You the firstfruits of our increase and pay You tithes of all, and then we will confess, "of your own have we given you."[1]

[1] 1 Chronicles 29:14

## Only let your manner of life be worthy of the gospel of Christ.

PHILIPPIANS 1:27

The apostle's concern is not simply with our talk and conversation with one another, but with the whole course of our life and behavior in the world. The Greek word translated "manner of life" signifies the actions and the privileges of citizenship: And in this way we are commanded to let our actions, as citizens of the New Jerusalem, be worthy of the Gospel of Christ. What "manner of life" is this? In the first place, *the Gospel is very simple*. So Christians should be simple and plain in their habits. There should be about our manner, our speech, our dress, our whole behavior that simplicity that is the very soul of beauty. The Gospel is *preeminently true*. It is gold without dross; and the Christian's life will be lusterless and valueless without the jewel of truth. The Gospel is a very *fearless Gospel*; it boldly proclaims the truth, whether men like it or not. We must be equally faithful and unflinching. But the Gospel is also *very gentle*. We see this in Jesus: "a bruised reed he will not break."[1] Some professing Christians are sharper than a thorn-hedge; such men are not like Jesus. Let us seek to win others by the gentleness of our words and deeds. The Gospel is *very loving*. It is the message of the God of love to a lost and fallen race. Christ's command to His disciples was, "Love one another." We need more real, hearty union with and love for all the saints, more tender compassion toward the souls of the worst and vilest of men! We must not forget that the Gospel of Christ is *holy*. It never excuses sin: It pardons it, but only through an atonement. If our life is to resemble the Gospel, we must shun not merely the grosser vices, but everything that would hinder our perfect conformity to Christ. For His sake, for our own sakes, and for the sake of others, we must strive day by day to let our manner of life be more in accordance with His Gospel.

[1]Matthew 12:20

> ### *And they rose that same hour and returned to Jerusalem. . . . Then they told what had happened on the road, and how he was known to them.*
>
> LUKE 24:33, 35

When the two disciples had reached Emmaus and were refreshing themselves at the evening meal, the mysterious stranger who had so enchanted them on the road took bread and broke it, made Himself known to them, and then vanished out of their sight. They had constrained Him to stay with them because the day was far spent; but now, although it was much later, their love was a lamp to their feet, indeed wings also. They forgot the darkness, their weariness was all gone, and immediately they headed back the seven miles to tell the wonderful news of a risen Lord who had appeared to them on the road. They reached the Christians in Jerusalem and were received by a burst of joyful news before they could tell their own tale. These early Christians were all on fire to speak of Christ's resurrection and to proclaim what they knew of the Lord; they happily shared their experiences. This evening let their example impress us deeply. We also must bear our witness concerning Jesus. John's account of the sepulcher needed to be supplemented by Peter; and Mary could speak of something further still; the combined accounts provide us with a complete testimony from which nothing necessary is missing. Each of us has peculiar gifts and personal experiences; but the one object God has in view is the maturing of the whole Body of Christ. We must, therefore, bring our spiritual possessions and lay them at the apostles' feet, that we may share all of what God has given to us. Withhold no part of the precious truth, but speak what you know and declare what you have seen. Do not allow the toil or darkness or possible unbelief of your friends to dissuade you. Let us rise and march to the place of duty, and there declare what great things God has shown to our soul.

## *Continue in the faith.*

ACTS 14:22

Perseverance is the badge of true saints. The Christian life is not only a beginning in the ways of God, but also means *continuing* in those ways as long as life lasts. It is with a Christian as it was with the great Napoleon: He said, "Conquest has made me what I am, and conquest must maintain me." So under God, dear believer in the Lord, conquest has made you what you are, and conquest must sustain you. Your motto must be, "Aim higher." The only true conqueror who shall be crowned in the end is he who continues until war's trumpet is blown no more. Perseverance is, therefore, the target of all our spiritual enemies. The *world* does not object to your being a Christian for a time, if she can tempt you to quit your pilgrimage and settle down to trade with her in Vanity Fair. The *flesh* will seek to ensnare you and to prevent your pressing on to glory. "Being a pilgrim is weary work and makes me wonder: Am I always to be mortified? Am I never to be indulged? Can I not have at least a holiday from this constant warfare?" *Satan* will make many a fierce attack on your perseverance; it will be the target for all his arrows. He will strive to hinder you in service: He will insinuate that you are doing no good and that you need to rest. He will endeavor to make you weary of *suffering*; he will whisper, "Curse God, and die." Or he will attack your *steadfastness*: "What is the good of being so zealous? Be quiet like the rest; sleep as others do, and let your lamp go out like the foolish virgins." Or he will assail your *doctrinal sentiments*: "Why do you hold to these doctrinal creeds? Sensible men are getting more liberal; they are removing the old landmarks: Fall in with the times." So, Christian, wear your shield close to your armor and cry earnestly to God, that by His Spirit you may endure to the end.

# What is your servant, that you should show regard for a dead dog such as I?

2 SAMUEL 9:8

If Mephibosheth was humbled by David's kindness, what shall we be in the presence of our gracious Lord? The more grace we have, the less we shall think of ourselves, for grace, like light, reveals our impurity. Eminent saints have scarcely known what to compare themselves to, their sense of unworthiness has been so clear and keen. "I am," says the godly Rutherford, "a dry and withered branch, a piece of dead carcass, dry bones, and not able to step over a straw." In another place he writes, "Apart from their open outbursts, I am too much like Judas and Cain." The meanest objects in nature appear to the humbled mind to have a preference above itself, because they have never contracted sin: A dog may be greedy, fierce, or filthy, but it has no conscience to violate, no Holy Spirit to resist. A dog may be appear to be worthless, and yet by a little kindness it is soon won to love its master and is faithful to death; but we forget the goodness of the Lord and do not follow His call. The term *dead dog* is the most expressive of all terms of contempt, but it is not too strong to express the self-abhorrence of well-taught believers. They do not display false modesty; they mean what they say; they have weighed themselves in the balances of the sanctuary and discovered the vanity of their nature. At best we are but clay, animated dust; but viewed as sinners, we are monsters indeed. Let it be published in heaven as a miracle that the Lord Jesus should set His heart's love upon people like us. Dust and ashes though we be, we must and will magnify the exceeding greatness of His grace. Could His heart not find rest in heaven? Does He need to come to these tents for a spouse and choose a bride from the children of men? Let the heavens and earth break forth into song and give all the glory to our sweet Lord Jesus.

## *This I call to mind, and therefore I have hope.*

### LAMENTATIONS 3:21

Memory is frequently the slave of despondency. Despairing minds remember every dark prediction in the past and expand upon every gloomy feature in the present; in this way memory, clothed in sackcloth, presents to the mind a cup of bitter-tasting herbs. There is, however, no necessity for this. Wisdom can readily transform memory into an angel of comfort. That same recollection that on the one hand brings so many gloomy omens may be trained instead to provide a wealth of hopeful signs. She need not wear a crown of iron; she may encircle her brow with a tiara of gold, all spangled with stars. Such was Jeremiah's experience: in the previous verse memory had brought him to deep humiliation of soul: "My soul continually remembers it and is bowed down within me"; but now this same memory restored him to life and comfort. "But this I call to mind, and therefore I have hope." Like a two-edged sword, his memory first killed his pride with one edge and then slew his despair with the other. As a general principle, if we would exercise our memories more wisely, we might, in our very darkest distress, strike a match that would instantaneously kindle the lamp of comfort. There is no need for God to create a new thing upon the earth in order to restore believers' joy; if they would prayerfully rake the ashes of the past, they would find light for the present; and if they would turn to the book of truth and the throne of grace, their candle would soon shine as before. Let us then remember the loving-kindness of the Lord and rehearse His deeds of grace. Let us open the volume of recollection, which is so richly illuminated with memories of His mercy, and we will soon be happy. Thus memory may be, as Coleridge calls it, "the bosom-spring of joy," and when the Divine Comforter bends it to His service, it is then the greatest earthly comfort we can know.

## Cursed before the LORD be the man who rises up and rebuilds this city, Jericho.

JOSHUA 6:26

If the man who rebuilt Jericho was cursed, how much more does the man who works to restore false religion among us deserve the same. In our fathers' days the gigantic walls of false religion fell by the power of their faith, the perseverance of their efforts, and the blast of their gospel trumpets; and now there are some who would like to rebuild those false systems upon their old foundations. Lord, we pray, be pleased to thwart these unrighteous endeavors, and pull down every stone that they build. It should be a serious business with us to be thoroughly purged of every error that tends to foster the spirit of falsehood, and when we have made a clean sweep at home we should seek in every way to oppose its all too rapid spread abroad in the church and in the world. This we may accomplish only in secret by fervent prayer and in public by faithful witness. We must warn with judicious boldness those who are inclined toward the errors of false religion; we must instruct the young in gospel truth and tell them of the dark doings of falsehood in earlier times. We must assist in spreading the light more thoroughly through the land, for false teachers, like owls, hate daylight. Are we doing all we can for Jesus and the Gospel? If not, our negligence plays into the hands of the heretics. What are we doing to spread the Bible, which is the antidote to falsehood? Are we sending out good, sound gospel writings? Luther once said, "The devil hates goose quills," and, no doubt, he has good reason; the writer's pen blessed by the Holy Spirit has damaged his evil kingdom greatly. If the thousands who read this short word tonight will do all they can to hinder the rebuilding of this accursed Jericho, the Lord's glory shall spread quickly among the sons of men. Reader, what can you do? What will you do?

## *. . . so that we would no longer be enslaved to sin.*

ROMANS 6:6

Christian, why would you play with sin? *Has it not cost you enough already?* Burnt child, will you play with the fire? What! When you have already been between the jaws of the lion, will you step a second time into his den? Have you not had enough of the old serpent? Did he not poison all your veins once, and will you play at the cobra's den and put your hand in the dragon's lair a second time? Do not be not so mad, so foolish! Did sin ever yield you real pleasure? Did you find solid satisfaction in it? If so, go back to your old drudgery, and wear the chain again, if it delights you. But inasmuch as sin never gave you what it promised to bestow but deluded you with lies, do not be snared by the old fowler: Be free, and let the memory of your enslavement prevent you from entering the net again! *It is contrary to the designs of eternal love*, which are all focused on your purity and holiness; therefore do not run counter to the purposes of your Lord. Another thought should restrain you from sin. *Christians can never sin cheaply*; they pay a heavy price for iniquity. Transgression destroys peace of mind, obscures fellowship with Jesus, hinders prayer, brings darkness over the soul; therefore do not be the serf and slave of sin. There is still a higher argument: Each time you serve sin you are "crucifying once again the Son of God . . . and holding him up to contempt."[1] Can you bear that thought? If you have fallen into any special sin during this day, it may be that my Master has sent this admonition this evening to bring you back before you have wandered very far. Turn to Jesus afresh. He has not forgotten His love for you; His grace is still the same. With weeping and repentance, come to His footstool, and you shall be reunited in His love; you will be set upon a rock again, and your goings shall be established.

[1]Hebrews 6:6

## . . . *who heals all your diseases.*

PSALM 103:3

Humbling as is the statement, yet the fact is certain that we are all more or less suffering under the disease of sin. What a comfort to know that we have a great Physician who is both able and willing to heal us! Let us think of Him for a moment tonight. His cures are very *speedy*—there is life for a look at Him; His cures are *radical*—He strikes at the center of the disease; and so His cures are sure and certain. He never fails, and *the disease never returns*. There is no relapse where Christ heals, no fear that His patients should be merely patched up for a season. He makes new men of them: He also gives them a new heart and puts a right spirit within them. He is well skilled in *all* diseases. Physicians generally have some *specialty*. Although they may know a little about almost all our pains and ills, there is usually one disease that they have studied more than others; but Jesus Christ is thoroughly acquainted with the whole of human nature. He is as much at home with one sinner as with another, and He never yet met an unusual case that was difficult for Him. He has had extraordinary complications of strange diseases to deal with, but He has known exactly with one glance of His eye how to treat the patient. He is the only universal doctor; and the medicine He gives is the only true panacea, healing in every instance. Whatever our spiritual malady may be, we should apply at once to this Divine Physician. There is no brokenness of heart that Jesus cannot bind up. "The blood of Jesus his Son cleanses us from all sin."[1] We have only to think of the myriads who have been delivered from all sorts of diseases through the power and virtue of His touch, and we will joyfully put ourselves in His hands. We trust Him, and sin dies; we love Him, and grace lives; we wait for Him, and grace is strengthened; we see Him as he is, and grace is perfected forever.

[1] 1 John 1:7

## For the LORD . . . makes her wilderness like Eden.

ISAIAH 51:3

In my mind's eye I see a howling wilderness, a great and terrible desert, like the Sahara. I perceive nothing in it to relieve the eye; all around I am wearied with a vision of hot and arid sand, on which are ten thousand bleaching skeletons of wretched men who have expired in anguish, having lost their way in the pitiless waste. What an appalling sight! How horrible! A sea of sand without boundary and without an oasis, a cheerless graveyard for a forlorn race. But look and wonder! All of a sudden, springing from the scorching sand I see a well-known plant; and as it grows it buds, the bud expands—it is a rose, and at its side a lily bows its modest head—and, miracle of miracles, as the fragrance of those flowers is diffused, the wilderness is transformed into a fruitful field, and all around it blossoms abundantly like the glory of Lebanon, the excellency of Carmel and Sharon. Do not call it Sahara; call it Paradise. Do not refer to it any longer as the valley of death, for where the skeletons lay bleaching in the sun, a resurrection is proclaimed, and up spring the dead, a mighty army, full of life immortal. Jesus is that well-known plant, and His presence makes everything new. The wonder is no less in each individual's salvation. I can see you, dear reader, cast out, an infant, unclothed, unwashed, defiled with your own blood, and left to be food for beasts of prey. But look, a jewel has been thrown into your bosom by a divine hand, and for its sake you have been pitied and guarded by divine providence; you are washed and cleansed from your defilement; you are adopted into heaven's family; the fair seal of love is upon your forehead, and the ring of faithfulness is on your hand—you are now a prince to God, though once an orphan and a castaway. Cherish then the matchless power and grace that changes deserts into gardens and makes the barren heart sing for joy.

## *Teacher.*

MATTHEW 19:16

If the young man in the Gospel used this title in speaking to our Lord, it is only right that we should address Him in this way. He is indeed my Teacher in that He rules and teaches me. I am glad to run His errands and to sit at His feet. I am both His servant and His disciple and count it my highest honor to serve Him in this way. He is a good teacher. If He should ask me why I call Him *"good,"* I could answer easily. It is true that "no one is good except God alone,"[1] but then He is God, and all the goodness of Deity shines in Him. In my experience I have found Him to be good, indeed so good that all the good I have has come to me through Him. He was good to me when I was dead in sin, for He raised me by His Spirit's power; He has been good to me in all my needs, trials, struggles, and sorrows. There could never be a better Teacher, for His service is freedom, His rule is love: I wish I were one thousandth part as good a servant. When He teaches me, He is unspeakably good, His doctrine is divine, His manner is gracious, His spirit is gentleness itself. There is no error in His instruction: Pure is the golden truth that He presents, and all His teachings lead to goodness, sanctifying as well as edifying the disciple. Angels know that He is good and delight to worship at His footstool. The ancient saints proved Him to be a good Teacher, and each of them rejoiced to sing, "I am Your servant, O Lord!" My own humble testimony must certainly be to the same effect. I will declare this before my friends and neighbors, for possibly they may be led by my testimony to seek my Lord Jesus as their Teacher. O I long that they might do so! They would never regret the decision. If they would submit to His easy yoke, they would find themselves in such royal service that they would never want to leave. The school of grace rejoices to have such a Teacher!

[1]Mark 10:18.

## He humbled Himself.

PHILIPPIANS 2:8

Jesus is the great teacher of lowliness of heart. Every day we need to learn from Him. Witness the Master taking a towel and washing His disciples' feet! Follower of Christ, will you not humble yourself? Consider Him the Servant of servants, and surely you cannot be proud! This sentence sums up His life: "He humbled Himself." Isn't it true to say that on earth he was always stripping off first one robe of honor and then another until, naked, He was fastened to the cross and emptied Himself, pouring out His life-blood, giving it up for all of us, until they laid Him penniless in a borrowed grave? Our dear Redeemer was brought low! How then can we be proud? Stand at the foot of the cross and count the purple drops by which you have been cleansed; see the crown of thorns; mark His scourged shoulders; see hands and feet given up to the rough iron, and His whole self to mockery and scorn; see the bitterness and the pains of inward grief, showing themselves in His outward frame; hear the beleaguered cry, "My God, my God, why have You forsaken me?" And if you do not lie prostrate on the ground before that cross, you have never seen it: If you are not humbled in the presence of Jesus, you do not know Him. You were so lost that nothing could save you but the sacrifice of God's only Son. Think of that, and as Jesus stooped for you, bow yourself in lowliness at His feet. A sense of Christ's amazing love for us has a greater tendency to humble us than even an awareness of our own guilt. May the Lord bring our thoughts to Calvary; then our position will no longer be that of the pompous man of pride, but we will take the humble place of one who loves much because he has been forgiven much. Pride cannot live beneath the cross. Let us sit there and learn our lesson, and then rise and carry it into practice.

## *. . . taken up in glory.*

### 1 TIMOTHY 3:16

We have seen the Lord Jesus in the days of His flesh, humiliated and scorned: "He was despised and rejected by men; a man of sorrows, and acquainted with grief."[1] He whose brightness is as the morning wore the sackcloth of sorrow as His daily dress: Shame was His belt, and reproach was His cloak. Yet now that He has triumphed over all the powers of darkness upon the bloody tree, our faith sees Him returning, robed in the splendor of victory. How glorious He must have been in the eyes of seraphs, when a cloud received Him out of sight and He ascended to heaven! Now He wears the glory that He had with God before creation, and yet another glory above all—that which He has earned in the fight against sin, death, and hell. As victor He wears the illustrious crown. Listen to the swelling song! It is a new and sweeter song: "Worthy is the Lamb who was slain, for by Your blood You ransomed people for God!" He wears the glory of an Intercessor who can never fail, of a Prince who can never be defeated, of a Conqueror who has defeated every foe, of a Lord who has the allegiance of every subject. Jesus wears all the glory that heaven can bestow upon Him, all that ten thousand times ten thousand angels can minister to Him. You cannot with the utmost stretch of imagination conceive of His exceeding greatness; yet there will be a further revelation of it when He shall descend from heaven in great power, with all the holy angels—"Then he will sit on his glorious throne."[2] The splendor of that glory seen will ravish the hearts of His people. This isn't the end, for eternity will sound His praise. "Your throne, O God, is forever and ever!"[3] Reader, if you would rejoice in Christ's glory *then*, He must be glorious in your sight *now*. So, is He?

[1]Isaiah 53:3  [2]Matthew 25:31  [3]Psalm 45:6

## *Anyone who does not love does not know God.*

1 JOHN 4:8

The distinguishing mark of a Christian is his confidence in Christ's love for him and in the offering of his love to Christ. First, faith sets her seal upon the man by enabling the soul to say with the apostle, "Christ loved me and gave himself for me."[1] Then love gives the countersign and stamps upon the heart gratitude and love to Jesus in return. "We love because he first loved us."[2] In those grand old ages, which are the heroic period of the Christian religion, this double mark was clearly seen in all believers in Jesus; they were men who knew the love of Christ and rested upon it as a man leans upon a staff whose trustiness he has proved. The love that they felt toward the Lord was not a quiet emotion that they hid within themselves in the secret place of their souls and that they only spoke about in private or when they met on the first day of the week and sang hymns in honor of Christ Jesus the crucified; it was a passion with them of such a vehement and all-consuming energy that it was visible in all their actions, evident in their conversation, and seen in their eyes, even in their casual glances. Love for Jesus was a flame that fed upon the core and heart of their being and therefore by its own force burned its way into their demeanor and shone there. Zeal for the glory of King Jesus was the seal and mark of all genuine Christians. Because of their dependence upon Christ's love they *dared* much, and because of their love for Christ they *did* much, and it is the same now. The children of God are ruled in their inmost powers by love. The love of Christ constrains them; they rejoice that divine love is set upon them, they feel it shed abroad in their hearts by the Holy Spirit, who is given to them, and then by force of gratitude they love the Savior with a pure and fervent heart. My reader, do you love Him? Before you sleep, give an honest answer to this weighty question!

[1]Galatians 2:20   [2]1 John 4:19

## *Are they Israelites? So am I.*

### 2 CORINTHIANS 11:22

We have here *a personal claim*, and one that *needs proof*. The apostle knew that his claim was indisputable, but there are many people who have no right to the title yet still claim to belong to the Israel of God. If we are confidently declaring, "I am also an Israelite," let us only say it after we have searched our hearts as in the presence of God. But if we can give proof that we are following Jesus, if we can say from the heart, "I trust Him wholly, trust Him only, trust Him simply, trust Him now, and trust Him ever," then the position that the saints of God hold also belongs to us. All their enjoyments are our possessions; we may be the very least in Israel, "least of all saints," but since the mercies of God belong to the saints as saints, and not as advanced saints or well-taught saints, we may put in our plea and say, "Are they Israelites? So am I. The promises are mine, grace is mine, and glory will be mine." The claim, rightfully made, is one that will yield untold comfort. When God's people are rejoicing that they are His, what a happiness to be able to say, "So am I!" When they speak of being pardoned and justified and accepted in the Beloved, how joyful to respond, "Through the grace of God, so am I." But this claim not only has its enjoyments and privileges, but also its conditions and duties. We must share with God's people in cloud as well as in sunshine. When we hear them spoken of with contempt and ridicule for being Christians, we must come boldly forward and say, "So am I." When we see them working for Christ, giving their time, their talent, their whole heart to Jesus, we must be able to say, "So do I." Let us then prove our gratitude by our devotion and live as those who, having claimed a privilege, are willing to take the responsibility connected with it.

## *Be zealous.*

### REVELATION 3:19

If you want to see souls converted, if you want to hear the cry that "the kingdom of the world has become the kingdom of our Lord,"[1] if you want to place crowns upon the head of the Savior and see His throne lifted high, then be filled with zeal. For under God, the way the world will be converted is by the zeal of the church. Every element of grace will do its work, but zeal will be first; prudence, knowledge, patience, and courage will follow in their places, but zeal must lead the charge. It is not the extent of your knowledge, though that is useful, it is not the extent of your talent, though that is not to be despised, it is your zeal that will do great exploits. This zeal is the fruit of the Holy Spirit: It draws its vital force from *the continued operations* of the Holy Spirit in the soul. If our inner life dwindles, if our heart beats slowly before God, we will not know zeal; but if everything inside is strong and vigorous, then we cannot but feel a loving urgency to see Christ's kingdom come, and His will done on earth, even as it is in heaven. A deep *sense of gratitude* will nourish Christian zeal. When we reflect on the miry pit from which we were lifted, we find plenty of reason for spending ourselves for God. And zeal is also stimulated *by the thought of the eternal future*. It looks with tearful eyes down to the flames of hell, and it cannot sleep: It looks up with anxious gaze to the glories of heaven, and it cannot stay still. It feels that time is short compared with the work to be done, and therefore it devotes all that it has to the cause of its Lord. And it is continually strengthened by *remembering Christ's example*. He was clothed with zeal as with a cloak. How swift the chariot-wheels of duty went with Him! He never loitered on the way. Let us prove that we are His disciples by displaying the same spirit of zeal.

[1]Revelation 11:15

## *Now you shall see whether my word will come true for you or not.*

NUMBERS 11:23

God had made a positive promise to Moses that for the space of a whole month He would feed the vast company in the wilderness with meat. Moses is then overtaken by a fit of unbelief, looks to the outward means, and is at a loss to know how the promise can be fulfilled. He looked to the creature instead of the Creator. But does the Creator expect the creature to fulfill His promise for Him? No; He who makes the promise always fulfills it by His own unaided omnipotence. If He speaks, it is done—done by Himself. His promises do not depend for their fulfillment upon the cooperation of the puny strength of man. We can immediately see the mistake that Moses made. And yet how routinely we do the same! God has promised to supply our needs, and we look to the creature to do what God has promised to do; and then, because we perceive the creature to be weak and feeble, we indulge in unbelief. Why do we look in that direction at all? Will you look to the North Pole to gather fruits ripened in the sun? You would be acting no more foolishly in doing this than when you look to the weak for strength, and to the creature to do the Creator's work. Let us, then, put the question on the right footing. The ground of faith is not the sufficiency of the visible means for the performance of the promise, but the all-sufficiency of the invisible God, who will definitely do what He has said. If after clearly seeing that the onus lies with the Lord and not with the creature we dare to indulge in mistrust, the question of God comes home forcefully to us: "Is the LORD's hand shortened?" May it also be that in His mercy the question will be accompanied by this blessed declaration: "Now you shall see whether my word will come true for you or not."

## *Search the Scriptures.*

JOHN 5:39

The Greek word translated *search* signifies a strict, close, diligent, curious search, the kind men make when they are seeking gold, or hunters when they are in pursuit of game. We must not be content with giving a superficial glance to one or two chapters, but with the candle of the Spirit we must deliberately seek out the meaning of the Word. Holy Scripture *requires searching*—much of it can only be learned by careful study. There is milk for babies, but also meat for strong men. The rabbis wisely say that a mountain of matter hangs upon every word, indeed, upon every title of Scripture. Tertullian declared, "I adore the fullness of the Scriptures." The person who merely skims the Book of God will not profit from it; we must dig and mine until we obtain the treasure. The door of the Word only opens to the key of diligence. The Scriptures *demand to be searched*. They are the writings of God, bearing the divine stamp and imprimatur—who shall dare to treat them casually? To despise them is to despise the God who wrote them. God forbid that any of us should allow our Bibles to become witnesses against us in the great day of account. The Word of God *will repay searching*. God does not ask us to sift through a mountain of chaff with only here and there a grain of wheat in it, but the Bible is sifted corn—we have only to open the granary door and find it. Scripture grows upon the student. It is full of surprises. Under the teaching of the Holy Spirit, to the searching eye, it glows with splendor of revelation, like a vast temple paved with gold and roofed with rubies, emeralds, and all manner of gems. There is no merchandise like the merchandise of scriptural truth. Finally, *the Scriptures reveal Jesus*: "They that bear witness about me." No more powerful motive can be urged upon Bible readers than this: He who finds Jesus finds life, heaven, and all things. Happy are they who, in searching the Bible, discover their Savior.

## *It is they that bear witness about me.*

JOHN 5:39

Jesus Christ is the Alpha and Omega of the Bible. He is the constant theme of its sacred pages; from beginning to end they bear witness to Him. At the creation we immediately recognize Him as one of the sacred Trinity; we catch a glimpse of Him in the promise of the woman's seed; we see Him pictured in the ark of Noah; we walk with Abraham as He sees Messiah's day; we live in the tents of Isaac and Jacob, feeding upon the gracious promise; and in the numerous types of the law, we find the Redeemer abundantly foreshadowed. Prophets and kings, priests and preachers all look one way—they all stand as the cherubs did over the ark, desiring to look within and to read the mystery of God's great propitiation. Even more obvious in the New Testament we discover that Jesus is the one pervading subject. It is not that He is mentioned every so often or that we can find Him in the shadows; no, the whole substance of the New Testament is Jesus crucified, and even its closing sentence sparkles with the Redeemer's name. We should always read Scripture in this light; we should consider the Word to be like a mirror into which Christ looks down from heaven; and then we, looking into it, see His face reflected—darkly, it is true, but still in such a way as to be a blessed preparation for one day seeing Him face to face. The New Testament contains Jesus Christ's letters to us, which are perfumed by His love. These pages are like the garments of our King, and they all bear His fragrance. Scripture is the royal chariot in which Jesus rides, and it is paved with love for the daughters of Jerusalem. The Scriptures are like the swaddling clothes of the holy child Jesus; unroll them, and there you find your Savior. The essence of the Word of God is Christ.

### *There he broke the flashing arrows, the shield, the sword, and the weapons of war.*

PSALM 76:3

Our Redeemer's glorious cry of "It is finished" was the death-knell of all the adversaries of His people, the breaking of "the weapons of war." Behold the hero of Golgotha using His cross as an anvil, and His wounds as a hammer, dashing to pieces bundle after bundle of our sins, those poisoned "flashing arrows," trampling on every indictment and destroying every accusation. What glorious blows the mighty Breaker gives with a hammer far more powerful than the fabled weapon of Thor! How the diabolical darts break in pieces, and the infernal swords are broken like old clay pots! Consider how He draws from its sheath of hellish workmanship the dreadful sword of satanic power! He snaps it across His knee as a man breaks dry sticks and throws it into the fire. Beloved, no sin of a believer can now be an arrow bringing death, no condemnation can now be a sword to kill him, for the punishment of our sin was borne by Christ, and a full atonement was made for all our iniquities by our blessed Substitute and Surety. Who now accuses? Who now condemns? Christ has died, yes, has risen again. Jesus has removed the weapons of hell, has quenched every fiery dart, and has broken the head off every arrow of wrath; the ground is covered with the splinters and relics of the weapons of hell's warfare, which are only visible to us to remind us of our former danger and of our great deliverance. Sin no longer has dominion over us. Jesus has made an end of it and put it away forever. Our enemy's destructions have come to a perpetual end. Declare all the wonderful works of the Lord, all you who make mention of His name; do not be silent, neither by day, nor when the sun goes down. Bless the Lord, O my soul.

## *. . . who saved us and called us to a holy calling.*

2 TIMOTHY 1:9

The apostle uses the perfect tense and says, "who saved us." Believers in Christ Jesus are saved. They are not looked upon as people who are in a hopeful state and may ultimately be saved, but they are already saved. Salvation is not a blessing to be enjoyed upon our dying bed and to be sung of in a future state above, but a matter to be obtained, received, promised, and enjoyed now. The Christian is perfectly saved *in God's purpose*; God has ordained him to salvation, and that purpose is complete. He is saved also as to *the price that has been paid for him*: "It is finished" was the cry of the Savior before He died. The believer is also perfectly saved *in His covenant Head*, for as he fell in Adam, so he lives in Christ. This complete salvation is accompanied by *a holy calling*. Those whom the Savior saved upon the cross are in due time effectually called by the power of God the Holy Spirit to holiness: They leave their sins; they endeavor to be like Christ; they choose holiness, not out of any compulsion, but from the power of a new nature, which leads them to rejoice in holiness just as naturally as when previously they delighted in sin. God neither chose them nor called them because they were holy, but He called them that they might be holy, and holiness is the beauty produced by His workmanship in them. The excellencies that we see in a believer are as much the work of God as the Atonement itself. In this way the fullness of the grace of God is beautifully displayed. Salvation must be of grace, because the Lord is the author of it: And what motive but grace could move Him to save the guilty? Salvation must be of grace because the Lord works in such a manner that our righteousness is forever excluded. Such is the believer's privilege—*a present salvation*; such is the evidence that he is called to it—*a holy life*.

## *Remove far from me falsehood and lying.*

PROVERBS 30:8

## *Do not forsake me, O LORD!*

PSALM 38:21

Here we have two great lessons—what to deprecate and what to supplicate. The happiest state of a Christian is the holiest state. Just as there is the most heat nearest to the sun, so there is the most happiness closest to Christ. No Christian enjoys comfort when his eyes are fixed on falsehood—he finds no satisfaction unless his soul is quickened in the ways of God. The world may find happiness elsewhere, but he cannot. I do not blame ungodly men for rushing to their pleasures. Why should I? Let them have their fill. That is all they have to enjoy. A converted wife who despaired of her husband was always very kind to him, for she said, "I fear that this is the only world in which he will be happy, and therefore I have made up my mind to make him as happy as I can in it." Christians must seek their delights in a higher sphere than the tasteless trifles or sinful enjoyments of the world. Empty pursuits are dangerous to renewed souls. We have heard of a philosopher who, while he looked *up* to the stars, fell into a pit; but how deeply do they fall who look *down*. Their fall is fatal. No Christian is safe when his soul is lazy, and his God is far from him. Every Christian is always safe as to the great matter of his standing in Christ, but he is not safe as regards his experience in holiness and communion with Jesus in this life. Satan does not often attack a Christian who is living near to God. It is when the Christian departs from God, becomes spiritually starved, and tries to feed on lies that the devil discovers his moment of advantage. He may sometimes stand foot to foot with the child of God who is active in his Master's service, but the battle is generally brief. He who slips as he goes down into the Valley of Humiliation will find that with every false step he invites the devil's attack. O for grace to walk humbly with our God!

## To us, O LORD, belongs open shame . . . because we have sinned against you.

DANIEL 9:8

A deep sense and clear view of sin, its dreadfulness, and the punishment that it deserves should make us lie low before the throne. We have sinned as Christians. It is sad that it should be so. We have been favored, and yet we have been ungrateful; privileged beyond most, but we have not brought forth fruit in proportion. Who is there, although he may have been engaged in the Christian warfare for years, who will not blush when he looks back upon the past? As for our days before we were born again, may they be forgiven and forgotten; but since then, though we have not sinned as before, yet we have sinned against light and against love—light that has really penetrated our minds, and love in which we have rejoiced. The sin of a pardoned soul is an atrocity! An unpardoned sinner sins cheaply compared with the sin of one of God's elect, who has had communion with Christ and leaned upon Him for his comfort. Look at David! Many will talk of his sin, but I ask you to look at his repentance and hear his broken bones as each one of them moans out its mournful confession! Consider his tears as they fall upon the ground, and the deep sighs with which he accompanies the softened music of his harp! We have strayed: Let us, therefore, seek the spirit of penitence. Look again at Peter! We often speak of how he denied Christ. Remember, it is written, "He wept bitterly." Do *we* have no denials of our Lord to be lamented with tears? These sins of ours, before and after conversion, would consign us to the place of inextinguishable fire if it were not for God's sovereign mercy, which snatched us like sticks from the fire. My soul, bow down under a sense of your natural sinfulness, and worship your God. Admire the grace that saves you—the mercy that spares you—the love that pardons you!

## . . . *who opens and no one will shut.*

REVELATION 3:7

Jesus is the keeper of the gates of paradise, and before every believing soul He sets an open door, which no man or devil will be able to close. What joy it will be to find that faith in Him is the golden key to the everlasting doors. My soul, do you carry this key close to you, or are you trusting in some dishonest locksmith who will fail you in the end? Pay attention to a parable of the preacher, and remember it. The great King has made a banquet, and He has proclaimed to all the world that no one will enter except those who bring with them the fairest flower that blooms. The spirits of men advance to the gate by thousands, and each one brings the flower that he esteems the queen of the garden; but in crowds they are driven from the royal presence and do not enter into the festive halls. Some are carrying the poisonous plant of superstition, others the flaunting poppies of empty religion, and some the hemlock of self-righteousness; but these are not precious to the King, and so those carrying them are shut out of the pearly gates. My soul, have you gathered the rose of Sharon? Do you wear the lily of the valley on your lapel constantly? If so, when you arrive at the gates of heaven you will know its value, for you only have to show this choicest of flowers, and the Porter will open and without a moment's delay, for to that rose the Porter always opens. You will find your way with the rose of Sharon in your hand up to the throne of God Himself, for heaven itself possesses nothing that excels its radiant beauty, and of all the flowers that bloom in paradise, none of them can rival the lily of the valley. My soul, get Calvary's blood-red rose into your hand by faith, by love wear it, by communion preserve it, by daily watchfulness make it your all in all, and you will be blessed beyond all bliss, happy beyond a dream. Jesus, be mine forever, my God, my heaven, my all.

### The LORD is my light and my salvation;
### whom shall I fear? The LORD is the stronghold
### of my life; of whom shall I be afraid?

PSALM 27:1

*T*he LORD is my light and my salvation." Here is personal interest: *"my light," "my salvation"*; the soul is assured of it, and therefore declares it boldly. Into the soul at the new birth divine light is poured as the forerunner of salvation; where there is not enough light to reveal our own darkness and to make us long for the Lord Jesus, there is no evidence of salvation. After conversion our God is our joy, comfort, guide, teacher, and in every sense our light: He is light within us, light around us, light reflected from us, and light to be revealed to us. Note, it does not just say that the Lord gives light, but that He is light; nor that He gives salvation, but that He is salvation; so, then, whoever by faith has laid hold upon God has all the covenant blessings in their possession. Once this fact is assured, the deduction from it is put in the form of a question, *"Whom shall I fear?"* A question that is its own answer. The powers of darkness are not to be feared, for the Lord, our light, destroys them; and we need not dread the damnation of hell, for the Lord is our salvation. This is a very different challenge from that of boastful Goliath, for it rests not upon the conceited vigor of human strength, but upon the real power of the omnipotent I AM. *"The LORD is the stronghold of my life."* Here is a third glowing quality showing that the writer's hope was fastened with a threefold cord that could not be broken. It is no surprise that we accumulate terms of praise where the Lord lavishes deeds of grace. Our life derives all its strength from God; and if He deigns to make us strong, we cannot be weakened by all the cunning movements of our adversary. *"Whom shall I fear?"* The bold question looks into the future as well as the present. "If God is for us, who can be against us,"[1] either now or in time to come?

[1]Romans 8:31

## *Then Israel sang this song:*
## *"Spring up, O well!—Sing to it!"*

NUMBERS 21:17

This well was famous in the wilderness because it was *the subject of a promise*: "That is the well of which the Lord said to Moses, 'Gather the people together, so that I may give them water.'" The people needed water, and it was promised by their gracious God. We need fresh supplies of heavenly grace, and in the covenant the Lord has pledged Himself to give us all we require. The well also became *the cause of a song*. Before the water gushed out, cheerful faith prompted the people to sing; and as they saw the crystal fountain bubbling up, the music grew more joyful. In similar fashion, we who believe the promise of God should rejoice in the prospect of divine revivals in our souls, and as we experience them our holy joy should overflow. Are we thirsting? Then let us not grumble but sing. Spiritual thirst is bitter to bear, but we need not bear it—the promise indicates a well; so let us be of good heart, and look for it. Moreover, the well was *the center of prayer*. "Spring up, O well." What God has promised to give, we must seek after, or we show that we have neither desire nor faith. This evening let us ask that the Scripture we have read, and our devotional exercises, may not be an empty formality but a channel of grace to our souls. May God the Holy Spirit work in us with all His mighty power, filling us with all the fullness of God. Lastly, the well was *the object of effort*. "The nobles of the people delved, with the scepter and with their staffs." The Lord wants us to be active in obtaining grace. Our implements are ill suited for digging in the sand, but we must use them to the best of our ability. Prayer must not be neglected; the gathering of God's people must not be forsaken; ordinances must not be set aside. The Lord will give us His peace most generously, but not on the path of laziness. Let us, then, stir ourselves to seek Him in whom we find all our fresh and flowing springs.

## *I came to my garden, my sister, my bride.*

SONG OF SOLOMON 5:1

The heart of the believer is Christ's garden. He bought it with His precious blood, and He enters it and claims it as His own. A garden *implies separation*. It is not the open field; it is not a wilderness; it is walled around or hedged in. If only we could see the wall of separation between the church and the world made broader and stronger. It is sad to hear Christians saying, "Well, there is no harm in this; there is no harm in that," and by this approach getting as near to the world as possible. Grace is at a low ebb in the soul that is always inquiring about how far it may go in worldly conformity. A garden is a place of beauty; it far surpasses the wild uncultivated lands. The genuine Christian must seek to be more excellent in his life than the best moralist, because Christ's garden ought to produce the best flowers in all the world. Even the best is poor compared with what Christ deserves; let us not disappoint Him with withering and feeble plants. The rarest, richest, choicest lilies and roses ought to bloom in the place that Jesus calls His own. The garden is *a place of growth*. The believer must not remain undeveloped, just mere buds and blossoms. We should grow in grace and in the knowledge of our Lord and Savior Jesus Christ. Growth should be rapid where Jesus is the gardener and the Holy Spirit the dew from heaven. A garden is *a place of retirement*. So the Lord Jesus Christ would have us reserve our souls as a place in which He can show Himself, in a way that He does not to the world. As Christians we should be far keener to keep our hearts closely shut up for Christ! We often worry and trouble ourselves, like Martha, with much serving, and like her we do not have the room for Christ that Mary had, and we do not sit at His feet as we ought. May the Lord grant the sweet showers of His grace to water His garden today.

> *My beloved is mine, and I am his;*
> *he grazes among the lilies. Until the day*
> *breathes and the shadows flee, turn, my beloved,*
> *be like a gazelle or a young stag on*
> *cleft mountains.*

SONG OF SOLOMON 2:16-17

Surely if there is a happy verse in the Bible it is this—"My beloved is mine, and I am his." It is so peaceful, so full of assurance, so overflowing with happiness and contentment, that it might well have been written by the same hand that penned the Twenty-third Psalm. Yet though the prospect is very bright and lovely—as fair a scene as earth can display—it is not an entirely sunlit landscape. There is a cloud in the sky, which casts a shadow over the scene. Listen: "Until the day breathes and the shadows flee."

There is a word, too, about the "cleft mountains," or "the mountains of division," and to our love, anything like division is bitterness. Beloved, this may be your present state of mind. You do not doubt your salvation, you know that Christ is yours, but you are not feasting with Him. You understand your vital interest in Him, so that you do not have a shadow of a doubt about being His and of His being yours, but still His left hand is not under your head, nor does His right hand embrace you. A shade of sadness is cast over your heart, perhaps by affliction, certainly by the temporary absence of your Lord, so that even while exclaiming, "I am his," you are forced to take to your knees and to pray, "Until the day breathes, and the shadows flee, turn, my beloved."

"Where is He?" asks the soul. And the answer comes, "He grazes among the lilies." If we would find Christ, we must get into communion with His people, we must come to the ordinances with His saints. Oh, for an evening glimpse of Him! Oh, to eat with Him tonight!

## *And immediately they left their nets and followed him.*

MARK 1:18

When they heard the call of Jesus, Simon and Andrew obeyed at once without hesitation. If we did likewise and punctually with resolute zeal put into practice what we hear immediately, then our attendance at the means of grace and our reading of good books could not fail to enrich us spiritually. He will not lose his loaf who has taken care to eat it immediately; neither can he be deprived of the benefit of the doctrine who has already acted upon it. Most readers and hearers become moved to decide to take action; but sadly, the proposal is a blossom that has not flowered, and as a result no fruit comes from it; they wait, they waver, and then they forget, until, like the ponds on frosty nights, when the sun shines by day, they are only thawed in time to be frozen again. That fatal tomorrow is blood-red with the murder of good resolutions; it is the slaughterhouse of the innocents. We are very concerned that our little book of "Evening Readings" should not be fruitless, and therefore we pray that readers may not be readers only, but doers of the Word. *The practice of truth is the fruit of profitable reading.* Should the reader be impressed with any duty while perusing these pages, let him be quick to fulfill it before the holy glow has departed from his soul, and let him leave his nets and all that he has rather than be found rebellious to the Master's call. Do not give place to the devil by delay! Act while opportunity and desire are working in happy partnership. Do not be caught in your own nets, but break the meshes of worldliness, and go where glory calls you. Happy is the writer who will meet with readers resolved to carry out his teachings: His harvest will be a hundredfold, and his Master will have great honor. We can only pray that this might be our reward from these brief meditations and hurried hints. Grant it, O Lord, to Your servant!

## But God's firm foundation stands.

2 TIMOTHY 2:19

The foundation upon which our faith rests is this, that "in Christ God was reconciling the world to himself, not counting their trespasses against them."[1] The great fact on which genuine faith relies is that "the Word became flesh and dwelt among us,"[2] and that "Christ also suffered once for sins, the righteous for the unrighteous, that he might bring us to God";[3] "He himself bore our sins in his body on the tree";[4] "Upon him was the chastisement that brought us peace, and with his stripes we are healed."[5] In one word, the great pillar of the Christian's hope is *substitution*. The vicarious sacrifice of Christ for the guilty, Christ being made sin for us that we might be made the righteousness of God in Him, Christ offering up a true and proper expiatory and substitutionary sacrifice in the room, place, and stead of as many as the Father gave Him, who are known to God by name and are recognized in their own hearts by their trusting in Jesus—this is the cardinal fact of the Gospel. If this foundation were removed, what could we do? But it stands firm as the throne of God. We know it; we rest on it; we rejoice in it; and our delight is to hold it, to meditate upon it, and to proclaim it, while we desire to be stirred and moved by gratitude for it in every part of our life and conversation. In these days a direct attack is made upon the doctrine of the Atonement. Men cannot bear substitution. They gnash their teeth at the thought of the Lamb of God bearing the sin of man. But we, who know by experience the preciousness of this truth, will proclaim it confidently and unceasingly and in defiance of them. We will neither dilute it nor change it, nor distort it in any shape or fashion. It shall still be Christ, a *positive substitute*, bearing human guilt and suffering in the place of men. We cannot, dare not give it up, for it is our life, and despite every controversy we affirm that "God's firm foundation stands."

[1] 2 Corinthians 5:19  [2] John 1:14  [3] 1 Peter 3:18  [4] 1 Peter 2:24
[5] Isaiah 53:5

### . . . *in order that the things that cannot be shaken may remain.*

HEBREWS 12:27

We have many things in our possession at the present moment that can be shaken, and it is not good for a Christian to rely upon them, for there is nothing stable beneath these rolling skies; change is written upon all things. Yet we have certain "things that cannot be shaken," and I invite you this evening to think of them—that if the things that can be shaken should all be taken away, you may derive real comfort from the things that cannot be shaken and that will remain. Whatever your losses have been, or may be, you enjoy present salvation. You are standing at the foot of Christ's cross, trusting alone in the merit of His precious blood, and no rise or fall of the markets can interfere with your salvation in Him; no breaking of banks, no failures and bankruptcies can touch that. Then you are *a child of God* this evening. God is your Father. No change of circumstances can ever rob you of that. Even if by loss you are brought to poverty and stripped bare, you can still say, "He is still my Father. In my Father's house are many rooms; therefore I will not be troubled." You have another permanent blessing, namely, *the love of Jesus Christ*. He who is God and man loves you with all the strength of His affectionate nature—nothing can affect that. The fig tree may not blossom, and the flocks may dwindle and wander from the field, but it does not matter to the man who can sing, "My Beloved is mine, and I am His." Our best portion and richest heritage we cannot lose. Whatever troubles come, let us play the man; let us show that we are not like little children cast down by what happens to us in this poor fleeting state of time. Our country is Immanuel's land, our hope is fixed in heaven, and therefore, calm as the summer's ocean, we will see the wreck of everything earthborn and yet rejoice in the God of our salvation.

## *We wait eagerly for adoption as sons.*

ROMANS 8:23

Even in this world saints are God's children, but the only way that people will discover this is by certain moral character- istics. The adoption is not displayed; the children are not yet openly declared. Among the Romans a man might adopt a child and keep it private for a long time; but there was a second adop- tion in public; when the child was brought before the constituted authorities, its old clothes were removed, and the father who took it to be his child gave it clothing suitable to its new status in life. "Beloved, we are God's children now, and what we will be has not yet appeared."[1] We are not yet clothed in the apparel of heaven's royal family; we are wearing in this flesh and blood just what we wore as the children of Adam. But we know that "when he appears" who is "the firstborn among many brothers,"[2] we will be like Him, for we will see Him as He is. Can't you imagine that a child taken from the lowest ranks of society and adopted by a Roman senator would say to himself, "I long for the day when I shall be publicly adopted. Then I shall discard these poor clothes and be dressed in clothes that depict my senatorial rank"? Glad for what he has already received, he still groans until he gets the fullness of what has been promised to him. So it is with us today. We are waiting until we put on our proper clothes and are declared as the children of God for all to see. We are young nobles and have not yet worn our crowns. We are young brides, and the marriage day has not arrived, but our fiancÉe's love for us leads us to long and sigh for the bridal morning. Our very happi- ness makes us long for more; our joy, like a swollen stream, longs to spring up like a fountain, leaping to the skies, heaving and groaning within our spirit for lack of space and room by which to reveal itself to men.

[1]1 John 3:2  [2]Romans 8:29

### Shadrach, Meshach, and Abednego answered and said . . . "be it known to you, O king, that we will not serve your gods."

DANIEL 3:16, 18

The narrative of the manly courage and marvelous deliverance of these three holy children, or rather champions, is well calculated to engender in the minds of believers firmness and steadfastness in upholding the truth in the teeth of tyranny and in the very jaws of death. Here is a wonderful example especially for young Christians, teaching them that when it comes to faith in action they must never sacrifice their consciences. Lose everything rather than lose your integrity, and when everything is gone, still hold fast a clear conscience as the rarest jewel that can adorn the bosom of a mortal. Do not be guided by expediency but by divine authority. Follow the right at every hazard. When you see no obvious advantage, then walk by faith and not by sight. Honor God by trusting Him when it comes to matters of loss for the sake of principle. See whether He will be your debtor! See if He does not even in this life prove His word that "there is great gain in godliness with contentment,"[1] and that for those who "seek first the kingdom of God and his righteousness . . . all these things will be added to you."[2] Should it happen that in the providence of God you are a loser for conscience's sake, you will find that if the Lord does not pay you back in the silver of earthly prosperity, He will discharge His promise in the gold of spiritual joy. Remember that a man's life does not consist in the abundance of what he possesses. To wear an honest spirit, to have a heart void of offense, to have the favor and smile of God is greater riches than all the gold and diamonds in the world. "Better is a dinner of herbs where love is than a fattened ox and hatred with it."[3] An ounce of contentment is worth a ton of gold.

[1] 1 Timothy 6:6   [2] Matthew 6:33   [3] Proverbs 15:17

## *But the dove found no place to set her foot.*

GENESIS 8:9

Reader, can you find rest apart from the ark, Christ Jesus? Then consider that your religion may be in vain. Are you satisfied with anything short of a conscious knowledge of your union and interest in Christ? Then woe to you. If you profess to be a Christian while finding full satisfaction in worldly pleasures and pursuits, your profession is probably false. If your soul can stretch herself at rest and find the bed long enough and the blanket broad enough to cover it in the chambers of sin, then you are a hypocrite and far away from any proper thoughts of Christ or awareness of His preciousness. But if, on the other hand, you feel that if you could indulge in sin without punishment, that would be a punishment itself, and that if you could have the whole world and live in it forever, it would be quite enough misery not to be separated from it, for your God—your God—is what your soul longs for, then be of good courage, you are a child of God. With all your sins and imperfections, take this for your comfort: If your soul has no rest in sin, you are not as the sinner is! If you are still crying after and craving after something better, Christ has not forgotten you, for you have not quite forgotten Him. The believer cannot do without his Lord; words are inadequate to express his thoughts of Him. We cannot live on the sands of the wilderness—we want the manna that drops from heaven; the pitchers of self-confidence cannot produce for us a drop of moisture, but we drink of the rock that follows us, and that rock is Christ. When you feed on Him, your soul can sing, "He who satisfies me with good so that my youth is renewed like the eagle's";[1] but if you don't have Him, your wine cellar and well-stocked pantry can give you no sort of satisfaction: Learn to lament over them in the words of wisdom, "Vanity of vanities, all is vanity!"

[1]See Psalm 103:5

## . . . *having escaped from the corruption that is in the world because of sinful desire.*

2 PETER 1:4

Banish forever any thought of indulging the flesh if you want to live in the power of your risen Lord. It is incongruous for a man who is alive in Christ to dwell in the corruption of sin. "Why do you seek the living among the dead?" said the angel to the women. Should the living dwell in the tombs? Should divine life be imprisoned in the burial ground of fleshly lust? How can we partake of the cup of the Lord and yet drink the cup of the devil? Surely, believer, from blatant lusts and sins you are delivered, but have you also escaped from those that are more secret and delusive? Have you left behind the lust of pride? Have you escaped from laziness? Have you given up trusting in earthly things? Are you seeking each day to live above worldliness, the pride of life, and the ensnaring grip of greed? Remember, it is in order that you might know such victory that you have been enriched with the treasures of God. If you are really the chosen of God, and beloved by Him, do not allow all this lavish treasure of grace to be wasted on you. Pursue holiness; it is the Christian's crown and glory. An unholy church is useless to the world and of no esteem among men. It is an abomination, hell's laughter, heaven's abhorrence. The worst evils that have ever come upon the world have been brought upon her by an unholy church. O Christian, the vows of God are upon you. You are God's servant: Act as such. You are God's king: Reign over your lusts. You are God's chosen: Do not associate with Satan. Heaven is your portion: Live like a heavenly spirit, and in this way you will prove that you have true faith in Jesus, for there cannot be faith in the heart unless there is holiness in the life.

*Lord, I desire to live as one*
*Who bears a blood-bought name,*
*As one who fears but grieving Thee,*
*And knows no other shame.*

## *Each one should remain in the condition in which he was called.*

1 CORINTHIANS 7:20

Some people have the foolish notion that the only way in which they can live for God is by becoming pastors, missionaries, or Bible teachers. How many would be excluded from any opportunity of spiritual usefulness if this were the case. Beloved, it is not office—it is sincerity; it is not position—it is grace that will enable us to serve and glorify God. God is definitely glorified at the workbench, where the godly worker fulfills his task singing of the Savior's love. In this humble setting God is glorified far more than in many a lofty pulpit where official religion performs its scanty duties. The name of Jesus is glorified by the taxicab driver as he blesses God and speaks to his passengers of the living hope. He will be more useful than the popular preacher who goes about peddling the Gospel for profit. God is glorified when we serve Him in our proper vocations. Take care, dear reader, that you do not neglect the path of duty by leaving your occupation, and take care you do not dishonor your profession while in it. Think little of yourselves, but do not think too little of your callings. Every lawful trade may be sanctified by the Gospel to noblest ends. Turn to the Bible, and you will find the most menial forms of labor connected either with most daring deeds of faith or with persons whose lives have been illustrations of holiness. Therefore do not be discontented with your calling. Whatever God has made your position or your work, remain in that, unless you are quite sure that He calls you to something else. Let your first concern be to glorify God to the best of your ability where you are. Fill your present sphere to His praise, and if He needs you in another, He will show it you. This evening lay aside anxious ambition, and embrace peaceful content.

## But Aaron's staff swallowed up their staffs.

EXODUS 7:12

This incident is an instructive illustration of the certain victory of God's handiwork over all opposition. Whenever a divine principle is set in the heart, even though the devil may create a counterfeit and produce swarms of opponents, we may be sure that God is in the work, and it will swallow up all its foes. If God's grace takes possession of a man, the world's magicians may throw down all their staffs, and every staff may be as cunning and poisonous as a serpent; but Aaron's staff will swallow up their staffs. The sweet attractions of the cross will woo and win the man's heart, so that although he had lived only for this deceitful earth, he will now have an eye for heaven, and his mind will be set on the things that are above. When grace has won the day, the unbeliever begins to seek the world to come. The same fact is to be observed in the life of the believer. A company of enemies assailed our faith—our old sins; the devil threw them down before us, and they turned to serpents. What numbers of them! But the cross of Jesus destroys them all. Faith in Christ makes short work of all our sins. Then the devil has launched another host of serpents in the form of worldly trials, temptations, unbelief; but faith in Jesus is more than a match for them and overcomes them all. The same absorbing principle shines in the faithful service of God! With an enthusiastic love for Jesus, difficulties are surmounted; sacrifices become pleasures; sufferings are honors. But if faith is a consuming passion in the heart, then it follows that there are many people who profess it but do not have it; for what they have will not bear this test. Examine yourself, my reader, on this point. Aaron's staff proved its heaven-given power. Is your faith doing so? If Christ is anything, He must be everything. Do not rest until love and faith in Jesus are the master passions of your soul!

***And so in the matter of the envoys of the princes
of Babylon, who had been sent to him to inquire
about the sign that had been done in the land,
God left him to himself, in order to test him
and to know all that was in his heart.***

2 CHRONICLES 32:31

Hezekiah was growing so inwardly great and priding himself
so much upon the favor of God that self-righteousness crept
in, and because he trusted in himself, the grace of God was for a
time, in its more active operations, withdrawn. If the grace of God
were to leave the best Christian, there is enough sin in his heart to
make him the worst of transgressors. If left to yourselves, you who
are warmest for Christ would cool down like Laodicea into sicken-
ing lukewarmness: You who are sound in the faith would be white
with the leprosy of false doctrine; you who now walk before the
Lord in excellency and integrity would reel to and fro and stagger
with a drunkenness of evil passion. Like the moon, we borrow
our light; bright as we are when grace shines on us, we are darkness itself when the Sun of Righteousness withdraws Himself.
*Therefore, let us cry to God to never leave us.* "Take not Your Holy
Spirit from me! Do not withdraw from us Your indwelling grace!
Have You not said, 'I, the LORD, am its keeper; every moment I
water it. Lest anyone punish it, I keep it night and day'?[1] Lord,
keep us everywhere. Keep us when we're in the valley so that
we do not grumble against Your humbling hand; keep us when
we're on the mountain, so we do not lose our balance by being
lifted up; keep us in youth, when our passions are strong; keep
us in old age, when becoming conceited in our wisdom, we may
therefore prove greater fools than those who are young and silly;
keep us when we come to die, in case at the very end we should
deny You! Keep us living, keep us dying, keep us working, keep us
suffering, keep us fighting, keep us resting, keep us everywhere,
for everywhere we need You, O our God!"

[1]Isaiah 27:3

> *Ah, Lord GOD! It is you who has made the heavens and the earth by your great power and by your outstretched arm! Nothing is too hard for you.*

JEREMIAH 32:17

At the very time when the Chaldeans surrounded Jerusalem, and when the sword, famine, and pestilence had desolated the land, Jeremiah was commanded by God to purchase a field and have the deed of transfer legally sealed and witnessed. This was a strange purchase for a rational man to make. Caution could not justify it, for it was buying with hardly a probability that the purchaser would ever enjoy the possession. But it was enough for Jeremiah that his God had instructed him, for he knew with certainty that God will be justified of all His children. He reasoned thus: "Lord God, You can make this plot of ground useful to me; You can rid this land of these oppressors; You can make me sit under my vine and my fig-tree in the heritage that I have bought; for You made the heavens and the earth, and there is nothing too hard for You." There was a majesty in the early saints, who dared to do at God's command things that human reason would condemn. Whether it be a Noah who is to build a ship on dry land, an Abraham who is to offer up his only son, a Moses who is to despise the treasures of Egypt, or a Joshua who is to besiege Jericho for seven days, using no weapons but the blasts of trumpets, they all act upon God's command, contrary to the dictates of human reason; and the Lord gives them a rich reward as the result of their obedient faith. Would to God we had in contemporary Christianity a more potent infusion of this heroic faith in God. If we would venture more upon the naked promise of God, we would enter a world of wonders to which as yet we are strangers. May Jeremiah's place of confidence become ours—nothing is too hard for the God that created the heavens and the earth.

## . . . *the sound of the LORD God walking in the garden in the cool of the day.*

GENESIS 3:8

My soul, now that the cool of the day has come, retire awhile and hearken to the voice of God. He is always ready to speak with you when you are prepared to hear. If there is any slowness to commune, it is not on His part, but altogether on yours, for He stands at the door and knocks, and if His people will but open, He rejoices to enter. But in what state is my heart, which is my Lord's garden? May I venture to hope that it is well trimmed and watered and is bringing forth fruit fit for Him? If not, He will have much to reprove, but still I pray Him to come to me, for nothing can so certainly bring my heart into a right condition as the presence of the Sun of Righteousness, who brings healing in His wings. Come, therefore, O Lord, my God, my soul invites You earnestly and waits for You eagerly. Come to me, O Jesus, my well-beloved, and plant fresh flowers in my garden, such as I see blooming in such perfection in Your matchless character! Come, O my Father, who is the Gardener, and deal with me in Your tenderness and prudence! Come, O Holy Spirit, and saturate my whole nature, as the herbs are now moistened with the evening dews. O that God would speak to me. Speak, Lord, for Your servant hears! O that He would walk with me; I am ready to give up my whole heart and mind to Him, and every other thought is hushed. I am only asking what He delights to give. I am sure that He will condescend to have fellowship with me, for He has given me His Holy Spirit to abide with me forever. Sweet is the cool twilight, when every star seems like the eye of heaven and the cool wind is as the breath of celestial love. My Father, my elder Brother, my sweet Comforter, speak now in loving-kindness, for You have opened my ear and I am not rebellious.

> *To you, O LORD, I call; my rock, be not deaf to me,*
> *lest, if you be silent to me, I become like those*
> *who go down to the pit.*

PSALM 28:1

A cry is the natural expression of sorrow, and a suitable utterance when all other modes of appeal fail us; but the cry must be alone directed to the Lord, for to cry to man is to waste our entreaties upon the air. When we consider the readiness of the Lord to hear and His ability to aid, we shall see good reason for directing all our appeals at once to the God of our salvation. It will be in vain to call to the rocks in the day of judgment, but our Rock attends to our cries.

"*Be not deaf to me.*" Mere formalists may be content without answers to their prayers, but genuine suppliants cannot; they are not satisfied with the results of prayer itself in calming the mind and subduing the will—they must go further and obtain actual replies from heaven or they cannot rest; and those replies they long to receive at once—they dread even a little of God's silence. God's voice is often so terrible that it shakes the wilderness; but His silence is equally full of awe to an eager suppliant. When God seems to close His ear, we must not therefore close our mouths but rather cry with more earnestness; for when our note grows shrill with eagerness and grief, He will not long deny us a hearing. What a dreadful case we would be in if the Lord should become forever deaf to our prayers. "*Lest, if you be silent to me, I become like those who go down to the pit.*" Deprived of the God who answers prayer, we would be in a more pitiable plight than the dead in the grave and would soon sink to the same level as the lost in hell. We *must* have answers to prayer: Ours is an urgent case of dire necessity; surely the Lord will speak peace to our agitated minds, for He never can find it in His heart to permit His own elect to perish.

## If we endure, we will also reign with him.

2 TIMOTHY 2:12

*W*e must not imagine that we are suffering for Christ and with Christ if we are not in Christ. Beloved friend, are you trusting in Jesus only? If not, whatever you may have to mourn over on earth, you are not suffering with Christ and have no hope of reigning with Him in heaven. Neither are we to conclude that all a Christian's sufferings are sufferings with Christ, *for it is essential that he be called by God to suffer*. If we are rash and imprudent and run into positions for which neither providence nor grace has fitted us, we ought to question whether we are not rather sinning than communing with Jesus. If we let passion take the place of judgment, and self-will reign instead of scriptural authority, we shall fight the Lord's battles with the devil's weapons, and if we cut our own fingers we must not be surprised. Again, *in troubles that come upon us as the result of sin, we must not dream that we are suffering with Christ*. When Miriam spoke evil of Moses, and the leprosy polluted her, she was not suffering for God. Moreover, suffering that God accepts must have God's glory as its end. If I suffer that I may earn a name or win applause, I shall get no other reward than that of the Pharisee. It is required also that *love for Jesus and love for His people should always be the mainspring of all our patience. We must manifest the Spirit of Christ* in meekness, gentleness, and forgiveness. Let us search and see if we truly *suffer with Jesus*. And if we do suffer in this way, what is our "slight momentary affliction"[1] compared with *reigning with Him*? Oh, it is so blessed to be in the furnace with Christ, and such an honor to stand in the jail with Him, that if there were no future reward, we might count ourselves happy in present honor; but when the recompense is so eternal, so infinitely more than we had any right to expect, shall we not take up the cross with enthusiasm and go on our way rejoicing?

[1] 2 Corinthians 4:16

### He who has clean hands and a pure heart, who does not lift up his soul to what is false and does not swear deceitfully.

PSALM 24:4

Outward practical holiness is a very precious mark of grace. It is to be feared that many professors have perverted the doctrine of justification by faith in such a way as to treat good works with contempt; if so, they will receive everlasting contempt at the last great day. If our hands are not clean, let us wash them in Jesus' precious blood, and so let us lift up pure hands unto God. But *"clean hands"* will not suffice unless they are connected with *"a pure heart."* True religion is heart-work. We may wash the outside of the cup and the plate as long as we please, but if the inward parts be filthy, we are filthy altogether in the sight of God, for our hearts are more truly ourselves than our hands are. The very life of our being lies in the inner nature, and hence the imperative need of purity within. The pure in heart shall see God; all others are but blind bats.

The man who is born for heaven *"does not lift up his soul to what is false."* All men have their joys by which their souls are lifted up. The worldling lifts up his soul in carnal delights, which are mere empty vanities; but the saint loves more substantial things; like Jehoshaphat, he is lifted up in the ways of the Lord. He who is content with husks will be reckoned with the swine. Does the world satisfy you? Then you have your reward and portion in this life; make much of it, for you will know no other joy.

*"Does not swear deceitfully."* The saints are men of honor still. The Christian man's word is his only oath; but that is as good as twenty oaths of other men. False speaking will shut any man out of heaven, for a liar shall not enter into God's house, whatever may be his professions or doings. Reader, does the text before us condemn you, or do you hope to ascend into the hill of the Lord?

## Trust in the LORD forever, for the LORD God is an everlasting rock.

ISAIAH 26:4

Seeing that we have such a God to trust, let us rest upon Him with all our weight; let us resolutely drive out all unbelief and endeavor to get rid of doubts and fears, which spoil our comfort, since there is no excuse for fear when God is the foundation of our trust. A loving parent would be sorely grieved if his child could not trust him; and how ungenerous, how unkind is our conduct when we put so little confidence in our heavenly Father, who has never failed us and who never will. It would be good if doubting was banished from the household of God; but it is to be feared that old Unbelief is as nimble today as when the psalmist asked, "Will the LORD spurn forever, and never again be favorable?"[1] David had not tested the mighty sword of the giant Goliath for long, and yet he said, "There is none like that."[2] He had tried it once in the hour of his youthful victory, and it had proved itself to be of the right metal, and therefore he praised it ever afterwards. Even so should we speak well of our God; there is none like unto Him in the heaven above or the earth beneath. "To whom will you liken me and make me equal, and compare me, that we may be alike?"[3] There is no rock like the rock of Jacob, our enemies themselves being judges. So far from tolerating doubts to live in our hearts, we will take the whole detestable crew, as Elijah did the prophets of Baal, and slay them over the brook; and for a stream to kill them at, we will select the sacred torrent that flows from our Savior's wounded side. We have been in many trials, but we have never yet been placed where we could not find in our God all that we needed. Let us then be encouraged to trust in the Lord forever, assured that His ever-lasting strength will be, as it has been, our deliverance and comfort.

[1]Psalm 77:7   [2]1 Samuel 21:9   [3]Isaiah 46:5

## *How many are my iniquities and my sins?*

JOB 13:23

Have you ever really weighed and considered how great the sin of God's people is? Think how heinous is your own transgression, and you will find that not only does a sin here and there tower up like an alp, but that your iniquities are heaped upon each other, as in the old fable of the giants who piled Pelian upon Ossa,[1] mountain upon mountain. What an aggregate of sin there is in the life of one of the most sanctified of God's children! Attempt to multiply this, the sin of one only, by the multitude of the redeemed, "a great multitude that no one could number,"[2] and you will have some conception of the great mass of the guilt of the people for whom Jesus shed His blood. But we arrive at a more adequate idea of the magnitude of sin by the greatness of the remedy provided. It is the blood of Jesus Christ, God's only and well-beloved Son. God's Son! Angels cast their crowns before Him! All the choral symphonies of heaven surround His glorious throne. "God over all, blessed forever. Amen."[3] And yet He takes upon Himself the form of a servant and is scourged and pierced, bruised and torn, and at last slain; nothing but the blood of the incarnate Son of God could make atonement for our offenses. No human mind can adequately estimate the infinite value of the divine sacrifice, for although the sin of God's people is great, the atonement that takes it away is immeasurably greater. Therefore, even when sin rolls in like a flood, and the remembrance of the past is bitter, the believer can still stand before the blazing throne of the great and holy God and cry, "Who is to condemn? Christ Jesus is the one who died—more than that, who was raised."[4] While the recollection of the believer's sin fills him with shame and sorrow, its very darkness serves to show the brightness of mercy; guilt is the dark night in which the fair star of divine love shines with serene splendor.

[1]The giant sons of Iphimedia who tried to reach Olympus by piling
  Mt. Pelian on Mt. Ossa (The Odyssey).
[2]Revelation 7:9   [3]Romans 9:5   [4]Romans 8:34

## *When I passed by you . . . I said to you . . . "Live!"*

EZEKIEL 16:6

Believer, consider gratefully this mandate of mercy. Note that this decree of God is *majestic*. In our text we find a sinner with nothing in him but sin, expecting nothing but wrath; but the eternal Lord passes by in His glory. He looks, He pauses, and He pronounces the solitary but royal word, "Live." Only God can speak in this way, dispensing life with a single syllable! Again, this decree is *manifold*. When He says "Live," it includes many things. Here is judicial life. The sinner is ready to be condemned, but the Mighty One says, "Live," and he rises pardoned and absolved. It is spiritual life. We did not know Jesus—our eyes could not see Christ, our ears could not hear His voice—but Jehovah said "Live," and we who were dead in trespasses and sins were quickened. Moreover, it includes glory-life, which is the perfection of spiritual life. "I said to you . . . 'Live,'" and that word rolls on through all the years of time till death comes; and even in the shadows of death, the Lord's voice is still heard—"Live!" In the morning of the resurrection it is that selfsame voice that is echoed by the archangel, "Live," and as holy spirits rise to heaven to be blessed forever in the glory of their God, it is in the power of this same word, "Live." Note again, that it is an *irresistible* decree. Saul of Tarsus is on the road to Damascus to arrest the saints of the living God. A voice is heard from heaven, and a light is seen above the brightness of the sun, and Saul is crying out, "Who are you, Lord?"[1] This decree is of *free grace*. When sinners are saved, it is only and solely because God will do it to magnify His free, unpurchased, unsought grace. Christians, see your position—debtors to grace; show your gratitude by earnest, Christlike lives; and as God has called you to live, see to it that you do so in sincerity.

[1]Acts 9:5

> *Lead me in your truth and teach me,*
> *for you are the God of my salvation;*
> *for you I wait all the day long.*

PSALM 25:5

When the believer has begun with trembling feet to walk in the way of the Lord, he still asks to be led onward like a little child upheld by its parent's helping hand, and he yearns to receive further instruction in the alphabet of truth. Experimental teaching is the burden of this prayer. David knew much, but he felt his ignorance and desired to be still in the Lord's school: four times over in two verses he applies for a scholarship in the college of grace. It would be better for many professors if instead of following their own devices and cutting out new paths of thought for themselves, they would inquire for the good old ways of God's own truth and beseech the Holy Ghost to give them sanctified understandings and teachable spirits. *"For you are the God of my salvation."* Jehovah is the Author and Perfecter of salvation to His people. Reader, is He the God of your salvation? Do you find in the Father's election, in the Son's atonement, and in the Spirit's quickening all the grounds of your eternal hopes? If so, you may use this as an argument for obtaining further blessings; if the Lord has ordained to save you, surely He will not refuse to instruct you in His ways. It is a happy thing when we can address the Lord with the confidence that David displays here; it gives us great power in prayer and comfort in trial. *"For you I wait all the day long."* Patience is the fair handmaid and daughter of faith; we cheerfully wait when we are certain that we shall not wait in vain. It is our duty and our privilege to wait upon the Lord in service, in worship, in expectancy, in trust all the days of our life. Our faith will be tried faith, and if it is of the true kind, it will bear continued trial without yielding. We shall not grow weary of waiting upon God if we remember how long and how graciously He once waited for us.

202

## *And God separated the light from the darkness.*

GENESIS 1:4

A believer has two principles at work within him. In his natural estate he was subject to one principle only, which was darkness; now light has entered, and the two principles disagree. Consider the apostle Paul's words in the seventh chapter of Romans: "I find it to be a law that when I want to do right, evil lies close at hand. For I delight in the law of God, in my inner being, but I see in my members another law waging war against the law of my mind and making me captive to the law of sin that dwells in my members."[1] How is this state of things occasioned? "God separated the light from the darkness." Darkness, by itself, is quiet and undisturbed, but when the Lord sends in light, there is a conflict, for the one is in opposition to the other, a conflict that will never end until the believer is altogether light in the Lord. If there is a division *inside* the individual Christian, there is certain to be *a division outside*. As soon as the Lord gives light to any man, he proceeds to separate himself from the darkness around; he withdraws from a merely worldly religion of outward ceremony, for nothing short of the Gospel of Christ will now satisfy him, and he removes himself from worldly society and frivolous amusements and seeks the company of the saints, for "We know that we have passed out of death into life, because we love the brothers."[2] The light gathers to itself, and the darkness to itself. What God has separated, let us never try to unite; but as Christ went outside the camp, bearing His reproach, let us come out from the ungodly and be a special people. He was holy, harmless, undefiled, separate from sinners; and as He was, so we are to be nonconformists to the world, dissenting from all sin, and distinguished from the rest of mankind by our likeness to our Master.

[1]Romans 7:21-23   [2]1 John 3:14

## And there was evening and there was morning, the first day.

GENESIS 1:5

The evening was "darkness," and the morning was "light," and *yet the two together are called by the name that is given to the light alone*! This is somewhat remarkable, but it has an exact analogy in spiritual experience. In every believer there is darkness and light, and yet he is not to be named a sinner because there is sin in him, but he is to be named a saint because he possesses some degree of holiness. This will be a most comforting thought to those who are mourning their infirmities and who ask, "Can I be a child of God while there is so much darkness in me?" Yes; like the "day," you do not take your name from the evening, but from the morning; and you are spoken of in the Word of God as if you were even now perfectly holy, as you will be soon. You are called the child of light, even though there is darkness in you still. You are named after what is the predominating quality in the sight of God, which will one day be the only principal remaining. Notice that *the evening comes first*. Naturally we are darkness first in order of time, and the gloom is often first in our mournful apprehension, driving us to cry out in deep humiliation, "God, be merciful to me, a sinner."[1] The place of the morning is second; it dawns when grace overcomes nature. It is a blessed maxim of John Bunyan, "That which is last, lasts forever." That which is first yields in due season to the last; but nothing comes after the last. So though you are naturally darkness, once you become light in the Lord, there is no evening to follow; "your sun shall no more go down."[2] The first day in this life is an evening and a morning; but the second day, when we shall be with God forever, shall be a day with no evening, but one, sacred, high, eternal noon.

[1]Luke 18:13  [2]Isaiah 60:20

# Tell your children of it, and let your children tell their children, and their children to another generation.

JOEL 1:3

In this simple way, by God's grace, a living testimony for truth is always to be kept alive in the land: The beloved of the Lord are to hand down their witness for the Gospel and the covenant to their heirs, and these again to their next descendants. This is our *first* duty; we are to begin at the family hearth: He is a bad preacher who does not commence his ministry at home. The heathen are to be sought by all means, and the highways and hedges are to be searched, but home has a prior claim, and woe to those who reverse the order of the Lord's arrangements. To teach our children is a *personal* duty; we cannot delegate it to Sunday school teachers or other friendly helpers. These can assist us but cannot deliver us from the sacred obligation; substitutes and sponsors are wicked devices in this case: Mothers and fathers must, like Abraham, command their households in the fear of God and talk with their offspring concerning the wondrous works of the Most High. Parental teaching is a *natural* duty. Who is better fitted to look after the child's well-being than those who are the authors of his actual being? To neglect the instruction of our children is worse than brutish. Family religion is *necessary* for the nation, for the family itself, and for the church of God. By a thousand plots empty religion is secretly advancing in our land, and one of the most effectual means for resisting its inroads is routinely neglected—namely, the instruction of our children in the faith. It is time for parents to awaken to a sense of the importance of this matter. It is a pleasant duty to talk of Jesus to our sons and daughters, and the more so because it has often proved to be an *accepted* work, for God has saved the children through the parents' prayers and admonitions. May every house into which this volume shall come honor the Lord and receive His smile.

## *His heavenly kingdom.*

2 TIMOTHY 4:18

The city of the great King is a place of *active service*. Ransomed spirits serve Him day and night in His temple. They never cease to fulfill the good pleasure of their King. They always rest, so far as ease and freedom from care is concerned, and never rest, in the sense of indolence or inactivity. Jerusalem the golden is the place of *communion* with all the people of God. We shall sit with Abraham, Isaac, and Jacob in eternal fellowship. We shall hold high converse with the noble host of the elect, all reigning with Him who by His love and His powerful arm has brought them safely home. We shall not sing solos, but in chorus shall we praise our King. Heaven is a place of *victory realized*. Whenever, Christian, you have achieved a victory over your lusts—whenever after hard struggling, you have laid a temptation dead at your feet—you have in that hour a foretaste of the joy that awaits you when the Lord shall soon tread Satan under your feet, and you shall find yourself more than a conqueror through Him who has loved you. Paradise is a place of *security*. When you enjoy the full assurance of faith, you have the pledge of that glorious security that shall be yours when you are a perfect citizen of the heavenly Jerusalem. O my sweet home, Jerusalem, happy harbor of my soul! Thanks, even now, to Him whose love has taught me to long for you; but louder thanks in eternity, when I shall possess you.

*My soul has tasted of the grapes,*
*And now it longs to go*
*Where my dear Lord His vineyard keeps*
*And all the clusters grow.*

*Upon the true and living vine,*
*My famish'd soul would feast,*
*And banquet on the fruit divine,*
*An everlasting guest.*

### Then my enemies will turn back in the day when I call. This I know, that God is for me.

PSALM 56:9

It is impossible for any human speech to express the full meaning of this delightful phrase, *"God is for me."* He was for us before the worlds were made. He was for us or He would not have given His well-beloved Son; He was for us when He smote the Only-begotten and laid the full weight of His wrath upon Him—He was for *us*, though He was against *Him*. He was "for us" when we were ruined in the Fall—He loved us notwithstanding all. He was for us when we were rebels against Him and with a high hand were bidding Him defiance. He was for us or He would not have brought us humbly to seek His face. He has been for us in many struggles; we have been summoned to encounter hosts of dangers; we have been assailed by temptations from without and within—how could we have remained unharmed to this hour if He had not been for us? He is for us with all the infinity of His being, with all the omnipotence of His love, with all the infallibility of His wisdom. Arrayed in all His divine attributes, He is for us—eternally and immutably for us; for us when the heavens shall be rolled up like a worn-out robe; for us throughout eternity. And because He is for us, the voice of prayer will always ensure His help. *"Then my enemies will turn back in the day when I call."* This is no uncertain hope, but a well-grounded assurance—*"this I know."* I will direct my prayer unto You and will look up for the answer, assured that it will come and that my enemies shall be defeated, for *"God is for me."* O believer, how happy you are with the King of kings on your side! How safe with such a Protector! How sure your cause pleaded by such an Advocate! If God be for you, who can be against you?

# Toward the dawn . . . Mary Magdalene . . . went to see the tomb.

MATTHEW 28:1

Let us learn from Mary Magdalene how to obtain fellowship with the Lord Jesus. Notice how she sought. She sought the Savior *very early* in the morning. If you can wait for Christ and be patient in the hope of having fellowship with Him at some distant season, you will never have fellowship at all; for the heart that is fitted for communion is a hungering and a thirsting heart. She sought Him also with *very great boldness*. Other disciples fled from the tomb, for they trembled and were amazed; but Mary, it is said, "stood"[1] at the tomb. If you would have Christ with you, seek Him boldly. Let nothing hold you back. Defy the world. Press on where others flee. She sought Christ *faithfully*—she stood *at the tomb*. Some find it hard to stand by a living Savior, but she stood by a dead one. Let us seek Christ after this mode, cleaving to the very least thing that has to do with Him, remaining faithful though all others should forsake Him. Note further, she sought Jesus *earnestly*—she stood "*weeping*." Those teardrops were as spells that led the Savior captive and made Him come forth and show Himself to her. If you desire Jesus' presence, weep after it! If you cannot be happy unless He come and say to you, "You are My beloved," you will soon hear His voice. Lastly, she sought the Savior *only*. What did she care about angels? She turned herself back from them; her search was only for her Lord. If Christ is your one and only love, if your heart has cast out all rivals, you will soon enjoy the comfort of His presence. Mary Magdalene sought thus *because she loved much*. Let us arouse ourselves to the same intensity of affection; let our heart, like Mary's, be full of Christ, and our love, like hers, will be satisfied with nothing short of Himself. O Lord, reveal Yourself to us this evening!

[1]John 20:11

## *He appeared first to Mary Magdalene.*

MARK 16:9

Jesus "appeared first to Mary Magdalene," probably not only on account of her great love and persevering seeking, but because, as the context intimates, she had been *a special trophy of Christ's delivering power.* Learn from this that the greatness of our sin before conversion should not make us imagine that we may not be specially favored with the very highest grade of fellowship. She was one who had left all to become *a constant attendant on the Savior.* He was her first, her chief, object. Many who were on Christ's side did not take up Christ's cross; *she* did. *She spent her substance in relieving His wants.* If we would see much of Christ, let us serve Him. Tell me who they are who sit most often under the banner of His love and drink the deepest from the cup of communion, and I am sure they will be those who give most, who serve best, and who abide closest to the bleeding heart of their dear Lord. But notice *how* Christ revealed Himself to this sorrowing one—by a *word*: "Mary."[1] It needed but one word *in His voice*, and at once she knew Him. *Her heart expressed allegiance by another word*, but her heart was too full to say more. That one word would naturally be the most fitting for the occasion. It implies obedience. She said, "*Master*" [KJV]. There is no state of mind in which this confession of allegiance will be too cold. When your spirit glows most with the heavenly fire, then you will say, "I am your servant. . . . You have loosed my bonds."[2] If you can say, "Master," if you feel that His will is your will, then you stand in a happy, holy place. He must have said, "Mary," or else you could not have said, "Rabboni," "Master." See, then, from all this how Christ honors those who honor Him, how love draws our Beloved, how it needs but one word of His to turn our weeping to rejoicing, how His presence makes the heart's sunshine.

[1]John 20:16   [2]Psalm 116:16

### You will arise and have pity on Zion; it is the time to favor her; the appointed time has come. For your servants hold her stones dear and have pity on her dust.

PSALM 102:13-14

A selfish man in trouble is exceedingly hard to comfort, because the springs of his comfort are entirely within himself, and when he is sad all his springs are dry. But a large-hearted man full of Christian generosity has other springs from which to supply himself with comfort beside those that lie within. He can go to his God first of all and there find abundant help; and he can discover arguments for consolation in things relating to the world at large, to his country, and, above all, to the Church. David in this Psalm was exceedingly sorrowful; he wrote, "I am like an owl of the waste places; I lie awake; I am like a lonely sparrow on the housetop."[1] The only way in which he could comfort himself was in the reflection that God would arise and have mercy upon Zion. Though he was sad, yet Zion should prosper; however low his own estate, yet Zion would arise. Christian man, learn to comfort yourself in God's gracious dealing toward the Church. That which is so dear to your Master, should it not also be supremely precious to you? Although your path be dark, can you not cheer your heart with the triumphs of His cross and the spread of His truth? Our own personal troubles are forgotten while we look not only upon what God has done and is doing for Zion, but on the glorious things He *will yet do* for His Church. Try this approach, O believer, whenever you are sad of heart and in heaviness of spirit: Forget yourself and your little concerns, and seek the welfare and prosperity of Zion. When you kneel in prayer to God, limit not your petition to the narrow circle of your own life, tried though it be, but send out your longing prayers for the church's prosperity. "Pray for the peace of Jerusalem,"[2] and your own soul shall be refreshed.

[1]Psalm 102:6-7  [2]Psalm 122:6

## *Let not one of them escape.*

### 1 KINGS 18:40

When the prophet Elijah had received the answer to his prayer, and the fire from heaven had consumed the sacrifice in the presence of all the people, he called upon the assembled Israelites to take the priests of Baal and sternly cried, "Let not one of them escape." He took them all down to the brook Kishon and slew them there. So must it be with our sins—they are all doomed; not one must be preserved. Our darling sin must die. Do not spare it because it cries. Strike though it be as dear as a beloved son. Strike, for God struck at sin when it was laid upon His own Son. With stern unflinching purpose you must condemn to death that sin that was once the idol of your heart. Do you ask how you are to accomplish this? Jesus will be your power. You have grace to overcome sin, given you in the covenant of grace; you have strength to win the victory in the crusade against inward lusts because Christ Jesus has promised to be with you even unto the end. If you would triumph over darkness, set yourself in the presence of the Sun of Righteousness. There is no place so well adapted for the discovery of sin and recovery from its power and guilt as the immediate presence of God. Job never knew how to get rid of sin half as well as he did when his eye of faith rested upon God, and then he abhorred himself and repented in dust and ashes. The fine gold of the Christian is often becoming dim. We need the sacred fire to consume the dross. Let us fly to our God. He is a consuming fire; He will not consume our spirit, but our sins. Let the goodness of God excite us to a sacred jealousy and to a holy revenge against those iniquities that are hateful in His sight. Go forth to battle in His strength and utterly destroy the accursed crew: "Let not one of them escape."

## *They [locusts] do not jostle one another;*
## *each marches in his path.*

JOEL 2:8

Locusts always keep their rank, and although their number is legion, they do not crowd upon each other, so as to throw their columns into confusion. This remarkable fact in natural history shows how thoroughly the Lord has infused the spirit of order into His universe, since the smallest animate creatures are as much controlled by it as are the rolling spheres or the angelic throng. It would be wise for believers to be ruled by the same influence in all their spiritual life. *In their Christian graces* no one virtue should usurp the sphere of another or feed off the rest for its own support. Affection must not smother honesty, courage must not elbow weakness out of the field, modesty must not jostle energy, and patience must not slaughter resolution. So also with *our duties*. One must not interfere with another; public usefulness must not injure private piety; church work must not push family worship into a corner. It is wrong to offer God one duty stained with the blood of another. Each thing is beautiful in its season, but not otherwise. The same rule applies to *our personal position*. We must take care to know our place, take it, and keep to it. We must minister as the Spirit has given us ability, and not intrude upon our fellow servant's domain. Our Lord Jesus taught us not to covet the high places, but to be willing to be the least among our brothers and sisters. Let us say no to an envious, ambitious spirit; let us feel the force of the Master's command and do as He bids us, keeping in step with the rest of the company. Tonight let us see whether we are keeping the unity of the Spirit in the bonds of peace, and let our prayer be that in all the churches of the Lord Jesus peace and order may prevail.

# *A bruised reed he will not break, and a smoldering wick he will not quench.*

MATTHEW 12:20

What is weaker than the bruised reed or the smoldering wick? A reed that grows in the marshland—let a wild duck land on it, and it snaps; let but the foot of man brush against it, and it is bruised and broken; every wind that flits across the river moves it to and fro. You can conceive of nothing more frail or brittle or whose existence is more in jeopardy than a bruised reed. Then look at the smoldering wick—what is it? It has a spark within it, it is true, but it is almost smothered; an infant's breath might blow it out; nothing has a more precarious existence than its flame. *Weak things* are here described; yet Jesus says of them, "The smoldering wick I will not quench; the bruised reed I will not break." Some of God's children are made strong to do mighty works for Him; God has His Samsons here and there who can pull up Gaza's gates and carry them to the top of the hill. He has a few mighties who are lionlike men, but the majority of His people are a timid, trembling race. They are like starlings, frightened at every passerby, a little fearful flock. If temptation comes, they are taken like birds in a snare; if trial threatens, they are ready to faint. Their frail craft is tossed up and down by every wave; they drift along like a seabird on the crest of the billows—weak things, without strength, without wisdom, without foresight. Yet, weak as they are, and *because* they are so weak, they have this promise made especially to them. Herein is grace and graciousness! Herein is love and loving-kindness! How it opens to us the compassion of Jesus—so gentle, tender, considerate! We need never shrink back from *His* touch. We need never fear a harsh word from *Him*; though He might well chide us for our weakness, He rebukes not. Bruised reeds shall have no blows from Him, and the smoldering wick no damping frowns.

## And now what do you gain by going to Egypt to drink the waters of the Nile?

JEREMIAH 2:18

By different miracles, by various mercies, by strange deliverances Jehovah had proved Himself to be worthy of Israel's trust. Yet they broke down the hedges with which God had enclosed them as a sacred garden; they forsook their own true and living God and followed after false gods. Constantly the Lord reproved them for this infatuation, and our text displays God's remonstrating with them, "And now what do you gain by going to Egypt to drink the waters of the Nile?" "Why are you wandering and leaving your own cool stream? Why do you forsake Jerusalem and turn aside to the wasteland? Why are you so strangely set on mischief that you cannot be content with what is good and healthy, but instead chase after what is evil and deceitful?" Is there not here a word of exposition and warning to the Christian? O true believer, called by grace and washed in the precious blood of Jesus, you have tasted a better drink than the muddy river of this world's pleasure. You have fellowship with Christ; you have obtained the joy of seeing Jesus and resting in His loving embrace. Do the trifles, the songs, the honors, the merriment of this earth content you after that? Have you eaten the bread of angels, and can you live on scraps? Good Rutherford once said, "I have tasted of Christ's own manna, and it has put my mouth out of taste for the brown bread of this world's joys." I think it should be so with you. If you are wandering after the waters of Egypt, O return quickly to the one living fountain: The waters of the Nile may be sweet to the Egyptians, but they will prove only bitterness to you. What have you to do with them? *Jesus asks you this question this evening*—what will you answer Him?

## *Why do I go mourning?*

PSALM 42:9

Can you answer this, believer? Can you find any reason why you are so often mourning instead of rejoicing? Why yield to gloomy anticipations? Who told you that the night would never end in day? Who told you that the sea of circumstances would ebb out till there should be nothing left but long stretches of the mud of horrible poverty? Who told you that the winter of your discontent would proceed from frost to frost, from snow and ice and hail to deeper snow and yet more heavy tempest of despair? Don't you know that day follows night, that flood comes after ebb, that spring and summer succeed winter? Be full of hope! Hope forever! For God does not fail you. Do you not know that God loves you in the midst of all this? Mountains, when in darkness hidden, are as real as in day, and God's love is as true to you now as it was in your brightest moments. No father chastens always. The Lord hates the rod as much as you do; He only cares to use it for that reason that would make you willing to receive it—namely, it brings about your lasting good. You will yet climb Jacob's ladder with the angels and behold Him who sits at the top of it—your covenant God. You will yet, amidst the splendors of eternity, forget the trials of time or only remember them to bless the God who led you through them and works your lasting good by them. Come, sing in the midst of tribulation. Rejoice even while passing through the furnace. Make the wilderness blossom like the rose! Cause the desert to ring with your exulting joys, for these light afflictions will soon be over, and then, forever with the Lord, your bliss shall never wane.

> *Faint not nor fear, His arms are near,*
> *He changeth not, and thou art dear;*
> *Only believe and you shalt see,*
> *That Christ is all in all to thee.*

## *"Behold the Man!"*

JOHN 19:5

If there be one place where our Lord Jesus most fully becomes the joy and comfort of His people, it is where He plunged deepest into the depths of woe. Come, gracious souls, and behold the Man in the garden of Gethsemane; behold His heart so brimming with love that He cannot hold it in—so full of sorrow that it must find expression. Behold the bloody sweat as it distills from every pore of His body and falls upon the ground. Behold the Man as they drive the nails into His hands and feet. Look up, repenting sinners, and see the sorrowful image of your suffering Lord. Consider Him as the ruby drops stand on the thorn-crown and adorn with priceless gems the diadem of the King of Misery. Behold the Man when all His bones are out of joint, and He is poured out like water and brought into the dust of death; God has forsaken Him, and hell surrounds Him. Look and see, was there ever sorrow like His sorrow that is done unto Him? All passersby pause and look upon this spectacle of grief, a wonder to men and angels, an unparalleled phenomenon. Behold the Emperor of Woe who had no equal or rival in His agonies! Gaze upon Him, you mourners, for if there is no consolation in a crucified Christ there is no joy in earth or heaven. If in the ransom price of His blood there is no hope, there is no joy in the harps of heaven, and the right hand of God shall know no pleasures forevermore. We need only sit more continually at the cross to be less troubled with our doubts and woes. We need only see *His* sorrows, and *our* sorrows we shall be ashamed to mention; we need only to gaze into His wounds and heal our own. If we would live properly, it must be by the contemplation of His death; if we would rise to dignity, it must be by considering His humiliation and His sorrow.

## *The blood of Jesus his Son cleanses us from all sin.*

1 JOHN 1:7

"Cleanses," says the text—not "*shall* cleanse." There are multitudes who think that as a dying hope they may look forward to pardon. Oh, how infinitely better to have cleansing now than to depend on the bare possibility of forgiveness when I come to die. Some imagine that a sense of pardon is an attainment only obtainable after many years of Christian experience. But forgiveness of sin is a *present* reality—a privilege for this day, a joy for this very hour. The moment a sinner trusts Jesus he is fully forgiven. The text, being written in the present tense, also indicates *continuance*; it was "cleanses" yesterday, it is "cleanses" today, it will be "cleanses" tomorrow. This is the way it will always be with you, Christian, until you cross the river; every hour you may come to this fountain, for it cleanses still. Notice, likewise, the *completeness* of the cleansing: "The blood of Jesus his Son cleanses us from all sin"—not only from sin, but "from *all* sin." Reader, I cannot convey the exceeding sweetness of this word, but I pray that God the Holy Ghost will give you a taste of it. Manifold are our sins against God. Whether the bill be little or great, the same receipt can discharge one as the other. The blood of Jesus Christ is as blessed and divine a payment for the transgressions of blaspheming Peter as for the shortcomings of loving John. Our iniquity is gone, all gone at once, and all gone forever. Blessed completeness! What a sweet theme to dwell upon as one gives himself to sleep.

> *Sins against a holy God;*
> *Sins against His righteous laws;*
> *Sins against His love, His blood;*
> *Sins against His name and cause;*
> *Sins immense as is the sea—*
> *From them all He cleanseth me.*

## *His camp is exceedingly great.*

JOEL 2:11

Consider, my soul, the mightiness of the Lord who is your glory and defense. He is a man of war; Jehovah is His name. *All the forces of heaven* are at His command; legions wait at His door; cherubim and seraphim, watchers and holy ones, principalities and powers are all attentive to His will. If our eyes were not blinded by the dust of sin, we should see horses of fire and chariots of fire round about the Lord's servants. *The powers of nature* are all subject to the absolute control of the Creator: Stormy wind and tempest, lightning and rain, snow and hail, and the soft dews and cheering sunshine come and go at His decree. The bands of Orion He looses, and He binds the sweet influences of the Pleiades.[1] Earth, sea, and air and the places under the earth are the barracks for Jehovah's great armies; space is His camping ground, light is His banner, and flame is His sword. When He goes forth to war, famine ravages the land, pestilence smites the nations, hurricane sweeps the sea, tornado shakes the mountains, and earthquake makes the solid world to tremble. As for *animate creatures*, they all own His dominion, and from the great fish that swallowed the prophet down to "all manner of flies," which plagued the field of Zoan,[2] all are His servants, and even the caterpillars and the worms are squadrons of His great army, for His camp is very great. My soul, see to it that you are at peace with this mighty King. Be sure to enlist under His banner, for to war against Him is madness, and to serve Him is glory. Jesus, Immanuel, God with us, is ready to receive recruits for the army of the Lord: If I am not already enlisted, let me go to Him before I sleep and beg to be accepted through His merits; and if I be already, as I hope I am, a soldier of the cross, let me be of good courage, for the enemy is powerless compared with my Lord, whose camp is very great.

[1]Job 38:31  [2]Psalm 78:43-45

## . . . *in their distress earnestly seek me.*

HOSEA 5:15

Losses and adversities are frequently the means that the Great Shepherd uses to bring home His wandering sheep; like fierce dogs they worry the wanderers back to the fold. Well-fed lions defy our attempts to tame them; they must be brought down from their great strength, and their stomachs must be lowered, and then they will submit to the tamer's hand. How often have we seen the Christian rendered obedient to the Lord's will by the absence of bread and the presence of difficulty. When rich and increased in goods, many professors carry their heads much too loftily and speak exceeding boastfully. Like David, they flatter themselves: "My mountain stands firm; I shall never be moved."[1] When the Christian grows wealthy, is in good repute, or has good health and a happy family, he too often admits Mr. Carnal-Security[2] to feast at his table, and then if he is a true child of God there is a rod preparing for him. Wait awhile, and perhaps you will see his substance melt away as a dream. There goes a portion of his estate—how soon the acres change hands. That debt, that dishonored bill—how fast his losses roll in—where will they end? It is a blessed sign of divine life if, when these embarrassments occur one after another, he begins to be distressed about his backslidings and turns afresh to God. Blessed are the waves that wash the mariner upon the rock of salvation! Losses in business are often sanctified to our soul's enriching. If the chosen soul will not come to the Lord full-handed, it shall come empty. If God, in His grace, finds no other means of making us honor Him among men, He will cast us into the deep; if we fail to honor Him on the pinnacle of riches, He will bring us into the valley of poverty. Yet do not faint, heir of sorrow, when you are rebuked in this fashion; rather, recognize the loving hand that chastens and say, "I will arise and go to my Father."[3]

[1]See Psalm 30:6-7  [2]*The Holy War* (John Bunyan)  [3]Luke 15:18

## . . . *to make them sit with princes.*

PSALM 113:8

Our spiritual privileges are of the highest order. "With princes" is *the place of select society.* "Indeed our fellowship is with the Father and with his Son Jesus Christ."[1] There is no more select society than this! "But you are a chosen race, a royal priesthood, a holy nation."[2] ". . . to the assembly of the firstborn who are enrolled in heaven."[3] The saints *have direct and immediate access:* Princes are admitted to royalty when common people must stand afar off. The child of God has free access to the inner courts of heaven. "For through him we both have access in one Spirit to the Father."[4] "Let us then with confidence draw near," says the apostle, "*to the throne* of grace."[5] Among princes there is *abundant wealth,* but what is the abundance of princes compared with the riches of believers? For "all are yours, and you are Christ's, and Christ is God's."[6] "He who did not spare his own Son but gave him up for us all, how will he not also with him graciously give us all things?"[7] Princes have *peculiar power.* A prince of heaven's empire has great influence: He wields a scepter in his own domain; he sits upon Jesus' throne, for "You have made them a kingdom and priests to our God, and they shall reign on the earth."[8] We reign over the united kingdom of time and eternity. Princes, again, have *special honor.* We may look down upon all earthborn dignity from the eminence upon which grace has placed us. For what is human grandeur to this: "[He] raised us up with him and seated us with him in the heavenly places in Christ Jesus"?[9] We share the honor of Christ, and compared with this, earthly splendors are not worth a thought. Communion with Jesus is a richer gem than ever glittered in a royal crown. Union with the Lord is an emblem of beauty outshining all the blaze of imperial pomp.

[1] 1 John 1:3  [2] 1 Peter 2:9  [3] Hebrews 12:23  [4] Ephesians 2:18  [5] Hebrews 4:16
[6] 1 Corinthians 3:22-23  [7] Romans 8:32  [8] Revelation 5:10  [9] Ephesians 2:6

## Who shall bring any charge against God's elect?

ROMANS 8:33

Most blessed challenge! How unanswerable it is! Every sin of the elect was laid upon the great Champion of our salvation, and by the atonement carried away. There is no sin in God's book against His people: He sees no sin in Jacob, neither iniquity in Israel; they are justified in Christ forever. When the guilt of sin was taken away, the punishment of sin was removed. For the Christian there is no stroke from God's angry hand—no, not so much as a single frown of punitive justice. The believer may be chastised by his Father, but God the Judge has nothing to say to the Christian except "I have absolved you: you are acquitted." For the Christian there is no penal death in this world, much less any second death. He is completely freed from all the punishment as well as the guilt of sin, and the power of sin is removed too. It may stand in our way and agitate us with perpetual warfare; but sin is a conquered foe to every soul in union with Jesus. There is no sin that a Christian cannot overcome if he will only rely upon his God to do it. They who wear the white robe in heaven overcame through the blood of the Lamb, and we may do the same. No lust is too mighty, no besetting sin too strongly entrenched; we can overcome through the power of Christ. Do believe it, Christian—your sin is a condemned thing. It may kick and struggle, but it is doomed to die. God has written condemnation across its brow. Christ has crucified it, nailing it to His cross. Go now and mortify it, and may the Lord help you to live to His praise, for sin with all its guilt, shame, and fear is gone.

*Here's pardon for transgressions past,*
*It matters not how black their cast;*
*And, O my soul, with wonder view,*
*For sins to come here's pardon too.*

### *He went about doing good.*

ACTS 10:38

Few words, but yet an exquisite miniature of the Lord Jesus Christ. There are not many touches, but they are the strokes of a master's pencil. Of the Savior and only of the Savior is this true in the fullest, broadest, and most unqualified sense. "He went about doing good." From this description it is evident that He did good *personally*. The evangelists constantly tell us that He touched the leper with His own finger, that He anointed the eyes of the blind, and that in cases where He was asked to speak the word only at a distance, He did not usually comply but went Himself to the sickbed and there personally worked the cure. A lesson to us, if we would do good, to do it ourselves. Give gifts with your own hand; a kind look or word will enhance the value of the gift. Speak to a friend about his soul; your loving appeal will have more influence than a whole library of tracts. Our Lord's mode of doing good sets forth His *constant activity*! He did not only the good that came close to hand, but He "went about" on His errands of mercy. Throughout the whole land of Judea there was scarcely a village or a hamlet that was not gladdened by the sight of Him. How this reproves the creeping, loitering manner in which many professors serve the Lord. Let us gird up the loins of our mind and not grow weary in doing good. Does the text not imply that Jesus Christ *went out of His way to do good*? "He went about doing good." He was never deterred by danger or difficulty. He sought out the objects of His gracious intentions. So must we. If old plans will not answer, we must try new ones, for fresh experiments sometimes achieve more than regular methods. Christ's *perseverance*, and the *unity* of His purpose, are also hinted at, and the practical application of the subject may be summed up in the words, "Christ . . . leaving you an example, so that you might follow in his steps."[1]

[1] 1 Peter 2:21

## *All that the Father gives me will come to me.*

JOHN 6:37

This declaration involves *the doctrine of election*: There are some whom the Father gave to Christ. It involves *the doctrine of effectual calling*: These who are given must and shall come; however stoutly they may set themselves against it, yet they shall be brought out of darkness into God's marvelous light. It teaches us *the indispensable necessity of faith*, for even those who are given to Christ are not saved except they come to Jesus. Even *they* must come, for there is no other way to heaven but by the door, Christ Jesus. All that the Father gives to our Redeemer *must come to Him*; therefore none can come to heaven except they come to Christ.

Oh, the power and majesty that rest in the words *"will come."* He does not say they have power to come, nor that they may come if they will, but they *"will come."* The Lord Jesus by His messengers, His Word, and His Spirit sweetly and graciously compels men to come in, that they may eat of His marriage supper; and this He does not by any violation of the free agency of man, but by the power of His grace. I may exercise power over another man's will, and yet that other man's will may be perfectly free, because the constraint is exercised in a manner accordant with the laws of the human mind. Jehovah Jesus knows how by irresistible arguments addressed to the understanding, by mighty reasons appealing to the affections, and by the mysterious influence of His Holy Spirit operating upon all the powers and passions of the soul so to subdue the whole man, whereas he was once rebellious, that he yields cheerfully to His government, subdued by sovereign love. But how shall those be known whom God has chosen? By this result: that they do willingly and joyfully accept Christ and come to Him with simple and unfeigned faith, resting upon Him as all their salvation and all their desire. Reader, have you come to Jesus in this way?

## *Whoever comes to me I will never cast out.*

JOHN 6:37

There is no *expiration date* on this promise. It does not merely say, "I will not cast out a sinner at his first coming," but "I will never cast him out." The original reads, "I will not, not cast out," or "I will never, never cast out." The text means that Christ will not at first reject a believer, and that as He will not do it at first, so He will not to the last.

But suppose the believer sins after coming? "If anyone does sin, we have an advocate with the Father, Jesus Christ the righteous."[1] But suppose that believers backslide? "I will heal their apostasy; I will love them freely, for my anger has turned from them."[2] But believers may fall under temptation! "God is faithful, and he will not let you be tempted beyond your ability, but with the temptation he will also provide the way of escape, that you may be able to endure it."[3] But the believer may fall into sin as David did! Yes, but He will "Purge me with hyssop, and I shall be clean; wash me, and I shall be whiter than snow."[4]

> *Once in Christ, in Christ forever,*
> *Nothing from His love can sever.*

Jesus said, "I give them eternal life, and they will never perish, and no one will snatch them out of my hand."[5] What do you say to this, O trembling, feeble mind? This is a precious mercy. Coming to Christ, you do not come to One who will treat you well for a little while and then send you about your business, but He will receive you and make you His bride, and you shall be His forever! Live no longer in the spirit of bondage to fear, but in the spirit of adoption, which cries, "Abba, Father!" Oh, the grace of these words: "I will never cast out."

[1] 1 John 2:1  [2] Hosea 14:4  [3] 1 Corinthians 10:13  [4] Psalm 51:7
[5] John 10:28

## Now these, the singers . . . were on duty day and night.

1 CHRONICLES 9:33

It was so well organized in the temple that the sacred refrain never ceased, for the singers constantly praised the Lord, whose mercy endures forever. As mercy did not cease to rule either by day or by night, so neither did music hush its holy sound. My heart, there is a lesson sweetly taught to you in the ceaseless song of Zion's temple. You are a constant debtor; therefore see to it that your gratitude, like charity, never fails. God's praise is constant in heaven, which is to be your final dwelling-place; so learn to practice the eternal hallelujah. Around the earth as the sun scatters its light, its beams awaken grateful believers to tune their morning hymn, so that by the priesthood of the saints perpetual praise is kept up at all hours; they surround our globe in a mantle of thanksgiving and girdle it with a golden belt of song.

The Lord always deserves to be praised for what He is in Himself, for His works of creation and providence, for His goodness toward His creatures, and especially for the transcendent act of redemption and all the marvelous blessings that flow from it. It is always beneficial to praise the Lord; such praise cheers the day and brightens the night; it lightens toil and softens sorrow; and over earthly gladness it sheds a sanctifying radiance that makes it less liable to blind us with its glare. Do we not have something to sing about at this moment? Can we not weave a song out of our present joys or our past deliverances or our future hopes? Earth yields her summer fruits: The hay is baled, the golden grain invites the scythe, and the sun tarries to shine upon a fruitful earth and shorten the interval of shade, that we may extend the hours of devoted worship. By the love of Jesus, let us be stirred up to close the day with a psalm of sanctified gladness.

## *You crown the year with your bounty.*

PSALM 65:11

All the year round, every hour of every day, God is richly bless-ing us; when we are asleep and when we awaken, His mercy waits upon us. The sun may leave us a legacy of darkness, but God never ceases to shine upon His children with beams of love. Like a river, His loving-kindness is always flowing, with a fullness as inexhaustible as His own nature. Like the atmosphere that con-stantly surrounds the earth and is always ready to support the life of man, the kindness of God surrounds all His creatures; in it, as in their element, they live and move and have their being. Just as the sun on summer days gladdens us with warmer and brighter rays than at other times, and as rivers in certain seasons are swol-len by the rain, and as the air itself is sometimes filled with fresher breezes than at other times, so is it with the mercy of God; it has its golden hours, its overflowing days, when the Lord magnifies His grace before the children of men. *The joyful days of harvest* are a special season of abundant favor. It is the glory of autumn that the ripe gifts of providence are then generously bestowed; it is the mellow season when we enjoy all that we had hoped for. The joy of harvest is great. The reapers are happy to fill their arms with the abundance of heaven. The psalmist tells us that the harvest is the crowning of the year. Surely these crowning mercies merit a crowning thanksgiving! Let us render it by *the inward emotions of gratitude*. Let our hearts be warmed; let our spirits remember, meditate, and think upon this goodness of the Lord. Then let us *praise Him with our lips* and honor and magnify His name who is the source of all this goodness. Let us glorify God by *offering our gifts* to His cause. A practical proof of our gratitude is a special thank-offering to the Lord of the harvest.

## *So she gleaned in the field until evening.*

RUTH 2:17

Let me learn from Ruth, the gleaner. As she went out to gather the ears of corn, so must I set out for the fields of prayer, meditation, the ordinances, and hearing the Word to gather spiritual food. The gleaner gathers her portion ear by ear; her gains are little by little: So I must be content to search for single truths, if they come just one at a time. Every ear helps to make a bundle, and every gospel lesson assists in making us wise for salvation. The gleaner keeps her eyes open: If she stumbled dream-like among the stubble, she would have no load to carry home rejoicingly at evening. I must be careful in religious exercises in case they become unprofitable to me; I fear I have lost quite a bit already. I need to estimate my opportunities properly and glean with greater diligence. The gleaner stoops for all she finds, and I must do the same. Proud minds criticize and object, but humble minds glean and receive benefit. A lowly heart is the key to profitably hearing the Gospel. The soul-saving Word is not received except with meekness. A stiff back makes for a bad gleaner. Pride is a vile robber and must not be tolerated for a moment. What the gleaner gathers, she keeps: If she dropped one ear to find another, the result of her day's work would be but meager; she is as careful to retain as to obtain, and so at last she makes great gains. How often do I forget all that I hear; the second truth pushes the first out of my head, and so my reading and hearing end in much ado about nothing! Do I understand the importance of storing up the truth? Hunger helps to make the gleaner wise; if she has no corn in her hand, there will be no bread on her table; she works under a sense of necessity, and consequently she moves swiftly and her grasp is firm. My need is even greater, Lord; help me to feel it, that it may urge me onward to glean in fields that yield to diligence a plenteous reward.

## *As Jesus went, the people pressed around him.*

LUKE 8:42

Jesus is passing through the crowd heading for the house of Jairus, so that he might raise the ruler's dead daughter. He is so extravagant in His goodness that He works another miracle on His way there. It is enough for most of us, if we have one purpose, to go immediately and accomplish it, without impulsively expending our energies on the way. Rushing to the rescue of a drowning friend, we cannot afford to use up our strength upon someone else in similar danger. It is enough for a tree to yield one sort of fruit and for a man to fulfill his own peculiar calling. But the Lord Jesus is not limited in His power or restricted in His mission. He is so prolific in grace that, like the sun that shines as it rolls onward in its orbit, His path is radiant with loving-kindness. He is a swift arrow of love that not only reaches its ordained target but perfumes the air through which it flies. Virtue is always going out of Jesus, just as sweet fragrance exudes from flowers; and it will always be emanating from Him, like water from a sparkling fountain. What delightful encouragement this truth affords us! If our Lord is so ready to heal the sick and bless the needy, then, my soul, do not be slow to put yourself in His path so that He may smile on you. Do not be lazy in asking, since He is so generous in giving. Pay careful attention to His Word now and at all times, so that Jesus may speak through it to your heart. Pitch your tent wherever He is so that you can obtain His blessing. When He is present to heal, may He not heal you? Be certain that He is present even now, for He always comes to hearts that need Him. And do you not need Him? He knows the extent of your need; so turn your gaze, look upon your distress, and call upon Him while He is near.

### I struck you and all the products of your toil with blight and with mildew and with hail.

HAGGAI 2:17

How destructive is the hail to the standing crops, beating out the precious grain upon the ground! How grateful we should be when the corn is spared so terrible a ruin! Let us offer to the Lord thanksgiving. Even more to be dreaded are those mysterious destroyers—fungus, rust, and mildew. They turn the ear into a mass of soot or render it putrid or dry up the grain, and all in a manner so beyond all human control that the farmer is compelled to cry, "This is the finger of God." Innumerable minute fungi cause the mischief, and if it weren't for the goodness of God, the rider on the black horse would soon scatter famine over the land. Infinite mercy spares the food of men, but in view of the active agents that are ready to destroy the harvest, wisdom teaches us to pray, "Give us this day our daily bread." The curse is everywhere, and we are in constant need of the blessing. When blight and mildew come, they are chastisements from heaven, and men must learn to deal with them accordingly.

Spiritually, mildew is not an uncommon evil. When our work is most promising, this blight appears. We hoped for many conversions, and instead we find a general apathy, an abounding worldliness, or a cruel hardness of heart! There may be no blatant sin in those for whom we are working, but there is a deficiency of sincerity and decision that is sadly disappointing. We learn from this to depend upon the Lord and the necessity of prayer so that no blight will fall upon our work. Spiritual pride or laziness will soon bring upon us the dreadful evil, and only the Lord of the harvest can remove it. Mildew may even attack our own hearts and shrivel our prayers and dampen our zeal. May it please the great Gardener to avert so serious a calamity. Shine, blessed Sun of Righteousness, and drive the diseases away.

# Shall your brothers go to the war while you sit here?

NUMBERS 32:6

Family brings its obligations. The people of Reuben and the people of Gad would have been unbrotherly if they had claimed the land that had been conquered and had left the rest of the people to fight for their portions alone. We have received great benefits as a result of the efforts and sufferings of the saints in years gone by, and if we do not make some return to the Church of Christ by giving her our best energies, we are unworthy to be enrolled in her ranks. Others are bravely combating the errors of the age or excavating the dying from amid the ruins of the Fall, and if we fold our hands in idleness we put ourselves in danger. The Master of the vineyard inquires, "Why do you stand here all day doing nothing?" What is the lazy man's excuse? Serving Jesus becomes the duty of all because it is cheerfully and generously rendered by some. The toils of devoted missionaries and fervent ministers shame us if we continue to sit in laziness. It is the residents of "easy street" who are tempted to run from trials: They would like to escape the cross but still wear the crown; to them the question for this evening's meditation is very relevant. If the most precious are tested in the fire, are we to escape the crucible? If the diamond must be cut and fashioned on the wheel, are we to be made perfect without suffering? Who has commanded the wind to stop blowing because our ship is on the ocean? Why should we be treated better than our Lord? The firstborn endured suffering, so why not His younger brothers? It is a cowardly pride that would choose a soft pillow and a silk couch for a soldier of the cross. Far wiser is the one who first resigns himself to God's will and then as he grows in grace learns to delight in it. So he picks berries on the path of duty, gathers lilies at the foot of the cross, and like Samson discovers honey in the lion.

## *May the whole earth be filled with his glory!*
## *Amen and Amen!*

PSALM 72:19

This is a large petition. To intercede for a whole city needs a stretch of faith, and there are times when praying for one man is more than we can handle. But how far-reaching was the psalmist's dying intercession! How comprehensive! How sublime! "May the whole earth be filled with his glory." Not a single country is exempt even if it is crushed by the foot of superstition; this does not exclude a single nation however uncivilized. For the terrorist as well as for the civilized, for all places and races this prayer is uttered: It encompasses the whole circle of the world and omits no one. We must be up and doing for our Master, or we cannot honestly offer such a prayer. The petition is not asked with a sincere heart unless we endeavor, with God's help, to extend the kingdom of our Master. Are there not some who *neglect* both to pray and to work? Reader, is it your prayer? Turn your eyes to Calvary. Look at the Lord of Life nailed to a cross, with a crown of thorns upon His brow, with bleeding head and hands and feet. What! Can you look upon this miracle of miracles, the death of the Son of God, without feeling within your heart a marvelous adoration that language never can express? And when you feel the blood applied to your conscience and know that He has blotted out your sins, you are not a man unless you jump from your knees to cry, "May the whole earth be filled with his glory! Amen, and Amen!" Can you bow before the Crucified in humble adoration and not wish to see your Monarch Master of the world? You only pretend to love your Prince if you do not desire to see Him the universal ruler. Your piety is worthless unless it leads you to wish that the same mercy that has been shown to you may bless the whole world. Lord, it is harvesttime; put in Your sickle and reap.

## *Satan hindered us.*

1 THESSALONIANS 2:18

Since the first hour in which goodness came into conflict with evil, it has never ceased to be true in spiritual experience that Satan hinders us. From all points of the compass, all along the line of battle, in the advance party or in the rear, at the dawn of day and in the midnight hour, Satan hinders us. If we work in the field, he seeks to break our implements; if we build a wall, he tries to cast down the stones; if we are serving God in suffering or in conflict—everywhere Satan hinders us. He hinders us when we are first coming to Jesus Christ. We had fierce conflicts with Satan when we first looked to the cross and lived. Now that we are saved, he tries to prevent our growth in Christian character. You may be congratulating yourself: "So far I have walked consistently; no one can challenge my integrity." Beware of boasting, for your virtue will soon be tested; Satan will direct his engines against the very virtue for which you are most famous. If you have to this point been a firm believer, your faith will soon be attacked; if you have been meek like Moses, expect to be tempted to speak unadvisedly with your lips. The birds will peck at your ripest fruit, and the wild boar will dash his tusks at your choicest vines. Satan is sure to hinder us when we are faithful in prayer. He hinders our persistence and weakens our faith in order that, if possible, we may miss the blessing. Satan is equally vigilant in obstructing Christian effort. There was never a revival of religion without a revival of his opposition. As soon as Ezra and Nehemiah began to work, Sanballat and Tobiah were stirred up to hinder them. What then? We are not alarmed because Satan hinders us, for it is a proof that we are on the Lord's side and are doing the Lord's work, and in His strength we will win the victory and triumph over our adversary.

### *All things are possible for one who believes.*

MARK 9:23

Many professed Christians are always doubting and fearing, and they forlornly think that this is the inevitable state of believers. This is a mistake, for "all things are possible for one who believes"; and it is possible for us to arrive at a place where a doubt or a fear shall be like a migrant bird flitting across the soul but never lingering there. When you read of the high and sweet communions enjoyed by favored saints, you sigh and murmur in the chamber of your heart, "Sadly, these are not for me." But, climber, if you exercise your faith, you will before long stand on the sunny pinnacle of the temple, for "all things are possible for one who believes." You hear of exploits that holy men have done for Jesus—what they have enjoyed of Him, how much they have been like Him, how they have been able to endure great persecutions for His sake—and you say, "But as for me, I am useless. I can never reach these heights." But there is nothing that one saint was that you may not be. There is no elevation of grace, no attainment of spirituality, no clearness of assurance, no place of duty, that is not open to you if you have but the power to believe. Lay aside your sackcloth and ashes, and rise to the dignity of your true position; you are impoverished not because you have to be but because you want to be. It is not right that you, a child of the King, should grovel in the dust. Rise! The golden throne of assurance is waiting for you! The crown of communion with Jesus is ready to adorn your brow. Wrap yourself in scarlet and fine linen, and eat lavishly every day; for if you believe, you can eat the royal portion, your land will flow with milk and honey, and your soul shall be satisfied in God. Gather golden sheaves of grace, for they await you in the fields of faith. "All things are possible for one who believes."

### *He appeared first to Mary Magdalene,*
### *from whom he had cast out seven demons.*

MARK 16:9

Mary of Magdala was *the victim of a fearful evil*. She was possessed not just by one demon, but by seven. These dreadful inmates caused much pain and pollution to the poor frame in which they had found a lodging. Hers was a hopeless, horrible case. She could not help herself, and no human power could set her free. But Jesus passed that way, and without being asked and probably while being resisted by the poor demoniac, He uttered the word of power, and Mary of Magdala became *a trophy of the healing power of Jesus*. All seven demons left her, left her never to return, forcibly ejected by the Lord of all. What a blessed deliverance! What a happy change! From delirium to delight, from despair to peace, from hell to heaven! Immediately she became *a constant follower of Jesus*, listening to His every word, following His winding steps, sharing His busy life; and in all this she became His generous helper, first among that band of healed and grateful women who ministered to Him out of their means. When Jesus was lifted up in crucifixion, Mary remained *the sharer of His shame*: We find her first watching from a distance and then drawing near to the foot of the cross. She could not die on the cross with Jesus, but she stood as near it as she could, and when His blessed body was taken down, she watched to see how and where it was laid. She was *the faithful and watchful believer*, last at the sepulcher where Jesus slept, first at the grave where He arose. Her loyalty and love made her *a favored beholder of her beloved Master*, who deigned to call her by her name and to make her *His messenger of good news* to the trembling disciples and Peter. Grace found her useless and made her useful, cast out her demons and gave her to behold angels, delivered her from Satan and united her forever to the Lord Jesus. May we also be such miracles of grace!

### The Son of Man has authority on earth to forgive sins.

MATTHEW 9:6

Consider here the Great Physician's mighty power: the power to forgive sin! While He lived here below, before the ransom had been paid, before the blood had been literally sprinkled on the mercy-seat, He had power to forgive sin. Has He no power to do it now that He has died? What power must dwell in Him who to the utmost penny has faithfully discharged the debts of His people! He has unlimited power now that He has finished transgression and made an end of sin. If you doubt it, see Him rising from the dead! Behold Him in ascending splendor, raised to the right hand of God! Hear Him pleading before the eternal Father, pointing to His wounds, declaring the merit of His sacred passion! What power to forgive is here! He ascended on high, and He gave gifts to men. He is exalted on high to give repentance and forgiveness of sins. The most crimson sins are removed by the crimson of His blood. At this moment, dear reader, whatever your sinfulness, Christ has power to pardon, power to pardon you, and millions just like you. A word will speak it. He has nothing more to do to win your pardon; all the atoning work is done. He can, in answer to your tears, forgive your sins today and make you know it. He can breathe into your soul at this very moment a peace with God that passes all understanding, which shall spring from perfect remission of your many iniquities. Do you believe that? I trust you believe it. May you even now experience the power of Jesus to forgive sin! Waste no time in applying to the Physician of souls; hasten to Him with words like these:

> Jesus! Master! hear my cry;
> Save me, heal me with a word;
> Fainting at Thy feet I lie,
> Thou my whisper'd plea has heard.

## *Eternal comfort.*

### 2 THESSALONIANS 2:16

"Comfort." There is music in the word: Like David's harp, it charms away the evil spirit of melancholy. It was a distinguished honor to Barnabas to be called "the son of encouragement";[1] it is one of the illustrious names of a greater than Barnabas, for the Lord Jesus is the comfort of Israel. "*Eternal* comfort"! This is the best of all, for the everlasting nature of comfort is its crown and glory. What is this "eternal comfort"? It includes a sense of pardoned sin. A Christian man has received in his heart the witness of the Spirit that his iniquities are put away like a cloud, and his transgressions like a thick cloud. If sin is pardoned, is that not an eternal comfort? Next, the Lord gives His people an abiding sense of being accepted in Christ. The Christian knows that God looks upon him as standing in union with Jesus. Union with the risen Lord is a comfort of the most abiding order; it is, in fact, everlasting. Let sickness prostrate us—haven't we seen hundreds of believers as happy in the weakness of disease as they would have been in the enjoyment of blooming health? If death's arrows pierce us to the heart, our comfort does not die, for we have often heard the songs of saints as they rejoiced because the living love of God was shed abroad in their hearts in dying moments. Yes, a sense of acceptance in the Beloved is an eternal comfort. Moreover, the Christian is convinced of his security. God has promised to save those who trust in Christ: The Christian does trust in Christ, and he believes that God will be as good as His word and will save him. He feels that he is safe by virtue of his being bound up with the person and work of Jesus. Herein is comfort such as can be found nowhere else and in no one else!

[1]Acts 4:36

## *The bow is seen in the clouds.*

GENESIS 9:14

The rainbow, the symbol of the covenant with Noah, foreshadows our Lord Jesus, who is the Lord's witness to the people. When may we *expect to see the token of the covenant?* The rainbow is only to be seen painted upon a cloud. When the sinner's conscience is dark with clouds, when he remembers his past sin and mourns and laments before God, Jesus Christ is revealed to him as the covenant Rainbow, displaying all the glorious hues of the divine character and declaring peace. To the believer, when his trials and temptations surround him, it is sweet to behold the person of our Lord Jesus Christ—to see Him bleeding, living, rising, and pleading for us. God's rainbow is hung over the cloud of our sins, our sorrows, and our woes, to prophesy deliverance. By itself a *cloud* does not give a rainbow; there must be *the crystal drops* to reflect the light of the sun. So, our sorrows must not only threaten, but they must really fall upon us. There would have been no Christ for us if the vengeance of God had been merely a threatening cloud: Punishment must fall in terrible drops upon Him. Until there is a *real* anguish in the sinner's conscience, there is no Christ for him; until the chastisement that he feels becomes grievous, he cannot see Jesus. But there must also be a sun; for clouds and drops of rain do not make rainbows unless the sun shines. Beloved, our God, who is as the sun to us, always shines, but we do not always see Him—clouds hide His face; but no matter what drops may be falling or what clouds may be threatening, if He shines there will be a rainbow at once. It is said that when we see the rainbow, the shower is over. It is certain that when Christ comes, our troubles withdraw; when we look on Jesus, our sins vanish, and our doubts and fears subside. When Jesus walks upon the waters of the sea, how profound the calm!

## *I will remember my covenant.*

GENESIS 9:15

Note the form of this promise. God does not say, "And when you shall look upon the bow, and *you* shall remember My covenant, *then* I will not destroy the earth," but it is gloriously put, not upon our memory, which is fickle and frail, but upon *God's* memory, which is infinite and immutable. "When . . . the bow is seen in the clouds, I will remember my covenant." It is not my remembering God—it is God's remembering *me* that is the ground of my safety; it is not my laying hold of His covenant, but His covenant's laying hold on me. Glory be to God! The ramparts of salvation are secured by divine power, and even the minor towers, which we could imagine being left to man, are guarded by almighty strength. Even the *remembrance* of the covenant is not left to our memories, for *we* might forget; but our Lord cannot forget the names of those whom He has graven on the palms of His hands. It is with us as it was with Israel in Egypt; the blood was upon the lintel and the two side-posts, but the Lord did not say, "When *you* see the blood I will pass over you," but "When *I* see the blood I will pass over you." My looking to Jesus brings me joy and peace, but it is God's looking to Jesus that secures my salvation and that of all His elect, since it is impossible for our God to look at Christ, our bleeding Surety, and then to be angry with us for sins already punished in Him. It is not left with us even to be saved by remembering the covenant. There is not a single thread of human effort in this fabric. It is not *of* man, neither *by* man, but of the Lord alone. We *should* remember the covenant, and we *shall* do it, through divine grace; but the hinge of our safety does not hang there—it is God's remembering *us*, not our remembering *Him*; and hence the covenant is *an everlasting covenant*.

# I know their sufferings.

EXODUS 3:7

The child is cheered as he sings, "This my father knows"; and shall we not be comforted as we discern that our dear and tender Friend knows all about us?

1. *He is the Physician*, and if He knows everything, there is no need for the patient to know. Calm down, you silly, fluttering heart, prying, peeping, and suspecting! What you don't know now, you will know later; and meanwhile Jesus, the beloved Physician, knows your soul in adversities. Why does the patient need to analyze all the medicine or estimate all the symptoms? This is the Physician's work, not mine; it is my business to trust, and His to prescribe. If He shall write His prescription in a fashion that I cannot read, I will not be uneasy on that account, but will rely upon His unfailing skill to make everything clear in the result, no matter how mysterious the process.

2. *He is the Master*, and His knowledge is to serve us instead of our own; we are to obey, not to judge: "The servant does not know what his master is doing."[1] Shall the architect explain his plans to every bricklayer on the job? If he knows his own intent, is it not enough? The pot upon the wheel cannot guess to what pattern it will be conformed, but if the potter understands his art, the ignorance of the clay is irrelevant. My Lord must not be cross-questioned any more by one so ignorant as I am.

3. *He is the Head.* All understanding centers there. What judgment has the arm? What comprehension has the foot? All the power to know lies in the head. Why should the member have a brain of its own when the head fulfills for it every intellectual office? Here, then, the believer must rest his comfort in sickness—not that he himself can see the end, but that Jesus knows all. Sweet Lord, be forever eye and soul and head for us, and let us be content to know only what You choose to reveal.

[1]John 15:15

## And I will give you a new heart . . . a heart of flesh.

EZEKIEL 36:26

A "heart of flesh" is known by its *tenderness concerning sin*. To have indulged a foul imagination or to have allowed a wild desire to linger even for a moment is quite enough to make a heart of flesh grieve before the Lord. The heart of stone calls a great iniquity nothing, but not so the heart of flesh.

*If to the right or left I stray,*
*That moment, Lord, reprove;*
*And let me weep my life away,*
*For having grieved Thy love.*

The heart of flesh is *tender to God's will*. Unlike a strong heart that refuses to bow before God's dictates, when the heart of flesh is given, the will quivers like an aspen leaf in every breath of heaven and bows like a willow in every breeze of God's Spirit. The natural will is cold, hard iron, which refuses to be hammered into form, but the renewed will, like molten metal, is quickly molded by the hand of grace. In the fleshy heart there is *a tenderness of the affections*. The hard heart does not love the Redeemer, but the renewed heart burns with affection toward Him. The hard heart is selfish and coldly demands, "Why should I weep for sin? Why should I love the Lord?" But the heart of flesh says, "Lord, You know that I love You; help me to love You more!" There are many privileges of this renewed heart. It is here the Spirit dwells; it is here that Jesus lives. It is fitted to receive every spiritual blessing, and every blessing comes to it. It is prepared to yield every heavenly fruit to the honor and praise of God, and therefore the Lord delights in it. A tender heart is the best defense against sin and the best preparation for heaven. A renewed heart stands on its watchtower looking for the coming of the Lord Jesus. Do you have this heart of flesh?

## . . . *ourselves, who have the firstfruits of the Spirit.*

ROMANS 8:23

Present possession is declared. At this present moment we have the firstfruits of the Spirit. We have repentance, that gem of the first water; faith, that priceless pearl; hope, the heavenly emerald; and love, the glorious ruby. We are already made new creatures in Christ Jesus by the effectual working of God the Holy Spirit. This is called the firstfruit because *it comes first.* As the wave-sheaf was the first of the harvest, so the spiritual life, and all the graces that adorn that life, are the first operations of the Spirit of God in our souls. *The firstfruits were the pledge of the harvest.* As soon as the Israelite had plucked the first handful of ripe ears, he looked forward with glad anticipation to the time when the wagon would creak beneath the sheaves. So, brethren, when God gives us things that are pure, lovely, and of good report, as the work of the Holy Spirit, these are to us the indications of the coming glory. *The firstfruits were always holy to the Lord,* and our new nature, with all its powers, is a consecrated thing. The new life is not ours that we should ascribe its excellence to our own merit; it is Christ's image and creation and is ordained for His glory. But *the firstfruits were not the harvest,* and the works of the Spirit in us at this moment are not the consummation—the perfection is still to come. We must not boast that we have attained, and so reckon the first sheaf to be all the produce of the year: We must hunger and thirst for righteousness and long for the day of full redemption. Dear reader, this evening open your mouth wide, and God will fill it. Let the blessing in present possession excite in you a sacred greed for more grace. Groan within yourself for higher degrees of consecration, and your Lord will grant them to you, for He is able to do far more abundantly than all that we ask or think.

## *This illness does not lead to death.*

JOHN 11:4

From our Lord's words we learn that there is a limit to illness. Here is a "lead to" within which its ultimate end is restrained and beyond which it cannot go. Lazarus might pass through death, but death was not to be the conclusion of his illness. In all illness the Lord says to the waves of pain, "You may go so far, but no further." His fixed purpose is not the destruction but the instruction of His people. Wisdom hangs up the thermometer at the furnace mouth and regulates the heat.

1. *The limit is encouragingly comprehensive.* The God of providence has limited the time, manner, intensity, repetition, and effects of all our sicknesses; each throb is decreed, each sleepless hour predestined, each relapse ordained, each depression of spirit foreknown, and each sanctifying result eternally purposed. Nothing great or small escapes the ordaining hand of Him who numbers the hairs of our head.

2. *This limit is wisely adjusted* to our strength, to the purpose designed, and to the grace apportioned. Affliction is not haphazard—the weight of every stroke of the rod is accurately measured. He who made no mistakes in balancing the clouds and stretching out the heavens commits no errors in measuring out the ingredients that compose the medicine of souls. We cannot suffer too much nor be relieved too late.

3. *The limit is tenderly appointed.* The knife of the heavenly Surgeon never cuts deeper than is absolutely necessary. "He does not willingly afflict or grieve the children of men."[1] A mother's heart cries, "Spare my child"; but no mother is more compassionate than our gracious God. When we consider how hardmouthed we are, it is a wonder that we are not driven with a sharper bit. The thought is full of comfort that He who has established the boundary lines of our lives has also determined the boundaries of our tribulation.

[1]Lamentations 3:33

### *And they offered him wine mixed with myrrh,*
### *but he did not take it.*

MARK 15:23

A golden truth is couched in the fact that the Savior pushed the myrrhed wine-cup from His lips. On the heights of heaven the Son of God stood of old, and as He looked down upon our globe He measured the long descent to the utmost depths of human misery. He considered the sum total of all the agonies that expiation would require and didn't shrink. He solemnly determined that to offer a sufficient atoning sacrifice He must go the whole way, from the highest to the lowest, from the throne of highest glory to the cross of deepest woe. This myrrhed cup, with its anesthetic influence, would have prevented Him from experiencing the utter limit of misery, and therefore He refused it. He would not stop short of all He had undertaken to suffer for His people. How many of us have cried for comfort in our grief to keep us from injury! Reader, did you never pray to be relieved of hard service or suffering with a petulant and willful eagerness? In a moment providence has taken from you the desire of your eyes. Say, Christian, if you were told, "If you want, your loved one will live, but God will be dishonored," could you have put away the temptation and said, "Your will be done"? It is good to be able to say, "My Lord, if for other reasons I do not need to suffer, yet if I can honor You more by suffering, and if the loss of my earthly goods will bring You glory, then let it be. I refuse the comfort if it stands in the way of Your honor." Let us learn to walk in the footsteps of our Lord, cheerfully enduring trial for His sake, promptly and willingly putting away the thought of self and comfort when it would interfere with our completing the work that He has given us to do. Great grace is needed, but great grace is provided.

### *You take me out of the net they have hidden for me, for you are my refuge.*

PSALM 31:4

Our spiritual foes belong to the serpent's brood and seek to ensnare us by subtlety. This prayer presupposes the possibility of the believer being caught like a bird. The catcher does his work so skillfully that simple souls are soon surrounded by the net. The request is that even out of Satan's snares the captive may be delivered; this is a proper petition, and one that can be granted: eternal love can rescue the saint from between the jaws of the lion and out of the depths of hell. It may need a sharp pull to save a soul from the net of temptations and a mighty pull to extricate a man from the snares of malicious cunning, but the Lord is equal to every emergency, and the most skillfully placed nets of the hunter will never be able to hold His chosen ones. There will be grief for those who are so clever at net laying; those who tempt others shall be destroyed themselves.

*"For you are my refuge."* What a wonderful encouragement is found in these few words! How joyfully may we encounter toils, and how cheerfully may we endure sufferings when we can lay hold upon the strength of the Lord. Divine power will thwart all the endeavors of our enemies, confound their politics, and frustrate their foolish tricks. Happy is the man who has such matchless might engaged upon his side. Our own strength would serve us poorly when trapped in the nets of our cunning enemy, but the Lord's refuge is always available; we have only to ask, and we will find it near at hand. If by faith we are depending solely on the strength of the mighty God of Israel, then our dependence may become the occasion of our prayer.

> *Lord, evermore Thy face we seek:*
> *Tempted we are, and poor, and weak;*
> *Keep us with lowly hearts, and meek.*
> *Let us not fall. Let us not fall.*

## *And they restored Jerusalem as far as the Broad Wall.*

NEHEMIAH 3:8

Well-fortified cities have broad walls, and so did Jerusalem in her glory days. The New Jerusalem must, similarly, be surrounded and preserved by a broad wall of nonconformity to the world and *separation* from its patterns and ideas. There is a tendency today to break down this holy barrier and make the distinction between the Church and the world merely nominal. Believers are no longer fixed on godliness, questionable literature is widely read, frivolous pastimes are eagerly indulged, and a general laxity threatens to deprive the Lord's special people of those sacred distinctives that separate them from sinners. It will be a bad day for the Church and the world when the proposed amalgamation is complete, and the sons of God and the daughters of men shall be united, and another deluge of wrath is ushered in. Beloved reader, make it your aim in heart, in word, in dress, in action to maintain the broad wall, remembering that the friendship of this world is enmity against God.

The Broad Wall provided a pleasant place of *relaxation* for the inhabitants of Jerusalem, from which they enjoyed sweeping views of the surrounding country. This reminds us of the Lord's exceeding broad commandments, which provide a pathway to freedom and communion with Jesus. From here we look upon the scenes of earth and gaze toward the glories of heaven. Separated from the world, and denying ourselves all ungodliness and fleshly lusts, we are not in prison, nor restricted within narrow boundaries; no, we walk in freedom, because we keep His commands. Come, reader; this evening walk with God in His statutes. As friend met friend upon the city wall, so meet your God on the path of holy prayer and meditation. You have every right to stand upon the walls of salvation, for you have been given the key to the King's city—you are a citizen of the metropolis of the universe.

## *I did not say to the offspring of Jacob, "Seek me in vain."*

ISAIAH 45:19

We can gain a great deal of comfort by considering what God has *not* said. What He has said is full of comfort and delight; but what He has not said is scarcely less rich in consolation. It was what God *had not said* that preserved the kingdom of Israel in the days of Jeroboam the son of Joash, for "the LORD had not said that he would blot out the name of Israel from under heaven" (2 Kings 14:27). In our text we have an assurance that God will answer prayer because He "did not say to the offspring of Jacob, 'Seek me in vain.'" Those of you who are prone to self-condemnation should remember that, let your doubts and fears say what they will, if God has not cut you off from mercy, there is no need for despair: Even the voice of conscience carries little weight if it is not seconded by the voice of God. We should tremble at what God *has* said! But do not allow your rambling thoughts to overwhelm you with despondency and sinful despair. Many timid persons have been vexed by the suspicion that there may be something in God's decree that shuts *them* out from hope, but we have here a complete rebuttal of that troublesome fear, for no true seeker can be decreed to wrath. "I did not speak in secret, in a land of darkness; I did not say [even in the secret of my unsearchable decree] . . . , 'Seek me in vain.'" God has clearly revealed that He *will* hear the prayer of those who call upon Him, and that declaration cannot be contradicted. He has spoken so firmly, so truthfully, so righteously that there can be no room for doubt. He does not reveal His mind in unintelligible words, but He speaks plainly and positively. "Everyone who asks receives."[1] Doubter, believe this sure truth—that prayer must and will be heard, and that never, even in the secrets of eternity, has the Lord said to any living soul, "Seek me in vain."

[1]Matthew 7:8

## *The unsearchable riches of Christ.*

EPHESIANS 3:8

My Master has riches beyond the calculation of arithmetic, the measurement of reason, the dream of imagination, or the eloquence of words. They are *unsearchable*! You may look and study and ponder, but Jesus is a greater Savior than you think Him to be even when your thoughts are at their best. My Lord is more ready to pardon than you are to sin, more able to forgive than you are to transgress. My Master is more willing to supply your needs than you are to confess them. Do not tolerate small thoughts of the Lord Jesus. When you put the crown on His head, you will only crown Him with silver when He deserves gold. *My Master has riches of happiness to bestow upon you now.* He can make you to lie down in green pastures and lead you beside still waters. There is no music like His music that He, the Shepherd, plays for His sheep as they lie down at His feet. There is no love like His; neither earth nor heaven can match it. To know Christ and to be found in Him is real life and true joy. My Master does not treat His servants meanly; He gives to them the way a king gives to a king. He gives them two heavens—a heaven below in serving Him here, and a heaven above in delighting in Him forever. *His unsearchable riches will be known best in eternity.* On the way to heaven He will give you all you need. He will defend you and provide for you en route, but it will be at the end of your journey when you will hear the songs of triumph, the shouts of salvation, and you will have a face-to-face view of the glorious and beloved One. "The unsearchable riches of Christ"! This is the tune for the minstrels of earth and the song for the musicians of heaven. Lord, teach us more and more of Jesus, and we will declare the good news to others.

## . . . *so that Christ may dwell in your hearts through faith.*

EPHESIANS 3:17

It is desirable beyond measure that we, as believers, should keep the person of Jesus constantly before us, to stir up our love for Him and to grow in our knowledge of Him. I would to God that my readers were all entered as diligent scholars in Jesus' college, students of *Corpus Christi*, or the body of Christ, resolved to get a good degree in the learning of the cross. But to have Jesus ever near, the heart must be full of Him, welling up with His love and even running over; so the apostle prays "that Christ may *dwell in your hearts.*" Look at how close he wants Jesus to be! You cannot get a subject closer to you than to have it in your heart. "*That Christ may dwell*"; not that He may call upon you sometimes, as a casual visitor may stay overnight, but that He may *dwell*; that Jesus may become the Lord and permanent resident of your inmost being, never to leave again.

Observe the words—that He may dwell *in your heart*, the best room in the house! Not in your thoughts alone, but in your affections; not merely in the mind's meditations, but in the heart's emotions. We should long to love Christ in an enduring way—not a love that flames up and then dies out into the darkness of a few embers, but a constant flame, fed by sacred fuel, like the fire upon the altar that never went out. This cannot be accomplished except by faith. Faith must be strong or love will not be fervent; the root of the flower must be healthy or we cannot expect the blossom to be glorious. Faith is the plant's root, and love is the plant's blossom. Now, reader, Jesus cannot be in your heart's love unless you have a firm hold of Him by your heart's faith; and, therefore, pray that you may always trust Christ in order that you may always love Him. If love is cold, be sure that faith is faltering.

> *If fire breaks out and catches in thorns
> so that the stacked grain or the standing grain
> or the field is consumed, he who started the fire
> shall make full restitution.*

EXODUS 22:6

But what restitution can be made by one who throws the firebrands of error or stirs the coals of lust and sets the souls of men ablaze with the fire of hell? The guilt is beyond estimate, and the result is irretrievable. Even if such an offender is forgiven, he will still experience grief in recognizing that he cannot undo the effects of his foolish behavior! A bad example may kindle a flame that years of amended character cannot quench. To burn the harvest is bad enough, but how much worse to destroy the eternal harvest! It may be useful for us to consider how guilty we may have been in the past, and to consider whether, even in the present, there might not be evil in us that has a tendency to cause damage to the souls of our relatives, friends, or neighbors.

The fire of conflict is a terrible evil when it breaks out in a Christian church. Where there are converts, and God is glorified, you will discover jealousy and envy doing the devil's work most effectively. Where the golden grain of blessing was being stored to reward the work of the servants, the fire of enmity comes in and leaves little else but smoke and a heap of blackness. Woe to those by whom offenses come. May they never come through us, for although we cannot make restitution, we shall certainly be the chief sufferers if we are the chief offenders. Those who feed the fire deserve fair criticism, but the one who first kindles it is most to blame. Discord usually takes hold first among the thorns; it is nurtured among the hypocrites and empty professors in the church and leaps among the righteous, blown by the winds of hell, until no one knows where it may end. O Lord, the giver of peace, make us peacemakers, and never let us aid and abet the men of strife, or even unintentionally cause the slightest division among Your people.

## *If you believe with all your heart,*
## *you may.*

ACTS 8:37

These words may address any hesitations the devout reader may have about *the ordinances*. Perhaps you say, "I am afraid to be baptized; it is such a solemn thing to declare myself to be dead with Christ and buried with Him. I do not feel at liberty to come to Communion; I am afraid of eating and drinking judgment to myself, of failing to discern the Lord's body." Come now, trembling one, Jesus has given you liberty—do not be afraid. If a stranger came to your house, he would stand at the door or wait in the hall; he would not dream of entering uninvited into your home—he is not at home. But your child enjoys complete freedom in the house; and so is it with the child of God. A stranger may not intrude where a child may venture. When the Holy Spirit has given you to feel the spirit of adoption, you may be baptized and take communion without apprehension. The same rule holds good for *the Christian's inward privileges*. Perhaps you think that you are not allowed to rejoice with joy unspeakable and full of glory; if you are permitted just to get inside Christ's door or sit at the end of His table, you will be content with that. But you will not have less privileges than the strongest saint. God makes no difference in His love to His children. A child is a child to Him; He will not make him a hired servant. The son will feast upon the fatted calf and have the music and dancing as much as if he had never wandered away. When Jesus comes into the heart, He issues a general permit to be glad in the Lord. No shackles are worn in the court of King Jesus. Our admission into full privileges may be gradual, but it is certain. Perhaps our reader is saying, "I wish I could enjoy the promises and walk at liberty in my Lord's commands." "If you believe with all your heart, you may." Loosen the chains at your neck and live in freedom, for Jesus makes you free!

### The crowd, when they saw him,
### were greatly amazed and ran up to him
### and greeted him.

MARK 9:15

How great the difference between Moses and Jesus! When Moses had been forty days upon the mountain, he underwent a kind of transfiguration, so that his face shone with exceeding brightness, and he put a veil over it because the people were not able to look upon his glory. Not so our Savior. He had been transfigured with a greater glory than that of Moses, and yet we do not read that the people were blinded by the blaze of His countenance, but rather they were amazed and ran to Him and greeted Him. The glory of the law repels, but the greater glory of Jesus attracts. Though Jesus is holy and just, yet blended with His purity there is so much truth and grace that sinners run to Him amazed at His goodness, fascinated by His love; they greet Him, become His disciples, and take Him to be their Lord and Master. Reader, it may be that just now you are blinded by the dazzling brightness of the law of God. You feel its claims on your conscience, but you cannot keep it in your life. Not that you find fault with the law; on the contrary, it commands your profoundest esteem. Still you are not drawn by it to God; you are rather hardened in heart and tending toward desperation. So turn your eye from Moses with all his repelling splendor, and look to Jesus, resplendent with milder glories. Look upon His flowing wounds and thorn-crowned head! He is the Son of God and greater than Moses, but He is the Lord of love and more tender than the lawgiver. He bore the wrath of God and in His death revealed more of God's justice than Sinai displayed, but that justice is now vindicated, and it is the guardian of believers in Jesus. Look, sinner, to the bleeding Savior, and as you feel the attraction of His love, run to His arms, and you will be saved.

### *Into your hand I commit my spirit;*
### *you have redeemed me, O LORD, faithful God.*

PSALM 31:5

These words have been frequently used by the godly in their hour of departure. We may profitably consider them this evening. The object of the believer's interest in life and death is not his body or his possessions but his spirit; this is his choice treasure: If this is safe, then all is well. What is our physical condition compared with the soul? The believer commits his soul to the hand of God; it came from Him, it is His own, He has until now sustained it, He is able to keep it, and it is fitting that He should receive it. All things are safe in Jehovah's hands; what we entrust to the Lord will be secure, both now and in that day of days toward which we are hastening. It is peaceful living and glorious dying to rest in the care of heaven. At all times we should commit everything to Jesus' faithful hand; then even if life should hang on a thread, and difficulties multiply like the sands of the sea, our soul shall live in safety and delight itself in quiet resting places.

"*You have redeemed me, O LORD, faithful God.*" Redemption is a solid basis for confidence. David did not know Calvary as we do, but even as redemption cheered him, so our eternal redemption will sweetly console us. Past deliverances are strong guarantees for present assistance. What the Lord has done He will do again, for He does not change. He is faithful to His promises and gracious to His saints; He will not turn away from His people.

> *Though Thou slay me I will trust,*
> *Praise Thou even from the dust,*
> *Prove, and tell it as I prove,*
> *Thine unutterable love.*
>
> *Thou may chasten and correct,*
> *But Thou never can neglect;*
> *Since the ransom price is paid,*
> *On Thy love my hope is stayed.*

## *Sing, O barren one.*

ISAIAH 54:1

Although we may have brought forth some fruit and have a joyful hope that we are abiding in the vine, yet there are times when we feel very barren. Prayer is lifeless, love is cold, faith is weak, each grace in the garden of our heart languishes and droops. We are like flowers in the hot sun, desperately needing the refreshing shower. In such a condition what are we to do? The text is addressed to us in just such a state. "*Sing, O barren one . . . break forth into singing and cry aloud.*" But what can I sing about? I cannot talk about the present, and even the past looks full of barrenness. I can sing of Jesus Christ. I can talk of visits that the Redeemer has paid to me in the past; or if not of these, I can magnify the great love with which He loved His people when He came from the heights of heaven for their redemption. I will go to the cross again. Come, my soul, you were once heavy-laden, and you lost your burden there. Go to Calvary again. Perhaps that very cross that gave you life may give you fruitfulness. What is my barrenness? It is the platform for His fruit-creating power. What is my desolation? It is the dark setting for the sapphire of His everlasting love. I will go to Him in my poverty, I will go in my helplessness, I will go in all my shame and backsliding; I will tell Him that I am still His child, and finding confidence in His faithful heart, even I, the barren one, will sing and cry aloud.

Sing, believer, for it will cheer your own heart and the hearts of others who are desolate. Sing on, for although you are presently ashamed of being barren, you will be fruitful soon; now that God makes you hate to be without fruit He will soon cover you with clusters. The experience of our barrenness is painful, but the Lord's visits are delightful. A sense of our own poverty drives us to Christ, and that is where we need to be, for in Him our fruit is found.

### All the days of his separation he shall eat nothing that is produced by the grapevine, not even the seeds or the skins.

NUMBERS 6:4

Nazirites had taken, among other vows, one that debarred them from the use of wine. In order that they might not violate the obligation, they were forbidden to drink the vinegar of wine or strong liquors; and to make the rule even clearer, they were not to touch the unfermented juice of grapes, nor even to eat the fruit either fresh or dried. In order to secure the integrity of the vow, they were not even allowed anything that had to do with the vine; they were, in fact, to avoid the appearance of evil. Surely this is a lesson to the Lord's separated ones, teaching them to come away from sin in every form, to avoid not merely its grosser shapes but even its spirit and likeness. Such strict walking is much despised in these days, but rest assured, dear reader, it is the safest and happiest path. He who yields a point or two to the world is in fearful peril; he who eats the grapes of Sodom will soon drink the wine of Gomorrah. A little crevice in the seawall in Holland lets in the sea, and the gap soon swells until a province is drowned. Worldly conformity, in any degree, is a snare to the soul and makes it more and more liable to presumptuous sins. The Nazirite who drank grape juice could not be completely certain whether or not it had fermented and consequently could not be clear in heart that his vow was intact. In a similar way the yielding, vacillating Christian cannot have a clear conscience but is constantly aware of his double standard. Doubtful things we need not wonder about; they are wrong for us. Tempting things we must not play with, but run from them speedily. Better to be sneered at as a Puritan than to be despised as a hypocrite. Careful walking may involve much self-denial, but it has pleasures of its own that are more than a sufficient reward.

### Heal me, O LORD, and I shall be healed.

JEREMIAH 17:14

### I have seen his ways, but I will heal him.

ISAIAH 57:18

It is the sole prerogative of God to remove spiritual disease. Natural disease may be instrumentally healed by men, but even then the honor is to be given to God who grants wisdom to doctors and bestows power to enable the human frame to cast off disease. As for spiritual sicknesses, these remain with the Great Physician alone; He claims it as His prerogative: "I kill and I make alive; I wound and I heal";[1] and one of the Lord's choice titles is Jehovah-Rophi, "the Lord who heals you." "I will heal your wounds" is a promise that could not come from the lips of man but only from the mouth of the eternal God. On this account the psalmist cried unto the Lord, "Heal me, O LORD, for my bones are troubled,"[2] and again, "Heal me, for I have sinned against you!"[3] For this also the godly praise the name of the Lord, saying, "[He] heals all your diseases."[4] He who made man can restore man; He who was at first the creator of our nature can re-create it. What a transcendent comfort it is that in the person of Jesus "the whole fullness of deity dwells bodily."[5] My soul, whatever your disease may be, this Great Physician can heal you. If He is God, there can be no limit to His power. Come then with the blind eye of darkened understanding; come with the limping foot of wasted energy; come with the disabled hand of weak faith, the fever of an angry temper, or the fit of shivering despondency; come just as you are, for He who is God can certainly restore you. No one can restrain the healing power that proceeds from Jesus our Lord. Legions of devils have attempted to overcome the power of the beloved Physician, and never once has He been hindered. All His patients have been cured in the past and shall be in the future, and you may be counted among them, my friend, if you will but rest yourself in Him tonight.

[1]Deuteronomy 32:39    [2]Psalm 6:2    [3]Psalm 41:4    [4]Psalm 103:3
[5]Colossians 2:9

## *If we walk in the light, as he is in the light . . .*

### 1 JOHN 1:7

As he is in the light"! Can we ever attain to this? Will we ever be able to walk as clearly in the light as He is whom we call "Our Father," of whom it is written, "God is light, and in him is no darkness at all" (verse 5)? Certainly this is the model that is set before us, for the Savior Himself said, "You therefore must be perfect, as your heavenly Father is perfect";[1] and although we may feel that we can never rival the perfection of God, yet we are to seek after it and not be satisfied until we attain to it. The youthful artist as he grasps his newly sharpened pencil can hardly hope to equal Raphael or Michelangelo; but still, if he did not have a noble *ideal* before his mind, he would only attain to something very mean and ordinary. But what is meant by the expression that the Christian is to walk in light as God is in the light? We conceive it to convey *likeness* but not *degree*. We are as truly in the light, we are as heartily in the light, we are as sincerely in the light, as honestly in the light, although we cannot be there in the same measure. I cannot dwell in the sun—it is too bright a place for my residence, but I can *walk* in the light of the sun; and so, though I cannot attain to that perfection of purity and truth that belongs to the Lord of hosts by nature as the infinitely good, yet I can set the Lord always before me and strive, by the help of the indwelling Spirit, to conform to His image. The famous old commentator John Trapp says, "We may be in the light as God is in the light for *quality*, but not for *equality*." We are to have the same light and are as truly to have it and walk in it as God does, though as for equality with God in His holiness and purity, that must be left until we cross the Jordan and enter into the perfection of the Most High. Notice how the blessings of sacred fellowship and perfect cleansing are bound up with walking in the light.

[1]Matthew 5:48

## *Trust in him at all times.*

PSALM 62:8

Faith is the rule of both temporal as well as spiritual life; we ought to have faith in God for our earthly affairs as well as for our heavenly business. It is only as we learn to trust in God for the supply of our daily needs that we will live above the world. We are not to be idle; *that* would show we did *not* trust in God, who is always working, but in the devil, who is the father of laziness. We are not to be hasty or rash; that would be to trust chance rather than the living God, who is a God of economy and order. Acting sensibly and honestly, we must rely simply and entirely on the Lord all the time.

Let me commend to you a life of trust in God in secular things. Trusting in God, you will not be compelled to mourn as a result of using sinful means to grow rich. Serve God with integrity, and if you are unsuccessful, at least sin will not lie upon your conscience. Trusting God, you will be free from self-contradiction. The one who trusts in craftiness, sails this way today and that way tomorrow, like a sailboat tossed about by the fickle wind; but the one who trusts in the Lord is like a powerful boat cutting through the waves, defying the wind, and making one bright silvery straightforward track to her desired haven. Be courageous as you act on principle; do not bow to the varying customs of worldly wisdom. Walk on the path of integrity with confidence, and show that you are invincibly strong in the strength that confidence in God alone confers. In this way you will be delivered from anxious care, you will be untroubled by evil tidings, and your heart will be fixed, trusting in the Lord. How pleasant to float along on the stream of providence! There is no more blessed way of living than a life of dependence upon a covenant-keeping God. We do not need to worry because He cares for us; we do not need to carry burdens because He invites us to cast them upon Him.

## *Unless you see signs and wonders you will not believe.*

JOHN 4:48

A craving for miracles was a symptom of the sickly condition of men's minds in our Lord's day; they refused solid nourishment and longed for mere wonders. The Gospel that they so greatly needed they would not have; the miracles that Jesus did not always choose to give they eagerly demanded. Even today there are many who must see signs and wonders or they will not believe. Some have said in their heart, "I must feel deep horror of soul or I never will believe in Jesus." But what if you never should feel it, as probably you never will? Will you go to hell out of spite against God because He did not treat you like someone else? One has said to himself, "If I had a dream, or if I could feel a sudden jolt of something, then I would believe." You undeserving mortals dream that my Lord is to be dictated to by you! You are beggars at His gate, asking for mercy, and you are drawing up rules and regulations as to how He will give that mercy. Do you think that He will submit to this? My Master has a generous spirit, but He also has a royal heart. He rejects all orders and maintains His sovereignty of action. Why, dear reader, if this is your case, do you crave signs and wonders? Isn't the Gospel its own sign and wonder? Isn't this the miracle of miracles, that "God so loved the world, that he gave his only Son, that whoever believes in him should not perish"? Surely that precious word, "Let the one who desires take the water of life without price"[1] and that solemn promise, "Whoever comes to me I will never cast out"[2] are better than signs and wonders! A truthful Savior ought to be believed. He is truth itself. Why will you ask the One who cannot lie for proof? The devils themselves declared Him to be the Son of God; will you mistrust Him?

[1]Revelation 22:17  [2]John 6:37

260

## The LORD tests the righteous.

PSALM 11:5

All events are under the control of providence; consequently all the trials of our outward life are ultimately traceable to God our Father. Out of the golden gate of God's ordinance the armies of trial march in rank, clad in their iron armor and armed with weapons of war. All providences are doors to testing. Even our mercies, like roses, have their thorns. Men may be drowned in prosperous seas as easily as in rivers of affliction. Our mountains are not too high, and our valleys are not too low for temptations: Trials lurk at every turn. Everywhere, above and below, we are confronted and surrounded with danger. Still no shower falls unpermitted from the threatening cloud; every drop has its order before it arrives on the earth. The trials that come from God are sent to prove and strengthen our graces and immediately illustrate the power of divine grace, to test the genuineness of our virtues and to add to their energy. Our Lord in His infinite wisdom and superabundant love sets such a high value upon His people's faith that He will not protect them from those trials by which faith is strengthened. You would never have possessed the precious faith that now supports you if the trial of your faith had not put you through the fire. You are a tree that never would have rooted as well if the wind had not rocked you to and fro and made you take a firm hold upon the precious truths of God's gracious covenant. Worldly ease is a great enemy to faith; it loosens the joints of holy zeal and snaps the sinews of sacred courage. The balloon never rises until the cords are cut; affliction provides this service for believing souls. While the wheat sleeps comfortably in the husk, it is useless to us; it must be threshed out of its resting place before its value can be known. Thus it is good that the Lord tests the righteous, for it causes them to grow rich toward God.

*September 4*

### You shall have just balances, just weights, a just ephah, and a just hin.

LEVITICUS 19:36

Weights and scales and measures were all to be according to the standard of justice. Surely no Christian will need to be reminded of this in his business, for if righteousness were banished from all the world beside, it would find a shelter in believing hearts. There are, however, other balances that weigh moral and spiritual things, and these need to be examined often.

Are the balances in which we weigh our own and other men's characters quite accurate? Do we not turn our own ounces of goodness into pounds, and other people's pounds of excellence into ounces? The scales in which we measure our trials and troubles—are they properly set? Paul, who had more to suffer than we have, called his afflictions light, and yet we often consider ours to be heavy—surely something must be wrong with the weights! We must see to this matter, before we get reported to the court above for unjust dealing. Those weights with which we measure our doctrinal belief—are they quite fair? The doctrines of grace should have the same weight with us as the precepts of the Word, no more and no less; but it is to be feared that with many, one scale or the other is unfairly weighted. It is a vital matter to give honest measure in truth. Christian, be careful here. Those measures in which we estimate our obligations and responsibilities look rather small. When a rich man gives to the work of God the same amount as the poor contribute, are things properly weighted? When pastors are neglected, is that honest dealing? When the poor are despised, while ungodly rich men are held in admiration, is that a just balance? Reader, we could extend the list, but we prefer to leave it as your evening's work to identify and destroy all unrighteous balances, weights, and measures.

## *Have you entered into the springs of the sea?*

JOB 38:16

Some things in nature remain a mystery even to the most intelligent and enterprising investigators. Human knowledge has boundaries beyond which it cannot pass. Universal knowledge is for God alone. If this is true in the things that are seen and temporal, I can be certain that it is even more so in spiritual and eternal matters. Why, then, have I been torturing my brain with speculations about divine sovereignty and human responsibility? These deep and dark truths I am no more able to comprehend than to discover the source from which the ocean draws her watery supplies. Why am I so curious to know the reason for my Lord's providences, the motive of His actions, the design of His visitations? Will I ever be able to clasp the sun in my fist or hold the universe in my palm? Yet these are as a drop in a bucket compared with the Lord my God. Do not let me strive to understand the infinite, but spend my strength in love. What I cannot gain by intellect I can possess by affection, and that should be enough for me. I cannot penetrate the heart of the sea, but I can enjoy the healthy breezes that sweep across it, and I can sail over its blue waves with propitious winds. If I could enter the springs of the sea, the feat would serve no useful purpose either to myself or to others; it would not save the sinking ship or restore the drowned sailor to his weeping wife and children. Neither would my solving deep mysteries avail me a single whit. The simplest act of obedience to Him is better than the profoundest knowledge. My Lord, I leave the infinite to You and ask You to put far from me a love for the tree of knowledge that would keep me from the tree of life.

## But if you are led by the Spirit, you are not under the law.

GALATIANS 5:18

The individual who looks at his character and position from a legal point of view will not only despair when he comes to the *end* of his reckoning, but if he is a wise man he will despair at the *beginning*; for if we are to be judged on the basis of the law, none of us will be justified. How blessed to know that we live in the realm of grace and not of law! When thinking of my standing before God, the question is not, "Am I perfect in myself before the law?" but "Am I perfect in Christ Jesus?" That is a very different matter. We need not ask ourselves, "Am I without sin naturally?" but "Have I been washed in the fountain opened for sin and for uncleanness?" It is not "Am I in myself well pleasing to God?" but "Am I accepted in the Beloved?" When the Christian views his evidences from the top of Sinai, he grows alarmed about his salvation; it is far better for him to view his position in the light of Calvary. "Why," he says, "my faith has unbelief in it; it is not able to save me." Suppose he had considered the *object* of his faith instead of his faith. Then he would have said, "There is no failure in *Him*, and therefore I am safe." He sighs over his hope: "My hope is spoiled and darkened by an anxious focusing on present things; how can I be accepted?" If he had regarded *the ground* of his hope, he would have seen that the promise of God stands sure and that whatever our doubts may be, God's oath and promise never fail. Believer, it is always safer for you to be led by the Spirit into gospel freedom than to wear legal fetters. Judge yourself on what *Christ* is rather than on what *you* are. Satan will try to spoil your peace by reminding you of your sinfulness and imperfections: You can only meet his accusations by faithfully holding to the Gospel and refusing to wear the yoke of slavery.

## They are troubled like the sea that cannot be quiet.

JEREMIAH 49:23

We are unaware of what sorrow may be upon the sea at this moment. We are safe in our quiet room, but far away out to sea the hurricane may be cruelly seeking the lives of men. Imagine the bitter winds howling through the rigging, the timbers heaving as the waves beat like battering rams upon the boat! God help you, poor drenched and wearied ones! I am praying to the great Lord of sea and land, that He will make the storm calm and bring you to your desired haven! I ought not simply to pray; I should try to help those brave men who risk their lives so constantly. Have I ever done anything for them? What can I do? How often does the boisterous sea swallow up the sailor! Thousands have died where pearls lie deep. There is sorrow on the sea, which is echoed in the sad lament of widows and orphans. The salt of the sea is in the eyes of many mothers and wives. Relentless billows, you have devoured the love of women and the strength of households. What a resurrection there will be from the caverns of the deep when the sea gives up her dead! Until then there will be sorrow on the sea. As if in sympathy with the woes of earth, the sea is always fretting along a thousand shores, wailing with a sorrowful cry, booming with a hollow crash of unrest, raving with uproarious discontent, chafing with hoarse rage, or jangling with the voices of ten thousand murmuring pebbles. The roar of the sea may be glorious to a rejoicing spirit, but to the son of sorrow, the wide, wide ocean is even more forlorn than the wide, wide world. This is not our comfort, and the restless billows tell us so. There is a land where there is no more sea—our faces are firmly set toward it; we are going to the place of which the Lord has spoken. Until then we cast our sorrows on the Lord who walked upon the sea of old and who makes a way for His people through the depths.

> *. . . and what is the immeasurable greatness*
> *of his power toward us who believe,*
> *according to the working of his great might*
> *that he worked in Christ when he raised him*
> *from the dead.*

EPHESIANS 1:19-20

The resurrection of Christ, and our salvation, was brought about by nothing less than *divine power*. What will we say of those who think that conversion is accomplished by the free will of man and is due to his own kindly disposition? When we begin to see the dead rise from the grave by their own power, then may we expect to see ungodly sinners turning to Christ by their own endeavors. It is not the word preached, nor the word read in itself; all quickening power proceeds from the Holy Spirit. This power was *irresistible*. All the soldiers and the high priests could not keep the body of Christ in the tomb; death itself could not hold Jesus in its grip: Just as irresistible is the power displayed in the believer when he is raised to newness of life. No sin, no corruption, no devils in hell nor sinners on earth can resist the hand of God's grace when it intends to convert a man. If God omnipotently says, "You shall," man will not say, "I shall not." Notice that the power that raised Christ from the dead was *glorious*. It reflected honor upon God and caused dismay in the hosts of evil. So there is great glory to God in the conversion of every sinner. It was everlasting power. "Christ being raised from the dead will never die again; death no longer has dominion over him."[1] So we, being raised from the dead, do not go back to our dead works or to our old corruptions, but we live to God. "Because I live, you also will live."[2] "For you have died, and your life is hidden with Christ in God."[3] "Just as Christ was raised from the dead by the glory of the Father, we too might walk in newness of life."[4] Finally, in the text note *the union of the new life to Jesus*. The same power that raised the Head works life in the members. What a blessing to be quickened together with Christ!

[1]Romans 6:9   [2]John 14:19   [3]Colossians 3:3   [4]Romans 6:4

### *Around the throne were twenty-four thrones, and seated on the thrones were twenty-four elders, clothed in white garments.*

REVELATION 4:4

These representatives of the saints in heaven are said to be *"around the throne."* In the passage in Solomon's Song where he sings of the King sitting at his table, some render it "a round table." From this, some expositors—I think, without straining the text—have said, "There is an equality among the saints." That idea is conveyed by the equal nearness of the twenty-four elders. The condition of glorified spirits in heaven is that of nearness to Christ, clear vision of His glory, constant access to His court, and familiar fellowship with His person. There is no difference in this respect between one saint and another, but all the people of God—apostles, martyrs, ministers, or private and obscure Christians—will all be seated *near the throne*, where they shall have a perfect view of their exalted Lord and be satisfied with His love. They will all be near Christ, all satisfied with His love, all eating and drinking at the same table with Him, all equally loved as His favorites and friends even if not all equally rewarded as His servants.

Believers on earth should imitate the saints in heaven in their nearness to Christ. We should be like the elders in heaven, sitting around the throne. Christ should be the object of our thoughts and the center of our lives. How can we endure to live at such a distance from Him? Lord Jesus, draw us nearer to Yourself. Say to us, "Abide in Me, and I in you"; and let us sing, "Holy, holy, holy is the Lord God Almighty, who was and is and is to come!"

> *O lift me higher, nearer Thee,*
> *And as I rise more pure and fit,*
> *O let my soul's humility*
> *Make me lie lower at Thy feet;*
> *Less trusting self, the more I prove*
> *The blessed comfort of Thy love.*

## *Evening wolves.*

HABAKKUK 1:8

While preparing the present volume, this particular expression recurred to me so frequently that in order to be rid of its constant demand I determined to give a page to it. The evening wolf, infuriated by a day of hunger, was fiercer and more ravenous than he would have been in the morning. This furious creature may promise a picture of our doubts and fears after a day of distraction of mind, losses in business, and perhaps ungenerous tauntings from our fellowmen. How our thoughts howl in our ears: "Where is your God now?" How voracious and greedy they are, swallowing up all suggestions of comfort and remaining as hungry as ever. Great Shepherd, slay these evening wolves, and bid Your sheep lie down in green pastures, undisturbed by unbelief. The fiends of hell seen just like evening wolves, for when the flock of Christ are in a cloudy and dark day, and their sun seems to be going down, they arrive to tear and to devour. They will scarcely attack the Christian in the daylight of faith, but in the gloomy night of the soul they fall upon him. O Lord who laid down Your life for the sheep, preserve them from the fangs of the wolf.

False teachers who craftily and industriously hunt for precious life, devouring men by their falsehoods, are as dangerous and detestable as evening wolves. Darkness is their element; deceit is their character; destruction is their end. They pose the greatest threat to our safety when they wear the sheep's skin. Blessed is he who is kept from them, for thousands become the prey of grievous wolves that enter within the fold of the church.

What a wonder of grace it is when fierce persecutors are converted, for then the wolf lives with the lamb, and men of cruel, ungovernable dispositions become gentle and teachable. O Lord, convert many like this: For this we will pray tonight.

## *Lead me, O Lord, in your righteousness because of my enemies.*

PSALM 5:8

The enmity of the world is bitter in its assault against the people of Christ. Men will forgive a thousand faults in others, but they will magnify the most trivial offense in the followers of Jesus. Instead of vainly regretting this, let us make it work for us, and since so many are watching for our collapse, let it be a special motive for walking very carefully before God. If we live carelessly, the watching world will soon see it, and multiple tongues will spread the story, exaggerated and emblazoned by the zeal of slander. They will shout triumphantly, "See! See how these Christians act! They are hypocrites to everyone." And so great damage will be done to the cause of Christ, and His name will be greatly maligned. The cross of Christ is in itself an offense to the world; let us take care that we add no offense of our own. It is "a stumbling block to Jews"[1]: Let us ensure that we put no stumbling blocks where there are enough already. "Folly to Gentiles": let us not add our folly to give apparent reason for the scorn with which the worldly deride the Gospel. How concerned we should be with ourselves! How rigid with our consciences! In the presence of adversaries who will misrepresent our best deeds and impugn our motives if they cannot censure our actions, we should be circumspect! Like pilgrims we travel under suspicion through Vanity Fair. Not only are we under surveillance, but there are more spies than we imagine, at home and at work. If we fall into the enemies' hands, we may sooner expect generosity from a wolf or mercy from a fiend than anything like patience with our infirmities from those who spice their infidelity toward God with scandals against His people. Lord, lead us always; do not allow our enemies to trip us up!

[1] 1 Corinthians 1:23.

# I will sing of steadfast love and justice.

PSALM 101:1

Faith is triumphant in trial. When reason has her feet fastened in the stocks of the inner prison, faith makes the dungeon walls ring with her happy notes as she cries, "I will sing of steadfast love and justice; to you, O Lord, I will make music." Faith pulls the dark mask from the face of trouble and discovers the angel beneath. Faith looks up at the cloud and sees that

> It is big with mercy and will break
> In blessings on her head.

There is a subject for song even in the judgments of God toward us. For, first, the trial is *not as difficult as it might have been*; next, the trouble is not as severe as we deserved; and our affliction is *not as crushing as the burden that others have to carry*. Faith sees that in her deepest sorrow there is no punishment. There is not a drop of God's wrath in it; it is all sent in love. Faith finds love gleaming like a jewel on the breast of an angry God. Faith wears her grief "like a badge of honor" and sings of the sweet result of her sorrows, because they work for her spiritual good. Faith says, "For this slight momentary affliction is preparing for us an eternal weight of glory beyond all comparison."[1] So faith rides out in victory, trampling down earthly wisdom and carnal knowledge, and singing songs of triumph where the battle rages.

> All I meet I find assists me
> In my path to heavenly joy:
> Where, though trials now attend me,
> Trials never more annoy.
>
> Blest there with a weight of glory,
> Still the path I'll not forget,
> But, exulting, cry, it led me
> To my blessed Savior's seat.

[1] 2 Corinthians 4:17

## *This man receives sinners.*

LUKE 15:2

Observe *the condescension* of this fact. Jesus, holy, harmless, undefiled, and separate from sinners, who towers above all other men—*this* Man receives sinners. This Man, who is no other than the eternal God, before whom angels veil their faces—*this* Man receives sinners. It requires an angel's tongue to describe such a mighty stoop of love. That any of us would be willing to reach the lost is nothing wonderful—they are, after all, our own race; but that He, the offended God, against whom the transgression has been committed, should take upon Himself the form of a servant and bear the sin of many and be willing to receive the worst of sinners—this is marvelous.

"This man receives sinners"; not in order for them to remain sinners, but He receives them in order that He may pardon their sins, justify their persons, cleanse their hearts by His purifying word, preserve their souls by the indwelling of the Holy Spirit, and enable them to serve Him, show forth His praise, and have communion with Him. Into His heart's love He receives sinners; He takes them from the refuse pile and wears them as jewels in His crown; He snatches them like branches from the fire and preserves them as costly monuments to His mercy. None are so precious in Jesus' sight as the sinners for whom He died. When Jesus receives sinners, He does not have an outdoor reception, no public square where He charitably entertains them in the way men treat passing beggars, but He opens the golden gates of His royal heart and receives the sinner right into Himself. He admits the humble penitent into personal union and makes Him a member of His body, of His flesh, and of His bones. There was never such a reception as this! This fact is certain. Even this evening, He is still receiving sinners: It is our prayer that sinners will receive Him.

> **I acknowledged my sin unto you, and I did not cover my iniquity; I said, "I will confess my transgressions to the LORD," and you forgave the iniquity of my sin.**
>
> PSALM 32:5

David's grief for sin was bitter. Its effects were visible on his outward frame: His bones wasted away; his strength dried up like the drought of summer. He was unable to find a remedy until he made a full confession before the throne of heavenly grace. He tells us that for a time he kept silent, and his heart was filled with grief and his lips with groaning: Like a mountain stream that is blocked, his soul was swollen with torrents of sorrow. He created excuses, he tried to divert his thoughts, but it was all to no purpose; like a festering sore his anguish gathered, and, unwilling to use the scalpel of confession, his spirit was tormented and knew no peace. At last it came to this, that he must return to God in humble penitence or die outright; so he hurried to the mercy-seat and there unrolled the volume of his iniquities before the all-seeing God, acknowledging all the evil of his ways in the terms of the Fifty-first and other penitential Psalms. Having confessed, a task so simple and yet so hard for the proud, he immediately received the token of divine forgiveness; the bones that had been wasted were made to rejoice, and he emerged from his prayers to sing the joyful songs of the one whose transgression is forgiven. Do you see the value of this grace-led confession of sin? It is to be prized above everything, for in every case where there is a genuine, gracious confession, mercy is freely given—not because the repentance and confession *deserve* mercy, but *for Christ's sake*. May God be praised, there is always healing for the broken heart; the fountain is ever flowing to cleanse us from our sins. Truly, O Lord, You are a God "ready to forgive."[1] Therefore will we humbly acknowledge our iniquities.

[1]Nehemiah 9:17

## . . . *for the people of Israel who are near to him.*

PSALM 148:14

Distance and separation were marks of the old covenant. When God appeared even to His servant Moses, He said, "Do not come near; take your sandals off your feet";[1] and when He revealed Himself on Mount Sinai to His own chosen and separated people, one of the first commands was, "You shall set limits for the people all around."[2] In the sacred worship of the tabernacle and the temple, the thought of distance was always prominent. The majority of the people did not even enter the outer court. Into the inner court none but the priests might dare to intrude, while into the innermost place, or the holy of holies, the high priest entered but only once in the year. It was as if the Lord in those early ages was teaching man that sin was so utterly loathsome to Him that He must treat men as lepers put outside the camp; and when He came closest to them, He still made them feel the extent of the separation between a holy God and an impure sinner. When the Gospel came, we were placed on quite another footing. The word "Go" was replaced with "Come"; distance was replaced with nearness, and we who previously were far away were brought near by the blood of Jesus Christ. Incarnate Deity has no fire wall around it. "Come to me, all who labor and are heavy laden, and I will give you rest"[3] is the joyful proclamation of God as He appears in human flesh. He no longer teaches the leper his leprosy by setting him at a distance, but by Himself suffering the penalty of the leper's defilement. What a state of safety and privilege is this proximity to God through Jesus! Do you know it by experience? If you know it, are you living in the power of it? This closeness is wonderful, and yet it is to be followed by a greater nearness still, when it shall be said, "The dwelling place of God is with man. He will dwell with them, and they will be his people."[4] Lord, haste the day!

[1]Exodus 3:5  [2]Exodus 19:12  [3]Matthew 11:28  [4]Revelation 21:3

## *Am I the sea, or a sea monster, that you set a guard over me?*

JOB 7:12

This was a strange question for Job to ask the Lord. He felt himself to be too insignificant to be so strictly watched and chastened, and he hoped that he was not so unruly as to need to be restrained. The inquiry was natural from one surrounded by such miseries, but after all, it is capable of a very humbling answer. It is true that man is not the sea, but he is even more troublesome and unruly. The sea obediently respects its boundary, and it does not overleap the limit, even though it is just a belt of sand. Mighty as it is, it hears the divine *"thus far,"* and when raging with tempest it still respects the word. Self-willed man, however, defies heaven and oppresses earth, and there is no end to his rebellious rage. The sea, obedient to the moon, ebbs and flows with ceaseless regularity and so renders an active as well as a passive obedience; but man, restless beyond his sphere, sleeps within the lines of duty, lazy where he should be active. He neither comes nor goes at the divine command but sullenly prefers to do what he should not and to leave undone what is required of him. Every drop in the ocean, every beaded bubble, and every yeasty foam-flake, every shell and pebble, feel the power of law and yield or move at once. If only our nature were but one thousandth as much conformed to the will of God! We call the sea fickle and false, but how constant it is! Since our fathers' days, and even before, the sea is where it was, beating on the same cliffs to the same tune. We know where to find it; it never hides, and its ceaseless pounding never fades; but where is man, fickle man? Can the wise man guess by what folly he will next be seduced from his obedience? We need more watching than the billowy sea and are far more rebellious. Lord, rule us for Your own glory. Amen.

274

## *Encourage him.*

DEUTERONOMY 1:38

God employs His people to encourage one another. He did not say to an angel, "Gabriel, My servant Joshua is about to lead My people into Canaan—go, encourage him." God never performs unnecessary miracles. If His purposes can be accomplished by ordinary means, He will not use miraculous agencies. Gabriel would not have been half so well fitted for the work as Moses. A brother's sympathy is more precious than an angel's prestige. The swift-winged angel knew more about the Master's desires than he did about the people's needs. An angel had never experienced the difficult journey, nor faced the fiery serpents, nor had he led the stiff-necked multitude in the wilderness as Moses had done. We should be glad that God usually works for man by man. This forms a bond of brotherhood, and being mutually dependent on one another, we are united more completely into one family. Brethren, take the text as God's message to you. Work at helping others, and especially strive to encourage them. Talk warmly to the young and anxious inquirer; lovingly try to remove stumbling blocks out of his way. When you find a spark of grace in the heart, kneel down and blow it into a flame. Leave the young believer to discover the roughness of the road by stages, but tell him of the strength that is found in God, of the certainty of the promise, and of the benefits of communion with Christ. Aim to comfort the sorrowful and to encourage the despondent. Speak a fitting word to the weary, and lift the spirits of those who are fearful to go on their way with gladness. God encourages you by His promises; Christ encourages you as He points to the heaven He has won for you; and the Spirit encourages you as He works in you to will and to do of His own purpose and pleasure. Imitate divine wisdom, and encourage others according to the Word this evening.

## *And they follow me.*

JOHN 10:27

We should follow our Lord as unhesitatingly as sheep follow their shepherd, for *He has a right to lead us wherever He pleases*. We are not our own, we are bought with a price—let us recognize the rights of the redeeming blood. The soldier follows his captain, the servant obeys his master, and so we must follow our Redeemer, to whom we are a purchased possession. We are not true to our profession of being Christians if we question the summons of our Leader and Commander. Submission is our duty; quibbling is our folly. Our Lord may say to us what he said to Peter, "What is that to you? You follow Me!"[1] Wherever Jesus may lead us, *He goes before us*. If we do not know where we go, we know with whom we go. With such a companion, who will dread the dangers of the journey? The road may be long, but His everlasting arms will carry us to the end. The presence of Jesus is the assurance of eternal salvation; because He lives, we will live also. We should follow Christ in simplicity and faith, because *the paths in which He leads us all end in glory and immortality*. It is true that they may not be smooth paths—they may be covered with sharp, flinty trials; but they lead to "the city that has foundations, whose designer and maker is God."[2] All the paths of the Lord are mercy and truth to those who keep His covenant. Let us put our complete trust in our Leader, since we know that in prosperity or adversity, sickness or health, popularity or contempt, His purpose will be worked out, and that purpose will be pure, unmingled good to every heir of mercy. We will find it sweet to go up the bleak side of the hill with Christ; and when rain and snow blow into our faces, His dear love will make us far more blessed than those who sit at home and warm their hands at the world's fire. When Jesus draws us, we will run after Him. No matter where He leads us, we follow the Shepherd.

[1]John 21:22   [2]Hebrews 11:10

## *For this child I prayed.*

### 1 SAMUEL 1:27

Devout souls delight to reflect upon those mercies that they have obtained in answer to prayer, for they can see God's special love in them. When we can name our blessings Samuel—that is, "asked of God"—they will be as dear to us as this child was to Hannah. Peninnah had many children, but they came as common blessings unsought in prayer. Hannah's one heaven-given child was far more precious, because he was the fruit of sincere pleadings. How sweet was the water that Samson found at "the spring of him who called."[1] Did we pray for the conversion of our children? How doubly sweet, when they are saved, to see in them our own petitions answered! Better to rejoice over them as the fruit of our pleadings than as the fruit of our bodies. Have we asked the Lord for some choice spiritual gift? When it comes to us, it will be wrapped up in the golden cloth of God's faithfulness and truth and will be doubly precious. Have we sought success in the Lord's work? How joyful is the prosperity that comes flying on the wings of prayer! It is always best to get blessings into our house in the legitimate way, by the door of prayer; then they are blessings indeed, and not temptations. Even when prayer is not speedy, the blessings grow all the richer on account of the delay; the child Jesus was all the more lovely in the eyes of Mary when she found Him after having searched for Him. What we gain by prayer we should dedicate to God, as Hannah dedicated Samuel. The gift came from heaven; let it go to heaven. Prayer brought it, gratitude sang over it—let devotion consecrate it. Here will be a special occasion for saying, "Of Your own I have given to You." Reader, is prayer your heartbeat or your weariness? Which?

[1]Judges 15:19, margin

## *At evening withhold not your hand.*

ECCLESIASTES 11:6

In *the evening of the day* opportunities are plentiful: Men return from their work, and the zealous soul-winner finds time to share widely the love of Jesus. Do I have no evening work for Jesus? If I have not, let me no longer withhold my hand from a service that requires wholehearted endeavor. Sinners are perishing for lack of knowledge; he who loiters may find his shoes red with the blood of souls. Jesus gave both His hands to the nails. How can I keep back one of mine from His blessed work? Night and day He toiled and prayed for me. How can I give a single hour to the pampering of my body with luxurious ease? Up, lazy heart; stretch out your hand to work, or lift it up to pray. Heaven and hell are serious; so must I be, and this evening I should sow good seed for the Lord my God.

*The evening of life* also has its calls. Life is so short that a morning of manhood's strength and an evening of decay make up the whole of it. To some it seems long, but a dollar is a great sum of money to a poor man. Life is so brief that no man can afford to lose a day. It has been well said that if a great king were to bring us a great heap of gold and bid us take as much as we could count in a day, we would make a long day of it; we would begin early in the morning, and in the evening we would not withhold our hand. Winning souls is far nobler work; so how is it that we quit so soon? Some are spared to a long evening of green old age; if such is my case, let me use any talents I still retain and serve my blessed and faithful Lord to the final hour. By His grace I will die with my boots on and lay down my commission only when I lay down my body. Age may instruct the young, cheer the faint, and encourage the despondent. If evening has less stifling heat, it should have more calm wisdom; therefore in the evening I will not withhold my hand.

## *Do not sweep my soul away with sinners.*

PSALM 26:9

Fear made David pray like this, for something whispered, *Perhaps, after all, you may be swept away with sinners.* That fear springs mainly from holy anxiety, arising from the recollection of past sin. Even the pardoned man will inquire, "What if at the end my sins should be remembered, and I should be left out of the company of the saved?" He thinks about his present condition—so little grace, so little love, so little holiness; and looking forward to the future, he considers his weakness and the many temptations that surround him, and he fears that he may fall and become a prey to the enemy. A sense of sin and present evil and his prevailing corruptions compel him to pray, in fear and trembling, "Do not sweep my soul away with sinners." Reader, if you have prayed this prayer, and if your character is correctly described in the Psalm from which it is taken, you need not be afraid that you will be swept away with sinners. Do you have the two virtues that David had—the outward walking in integrity and the inward trusting in the Lord? Are you resting upon Christ's sacrifice, and can you approach the altar of God with humble hope? If so, rest assured, you will never be swept away with sinners, for that calamity is impossible. At the judgment the command will be given, "Gather the weeds first and bind them in bundles to be burned, but gather the wheat into my barn."[1] If, then, you are *like* God's people, you will be *with* God's people. You cannot be swept away with sinners, for you have been purchased at too high a price. Redeemed by the blood of Christ, you are His forever, and where He is, there His people must be. You are loved too much to be swept away with reprobates. Will one who is dear to Christ perish? Impossible! Hell cannot hold you! Heaven claims you! Trust in Christ, and do not fear!

[1]Matthew 13:30

## *When my heart is faint . . . lead me to the rock that is higher than I.*

PSALM 61:2

Most of us know what it is to be overwhelmed in heart, emptied like when a man wipes a dish and turns it upside down, submerged and thrown on our beam-ends like a boat mastered by the storm. Discoveries of inward corruption will do this, if the Lord permits the depth of our depravity to become troubled and cast up mire and dirt. Disappointments and heartbreaks will do this when billow after billow rolls over us, and we are like a broken shell thrown to and fro by the surf. Blessed be God, at such seasons we are not left without a sufficient solace: Our God is the harbor of weather-beaten sails, the hostel for forlorn pilgrims. He is higher than we are, His mercy higher than our sins, His love higher than our thoughts. It is pitiful to see men putting their trust in something lower than themselves; but our confidence is fixed on an exceeding high and glorious Lord. He is a Rock since He doesn't change, and a high Rock because the tempests that overwhelm us roll far beneath His feet; He is not disturbed by them but rules them at His will. If we get under the shelter of this lofty Rock, we may defy the hurricane; all is calm under the lee of that towering cliff. Sadly, the confusion in which the troubled mind is often cast is such that we need piloting to this divine shelter. Hence the prayer of the text. O Lord, our God, by Your Holy Spirit, teach us the way of faith; lead us into Your rest. The wind blows us out to sea—the helm does not answer to our puny hand; You alone can steer us over the bar between the sunken rocks and safe into the fair haven. We are totally dependent upon You—we need You to bring us to You. To be wisely directed and steered into safety and peace is Your gift, and Yours alone. Tonight be pleased to deal kindly with Your servants.

### And Jesus said to him, "If you can!
### All things are possible for one who believes."

MARK 9:23

A certain man had a deeply troubled son who was afflicted with a spirit that struck him dumb. The father, having seen the futility of the attempts of the disciples to heal his child, had little or no faith in Christ. Therefore, when he was invited to bring his son to Him, he said to Jesus, "If You can do anything, have compassion on us and help us." Now there was an "if" in the question, but the poor trembling father had put the "if" in the wrong place. Jesus Christ, therefore, without commanding him to retract the "if," kindly puts it in its legitimate position. "Actually, " He seemed to say, "there should be no 'if' about My power, nor concerning My willingness; the 'if' lies somewhere else. *If you can believe,* 'all things are possible for one who believes.'" The man's trust was strengthened, he offered a humble prayer for an increase of faith, and instantly Jesus spoke the word, and the devil was cast out, with an injunction never to return. There is a lesson here that we need to learn. We, like this man, often see that there is an "if" somewhere, but we are continually blundering by putting it in the wrong place. "*If* Jesus can help me"—"*if* He can give me grace to overcome temptation"—"*if* He can grant me pardon"—"*if* He can make me successful." No; if you can believe, He both can and will. You have misplaced your "if." If you can confidently trust, even as all things are possible to Christ, so will all things be possible to you. Faith stands in God's power and is robed in God's majesty; it wears the royal apparel and rides on the King's horse, for it is the grace that the King delights to honor. Girding itself with the glorious might of the all-working Spirit, it becomes, in the omnipotence of God, mighty to do, to dare, and to suffer. All things, without limit, are possible to one who believes. My soul, can you believe your Lord tonight?

## *I slept, but my heart was awake.*

SONG OF SOLOMON 5:2

Paradoxes abound in Christian experience, and here is one: The spouse was asleep, and yet she was awake. The only one who can read the believer's riddle is he who has lived through this experience. The two points in this evening's text are: a mournful sleepiness and a hopeful wakefulness. "I *slept.*" Through sin that dwells in us we may become lax in holy duties, lazy in religious exercises, dull in spiritual joys, and completely indolent and careless. This is a shameful state for one in whom the quickening Spirit dwells; and it is dangerous in the highest degree. Even wise virgins sometimes slumber, but it is high time for all to shake off the chains of idleness. It is to be feared that many believers lose their strength as Samson lost his hair, while sleeping on the lap of carnal security. With a perishing world around us, to sleep is cruel; with eternity so close at hand, it is madness. Yet none of us are as awake as we should be; a few thunderclaps would do us all good, and it may be, unless we soon stir ourselves, we will have them in the form of war or disease or personal bereavements and loss. May we leave forever the couch of fleshly ease, and go out with flaming torches to meet the coming Bridegroom! "*My heart was awake.*" This is a happy sign. Life is not extinct, though sadly smothered. When our renewed heart struggles against our natural heaviness, we should be grateful to sovereign grace for keeping a little vitality within this body of death. Jesus will hear our hearts, will help our hearts, will visit our hearts; for the voice of the wakeful heart is really the voice of our Beloved, saying, "Open to me." Holy zeal will surely unlock the door.

> *Oh lovely attitude! He stands*
> *With melting heart and laden hands;*
> *My soul forsakes her every sin;*
> *And lets the heavenly stranger in.*

September 25

## Whom God made our wisdom.

1 CORINTHIANS 1:30

Man's intellect seeks for peace and by nature seeks it apart from the Lord Jesus Christ. Men of education are apt, even when converted, to look upon the simplicities of the cross of Christ with too little reverence and love. They are trapped in the old net in which the Greeks were taken and have a hankering to mix philosophy with revelation. The temptation with a man of refined thought and high education is to depart from the simple truth of Christ crucified and to invent, as the term is, a more *intellectual* doctrine. This led the early Christian churches into Gnosticism and bewitched them with all sorts of heresies. This is the root of unorthodoxy and the other high-sounding notions that in the past were so fashionable in Germany and are now so enthralling to certain classes of divines. Whoever you are, good reader, and whatever your education may be, if you are the Lord's, rest assured that you will find no peace in philosophizing divinity. You may receive the dogma of one great thinker or the dream of another profound reasoner, but what the chaff is to the wheat is what these notions are to the pure Word of God. Reason at its best can only discover the ABC's of truth, and even that lacks certainty, while in Christ Jesus there is treasured up all the fullness of wisdom and knowledge. All attempts on the part of Christians to be content with the systems that Unitarian and liberal-church thinkers approve of must fail; true heirs of heaven must come back to the grandly simple reality that makes the plowboy's eye flash with joy and rejoices the pious pauper's heart—"Christ Jesus came into the world to save sinners."[1] Jesus satisfies the most elevated intellect when He is believingly received, but apart from Him the mind of the regenerate discovers no rest. "The fear of the LORD is the beginning of knowledge."[2] "All those who practice it have a good understanding."[3]

[1] 1 Timothy 1:15  [2] Proverbs 1:7  [3] Psalm 111:10

283

## *Wail, O cypress, for the cedar has fallen.*

ZECHARIAH 11:2

W hen in the forest there is heard the crash of a falling oak, it is a sign that the woodman is around, and every tree in the whole company may tremble lest tomorrow the sharp edge of the axe should find it out. We are all like trees marked for the axe, and the fall of one should remind us that for every one, whether as great as the cedar or as humble as the cypress, the appointed hour is fast approaching. I trust we do not, by often hearing of death, become callous to it. May we never be like the birds in the steeple, which build their nests when the bells are tolling and sleep quietly when the solemn funeral peals are startling the air. May we regard death as the most serious of all events and be sobered by its approach. It ill behooves us to play while our eternal destiny hangs on a thread. The sword is out of its sheath—let us not trifle; it is ready, and the edge is sharp—let us not play with it. He who does not prepare for death is more than an ordinary fool—he is a madman. When the voice of God is heard among the trees of the garden, let fig tree and sycamore and elm and cedar all hear the sound.

Be ready, servant of Christ, for your Master comes suddenly, when an ungodly world least expects Him. See to it that you are faithful in His work, for the grave shall soon be prepared for you. Be ready, parents, see to it that your children are brought up in the fear of God, for they will soon be orphans. Be ready, businessmen, make sure that your affairs are in order and that you serve God with all your hearts, for the days of your earthly service will soon be over, and you will be called to give account for the deeds done in the body, whether they are good or bad. May we all prepare for the tribunal of the great King with a care that will be rewarded with the gracious commendation, "Well done, good and faithful servant."[1]

[1]Matthew 25:21

# *My beloved put his hand to the latch, and my heart was thrilled within me.*

SONG OF SOLOMON 5:4

Knocking was not enough, for my heart was too full of sleep, too cold and ungrateful to rise and open the door; but the touch of His effectual grace has caused my soul to stir. How patient of my Beloved to wait when He found Himself shut out, and me asleep upon the bed of indolence! How great His patience to knock and knock again, and to add His voice to His knockings, beseeching me to open to Him! How could I have refused Him! My heart is base; I blush and without excuse! But the greatest kindness of all is this, that He becomes His own porter and unlocks the door Himself. Blessed is the hand that condescends to lift the latch and turn the key. Now I see that nothing but my Lord's own power can save such a naughty mass of wickedness as I am; ordinances fail, and even the Gospel has no effect upon me, until His hand is stretched out. I also see that His hand is good where everything else is unsuccessful; He can open when nothing else will. Blessed be His name, I feel His gracious presence even now. Well may my heart be thrilled within me when I think of all that He has suffered for me and of my ungenerous response. I have allowed my affections to wander. I have tolerated rivals. I have grieved Him. Sweetest and dearest of all lovers, I have treated You as an unfaithful wife treats her husband. Oh, my cruel sins, my cruel self. What can I do? Tears are a poor evidence of my repentance; my whole heart palpitates with indignation at myself. I am wretched to treat my Lord, my All in All, my exceeding great joy, as though He were a stranger. Jesus, You freely forgive, but this is not enough; prevent my unfaithfulness in the future. Kiss away these tears, and then purge my heart and bind it with sevenfold cords to Yourself, so that I may never wander from You again.

### *And he said, "Go again," seven times.*

1 KINGS 18:43

Success is certain when the Lord has promised it. Although you may have pleaded month after month without evidence of response, it is not possible that the Lord should be deaf when His people are serious about a matter that concerns His glory. The prophet on the top of Carmel continued to wrestle with God and never for a moment gave way to the fear that he would not be suited for Jehovah's courts. Six times the servant returned, but on each occasion no word was spoken but "Go again." We must not dream of unbelief but hold to our faith even to seventy times seven. Faith sends expectant hope to look from Carmel's peak, and if nothing is seen, she sends again and again. So far from being crushed by repeated disappointment, faith is quickened to plead more fervently with her God. She is humbled but not crushed: Her groans are deeper, and her sighings more vehement, but she never relaxes her hold or stays her hand. It would be more agreeable to flesh and blood to have a speedy answer, but believing souls have learned to be submissive and to find it good to wait *for* as well as *upon* the Lord. Delayed answers often set the heart searching itself and so lead to contrition and spiritual reformation: Deadly blows are then struck at our corruption, and the sinful images are cleansed. The great danger is that men should faint and miss the blessing. Reader, do not fall into that sin, but continue to watch and pray. At last the little cloud was seen, the sure forerunner of torrents of rain; and even so with you, the token for good will surely be given, and you will rise as a prevailing prince to enjoy the mercy you have sought. Elijah was a man with passions just like us: His power with God did not lie in his own merits. If his believing prayer availed so much, why not yours? Plead the precious blood with unceasing persistence, and it will be with you according to your desire.

# I found him whom my soul loves. I held him, and would not let him go.

SONG OF SOLOMON 3:4

Does Christ receive us when we come to Him despite all our past sinfulness? Does He never chide us for having tried all other refuges first? And is there none on earth like Him? Is He the best of all the good, the fairest of all the fair? Then let us praise Him! Daughters of Jerusalem, extol Him with tambourine and harp! Down with your idols; up with the Lord Jesus. Let the standards of pomp and pride be trampled underfoot, but let the cross of Jesus, which the world frowns and scoffs at, be lifted on high. O for a throne of ivory for our King. Let Him be set on high forever, and let my soul sit at His footstool and kiss His feet and wash them with my tears. How precious is Christ! How can it be that I have thought so little of Him? How is it I can go anywhere else for joy or comfort when He is so full, so rich, so satisfying? Fellow believer, make a covenant with your heart that you will never depart from Him, and ask the Lord to ratify it. Bid Him set you as a ring on His finger and as a bracelet on His arm. Ask Him to bind you to Him as the bride adorns herself with ornaments and as the bridegroom puts on his jewels. I would live in Christ's heart; in the hollow of that rock my soul would eternally abide. The sparrow has made a house, and the swallow a nest for herself where she may lay her young, even your altars, O Lord of hosts, my King and my God. And in the same way I would make my nest, my home, in You, and may this soul never leave again, but let me nestle close to You, Lord Jesus, my true and only rest.

*When my precious Lord I find,*
*All my ardent passions glow;*
*Him with cords of love I bind,*
*Hold and will not let Him go.*

## *A living dog is better than a dead lion.*

### ECCLESIASTES 9:4

Life is a precious thing, and in even its humblest form it is superior to death. This is eminently true in spiritual matters. It is better to be the least in the kingdom of heaven than the greatest out of it. The lowest degree of grace is superior to the noblest development of unregenerate nature. Where the Holy Spirit implants divine life in the soul, there is a precious deposit that none of the refinements of education can equal. The thief on the cross excels Caesar on his throne; Lazarus among the dogs is better than Cicero among the senators; and the most unlettered Christian is in the sight of God superior to Plato. Life is the badge of nobility in the realm of spiritual things, and men without it are only coarser or finer specimens of the same lifeless material, needing to be made alive, for they are dead in trespasses and sins.

A living, loving gospel sermon, however unlearned in matter and lacking in style, is better than the finest discourse devoid of unction and power. A living dog keeps better watch than a dead lion and is of more service to his master; and so the poorest spiritual preacher is infinitely to be preferred to the exquisite orator who has no wisdom but that of words, no energy but that of self. The same holds true of our prayers and other religious exercises: If we are quickened in them by the Holy Spirit, they are acceptable to God through Jesus Christ, though we may think them to be worthless things, while our grand performances in which our hearts were absent, like dead lions, are mere carcasses in the sight of the living God. We need living groans, living sighs, living despondencies rather than lifeless songs and dead calms. Anything is better than death. The snarlings of the dog of hell will at least keep us awake, but dead faith and dead profession—what greater curses can a man have? Quicken us, quicken us, O Lord!

## The LORD *bestows favor and honor.*

PSALM 84:11

God is wonderfully generous by nature; to give is His delight. His gifts are immeasurably precious and are given as freely as the light of the sun. He gives grace to His own because He wills it, to His redeemed because of His covenant, to the called because of His promise, to believers because they seek it, to sinners because they need it. He gives grace abundantly, seasonably, constantly, readily, sovereignly; the value of the blessings is doubled by the manner in which it is given. Grace in all its forms He freely supplies to His people: Comforting, preserving, sanctifying, directing, instructing, assisting grace He generously and constantly pours into their souls, and He will always do so, whatever may happen. Sickness may come, but the Lord will give grace; poverty may descend on us, but grace will definitely be supplied; death must come, but grace will light a candle in the darkest hour. Reader, how blessed it is as years roll on, and the leaves again begin to fall, to enjoy this unfading promise, "The LORD bestows favor and honor."

The little conjunction "and" in this verse is a diamond rivet binding the present with the future: Favor and honor always go together. God has married them, and no one can separate them. The Lord will never deny a soul honor to whom He has freely granted favor; indeed, honor is nothing more than favor in its Sunday best, favor in full bloom, favor like autumn fruit, mellow and perfected. How soon we may have honor none can tell! It may be that before this month of October has run out we will see the Holy City; but if the interval is longer or shorter, we shall be honored before long. The honor of heaven, the honor of eternity, the honor of Jesus, the honor of the Father—the Lord will certainly give all this to His chosen. What a wonderful promise from a faithful God!

> *Two golden links of one celestial chain:*
> *Who owns favor shall surely honor gain.*

## . . . *man greatly loved.*

DANIEL 10:11

Child of God, do you hesitate to appropriate this title? Has your unbelief made you forget that you are also greatly loved? Surely you must have been greatly loved, to have been bought with the precious blood of Christ, as of a lamb without blemish and without spot? When God crushed His only Son for you, what was this but being greatly loved? You lived in sin and rioted in it; surely you were greatly loved for God to have been so patient with you. You were called by grace and led to a Savior and made a child of God and an heir of heaven. Doesn't this all prove a very great and superabounding love? Since that time, whether your path has been rough with troubles or smooth with mercies, it has been full of proofs that you are greatly loved. If the Lord has chastened you, it was not in anger; if He has made you poor, still in grace you have been rich. The more unworthy you feel yourself to be, the more evidence you have that nothing but unspeakable love could have led the Lord Jesus to save a soul like yours. The more disapproval you feel, the clearer is the display of God's abounding love in choosing you and calling you and making you an heir of heaven. Now, if such love exists between God and us, let us live in the influence and sweetness of it and use the privilege of our position. We should not approach our Lord as though we were strangers or as though He were unwilling to hear us—for we are greatly loved by our loving Father. "He who did not spare his own Son but gave him up for us all, how will he not also with him graciously give us all things?"[1] Come boldly, believer, for despite the whispers of Satan and the doubts of your own heart, you are greatly loved. Meditate on the exceeding greatness and faithfulness of divine love this evening, and then go to your bed in peace.

[1]Romans 8:32

## *He himself has suffered when tempted.*

HEBREWS 2:18

It is a common thought, and yet it tastes like honey to the weary heart—Jesus was tempted as I am. You have heard that truth many times, but have you grasped it? He was tempted by the very same sins into which we fall. Do not separate Jesus from our common humanity. If you are going through a dark room, remember Jesus went through it before you. If you are engaged in s a sore fight, remember that Jesus has stood foot to foot with the same enemy. Let us be encouraged—Christ has borne the load before us, and the blood-stained footsteps of the King of glory can be seen along the road that we travel at this hour. There is something sweeter yet—Jesus was tempted, but Jesus never sinned. My soul, it is not necessary for you to sin, for Jesus was a man, and if one man endured these temptations without sin, then in His power His followers may also flee from sin. Some new believers think that they cannot be tempted without sinning, but they are mistaken; there is no sin in *being* tempted, but there *is* sin in *yielding to temptation.* Here is comfort for those who are greatly tempted. There is still more to encourage them if they recall that the Lord Jesus, though tempted, gloriously triumphed; and as He overcame, so may His followers also, for Jesus is the representative man for His people. The Head has triumphed, and the members share in the victory. Fears are unnecessary, for Christ is with us, armed for our defense. Our place of safety is the embrace of the Savior. Perhaps we are tempted just now in order to drive us nearer to Him. Blessed be any wind that blows us into the harbor of our Savior's love! Happy wounds that make us seek the beloved Physician. Tempted ones, come to your tempted Savior, for He can sympathize with your weaknesses and will comfort every tried and tempted one.

## But if anyone does sin,
## we have an advocate with the Father,
## Jesus Christ the righteous.

1 JOHN 2:1

If anyone does sin, we have an advocate." Yes, though we sin, we have Him still. John does not say, "If anyone sins, they have forfeited their advocate," but "we have an advocate," even though we are sinners. All the sin that a believer ever did or can be allowed to commit cannot destroy his interest in the Lord Jesus Christ as his advocate. The name given here to our Lord is suggestive. "*Jesus.*" He is the kind of advocate we need, for Jesus is the name of one whose business and delight it is to save. "You shall call his name Jesus, for *he will save his people* from their sins."[1] His sweetest name implies His success. Next, it is "Jesus *Christ*"—*Christos*, the anointed. This shows *His authority* to plead. Christ has a right to plead, for He is the Father's own appointed advocate and elected priest. If He were our choice He might fail, but if God has laid help on one who is mighty, we may safely place our trouble where God has laid His help. He is Christ, and therefore authorized; He is Christ, and therefore *qualified*, for the anointing has fitted Him fully for His work. He can plead in such a way as to move the heart of God and prevail. What words of tenderness, what sentences of persuasion will the anointed use when He stands up to plead for me! One more aspect of His name remains: "Jesus Christ *the righteous.*" This is not only His character but His plea. It is His character, and if the Righteous One is my advocate, then my cause is good or He would not have represented it. It is His plea, for He meets the charge of unrighteousness against me by the plea that He *is* righteous. He declares Himself my substitute and puts His obedience to my account. My soul, you have a friend perfectly fitted to be your advocate—He cannot but succeed; leave yourself entirely in His hands.

[1]Matthew 1:21

## *Whoever believes and is baptized will be saved.*

MARK 16:16

Mr. MacDonald asked the inhabitants of the island of St. Kilda how a man must be saved. An old man replied, "We will be saved if we repent and forsake our sins and turn to God." "Yes," said a middle-aged woman, "and with a true heart too." "Yes," rejoined a third, "and with prayer"; and a fourth added, "It must be the prayer of the heart." "And we must be diligent too," said a fifth, "in keeping the commandments." When each of them made their contribution, feeling that a very decent creed had been made up, they all looked and listened for the preacher's approval, but they had aroused his deepest pity. The secular mind always maps out for itself a way in which self can work and become great, but the Lord's way is quite the reverse. Believing and being baptized are not matters of merit to be gloried in—they are so simple that boasting is excluded. It may be that the reader is unsaved—what is the reason? Do you think the way of salvation as laid down in the text is dubious? How can that be when God has pledged His own word for its certainty? Do you think it too easy? Why, then, do you not obey it? Those who neglect it are without excuse. To believe is simply to trust, to depend, to rely upon Christ Jesus. To be baptized is to submit to the ordinance that our Lord fulfilled at Jordan, to which the converted ones submitted at Pentecost, to which the jailer yielded obedience on the very night of his conversion. The outward sign does not save, but it portrays our death, burial, and resurrection with Jesus and, like the Lord's Supper, is not to be neglected. Reader, do you believe in Jesus? Then, dear friend, dismiss your fears—you will be saved. Are you still an unbeliever? Then remember there is only one door, and if you will not enter by it you will perish in your sins.

## *He had married a Cushite woman.*

NUMBERS 12:1

Moses made a strange choice, but not as surprising as the choice of Him who is a prophet like Moses but greater than him—even our Lord Jesus! It is the wonder of angels that the love of Jesus should be set upon poor, lost, guilty men. Each believer must, when filled with a sense of Jesus' love, also be overwhelmed with astonishment that such love should be lavished on an object so utterly unworthy of it. Knowing as we do our secret guiltiness, unfaithfulness, and halfheartedness, we are dissolved in grateful admiration for the matchless freeness and sovereignty of grace. Jesus must have found the cause of His love in His own heart; He could not have found it in us, for it is not there. Even since our conversion we have been poor, though grace has made us rich. Holy Rutherford said of himself what we must each subscribe to: "His relation to me is that I am sick, and He is the Physician of whom I stand in need. Sadly how often I play fast and loose with Christ! He binds, I loose; He builds, I tear down; I quarrel with Christ, and He agrees with me twenty times a day!" Most tender and faithful Husband of our souls, pursue Your gracious work of conforming us to Your image, until You will present even us in our poverty to Yourself without spot or wrinkle or any such thing. Moses met with opposition because of his marriage, and both himself and his spouse were the subjects of disapproval. Can we be surprised if this empty world opposes Jesus and His church, and particularly when notorious sinners are converted? For this is always the basis of the Pharisee's objection: "This man receives sinners."[1] Of course He does; after all, He did not come to call the righteous but sinners to repentance.

[1]Luke 15:1.

## In whom do you now trust?

ISAIAH 36:5

Reader, this is an important question. Listen to the Christian's answer, and see if it is yours. "In whom do you now trust?" "I trust," says the Christian, "in a triune God. I trust *the Father*, believing that He has chosen me from before the foundations of the world; I trust Him to provide for me in providence, to teach me, to guide me, to correct me if need be, and to bring me home to His own house where there are many rooms. I trust *the Son*. He is very God of very God—the man Christ Jesus. I trust in Him to take away all my sins by His own sacrifice and to clothe me with His perfect righteousness. I trust Him to be my Intercessor, to present my prayers and desires before His Father's throne, and I trust Him to be my Advocate at the last great day, to plead my cause, and to justify me. I trust Him for what He is, for what He has done, and for what He has promised still to do. And I trust *the Holy Spirit*—He has begun to save me from my inbred sins; I trust Him to drive them all out; I trust Him to curb my temper, to subdue my will, to enlighten my understanding, to check my passions, to comfort my despondency, to help my weakness, to illuminate my darkness. I trust Him to dwell in me as my life, to reign in me as my King, to sanctify me completely, spirit, soul, and body, and then to take me up to dwell with the saints in light forever."

What blessed trust—to trust Him whose power will never be exhausted, whose love will never weaken, whose kindness will never change, whose faithfulness will never fail, whose wisdom will never be overruled, and whose perfect goodness can never be impaired! You are happy, reader, if this trust is yours! So trusting, you will enjoy sweet peace now and glory later, and the foundation of your trust will never be removed.

## *Pray in the Holy Spirit.*

JUDE 20

Note the key characteristic of true prayer—"*in the Holy Spirit.*" The seed of acceptable devotion must come from heaven's storehouse. Only the prayer that comes from God can go to God. We must shoot the Lord's arrows back to Him. The desire that He writes upon our heart will move His heart and bring down a blessing, but the desires of the flesh have no power with Him.

Praying in the Holy Spirit is praying in *fervency*. Cold prayers ask the Lord not to hear them. Those who do not plead with fervency do not plead at all. We might as well talk of lukewarm fire as of lukewarm prayer—it is essential that it be red-hot. It is praying *perseveringly*. The true petitioner gathers force as he proceeds and grows more fervent when God delays to answer. The longer the gate is closed, the louder the knocking becomes; and the longer the angel lingers, the more determined he becomes to never let him go without the blessing. In God's sight tearful, agonizing, unconquerable importunity is commendable. It means praying *humbly*, for the Holy Spirit never puffs us up with pride. It is His part to convince of sin and to cause us to bow down in contrition and brokenness of spirit. We will never sing *Gloria in excelsis* except we pray to God *de profundis*: Out of the depths must we cry, or we will never behold glory in the highest. It is *loving* prayer. Prayer should be perfumed with love, saturated with love—love for our fellow believers and love for Christ. Moreover, it must be a prayer *full of faith*. A man prevails only to the extent that he believes. The Holy Spirit is the author of faith and strengthens it, so that we pray believing God's promise. Now our prayer is that this blessed combination of excellent graces, as priceless and sweet as rare spices, might be fragrant within us because the Holy Spirit is in our hearts! Blessed Comforter, exert Your mighty power within us, helping our weaknesses in prayer.

## *But he did not answer her a word.*

MATTHEW 15:23

Genuine seekers who as yet have not obtained the blessing may find comfort in this story. The Savior did not immediately bestow the blessing, even though the woman had great faith in Him. He intended to give it, but He waited awhile. "He did not answer her a word." Were her prayers no good? Never better in the world. Was she not needy? Dreadfully needy. Did she not *feel* her need sufficiently? She felt it overwhelmingly. Was she not sincere enough? She was intensely so. Did she have no faith? She had such a high degree of it that even Jesus wondered and said, "O woman, great is your faith!" Notice then, although it is true that faith brings peace, it does not always bring it instantaneously. There may be certain reasons for faith to be tested rather than rewarded. Genuine faith may be in the soul like a hidden seed, but so far it may not have budded and blossomed into joy and peace. Silence from the Savior is the painful trial of many a seeking soul, but heavier still is the affliction of a harsh, cutting reply such as, "It is not right to take the children's bread and throw it to the dogs." Many in waiting upon the Lord find immediate delight, but this is not the case with all. Some, like the jailer, are in a moment turned from darkness to light, but others are plants of slower growth. A deeper sense of sin may be given to you instead of a sense of pardon, and in such a case you will need patience to bear the heavy blow. Poor heart, though Christ beat and bruise you, or even slay you, trust Him; even if He should give you an angry word, believe in the love of His heart. I urge you, do not give up seeking or trusting my Master because you have not yet obtained the conscious joy that you long for. Cast yourself on Him, and perseveringly depend even when you cannot rejoicingly hope.

> *I will deliver you out of the hand of the wicked,*
> *and redeem you from the grasp of the ruthless.*

JEREMIAH 15:21

Notice the personal nature of this promise: "*I* will." The Lord Jehovah Himself intervenes to deliver and redeem His people. He pledges Himself personally to rescue them. His own arm shall do it, in order that He may have the glory. Not a word is said of any effort of our own that may be needed to assist the Lord. Neither our strength nor our weakness is taken into account, but the lone "*I*," like the sun in the heavens, shines out resplendent in complete sufficiency. Why then do we allow ourselves to be wounded by calculating our forces and consulting with mere men? God has enough power without borrowing from our puny arm. To enjoy peace, our unbelieving thoughts must be stilled, and we must learn that the Lord reigns. There is not even a hint of help from any secondary source. The Lord says nothing of friends and helpers: He undertakes the work alone and feels no need of human arms to aid Him. All our lookings around to companions and relatives are vain; they are broken reeds if we lean upon them—often unwilling when able, and unable when they are willing. Since the promise comes from God alone, it is best for us to wait only on Him; and when we do so, our expectation never fails us. Who are the wicked, that we should fear them? The Lord will utterly consume them; they are to be pitied rather than feared. As for terrible ones, they are only terrors to those who have no God to turn to, for when the Lord is on our side, whom shall we fear? If we run into sin to please the wicked, we have cause to be alarmed; but if we maintain our integrity, the rage of tyrants will be overruled for our good. When the fish swallowed Jonah, he found him a morsel that he could not digest; and when the world devours the church, it is glad to be rid of it again. In all occasions of fiery trial, let us maintain our souls in patience.

## *And those whom he predestined he also called.*

ROMANS 8:30

In the second letter to Timothy, first chapter and ninth verse, we read these words: "who saved us and called us to a *holy* calling." Now here is a touchstone by which we may test our calling. It is "a holy calling, not because of our works, but because of his own purpose and grace." This calling forbids all trust in our own doings and turns us to Christ alone for salvation, but it afterwards purges us from dead works to serve the living and true God. As He who called you is holy, so must you be holy. If you are living in sin, you are not called; but if you are truly Christ's, you can say, "Nothing pains me so much as sin; I desire to be rid of it. Lord, help me to be holy." Is this the longing of your heart? Is this the substance of your life toward God and His divine will? Again, in Philippians 3:13-14 we are told of "the *upward* call of God in Christ Jesus." Is your calling an upward call? Has it refined your heart and focused it upon heavenly things? Has it elevated your hopes, your tastes, your desires? Has it raised the constant tenor of your life, so that you spend it with God and for God? We find another test in Hebrews 3:1—"you who share in a *heavenly* calling." "Heavenly calling" means a call from heaven. If your call comes from man alone, you are uncalled. Is your calling from God? Is it a call *to* heaven as well as *from* heaven? Unless you are a stranger here, and heaven is your home, you have not been called with a heavenly calling, for those who have been called from heaven declare that they look for a city that has foundations, whose builder and maker is God, and they find themselves strangers and pilgrims on the earth. Is your calling holy, high, heavenly? Then, beloved, you have been called of God, for such is the calling by which God calls His people.

## *The Helper, the Holy Spirit.*

JOHN 14:26

This age is peculiarly the dispensation of the Holy Spirit, in which Jesus cheers us not by His personal presence, as He will do soon enough, but by the indwelling and constant abiding of the Holy Spirit, who is forever the Comforter of the church. It is the Spirit's role to console the hearts of God's people. He convinces of sin; He illumines and instructs; but the main part of His work still lies in gladdening the hearts of the renewed, confirming the weak, and lifting up all those who are bowed down. He does this by revealing Jesus to them. The Holy Spirit consoles, but Christ *is the consolation.* If we may use the figure, the Holy Spirit is the Physician, but Jesus is the medicine. He heals the wound, but it is by applying the holy ointment of Christ's name and grace. He does not take of His own things, but of the things of Christ. So if we give to the Holy Spirit the Greek name of *Paraclete,* as we sometimes do, then our heart confers on our blessed Lord Jesus the title of *Paraclesis.* If one is the Comforter, the other is the Comfort. Now, with such rich provision for his need, why should the Christian be sad and despondent? The Holy Spirit has graciously committed to be your Comforter: Do you imagine, weak and trembling believer, that He will neglect this sacred trust? Do you suppose that He has undertaken what He cannot or will not perform? If it is His special work to strengthen you and to comfort you, do you suppose He has forgotten His business or that He will fail in fulfilling His loving task of sustaining you? Don't think so poorly of the tender and blessed Spirit whose name is the Comforter. He delights to give the oil of joy for mourning and the garment of praise for the spirit of heaviness. Trust in Him, and He will surely comfort you until the house of mourning is closed forever, and the marriage feast has begun.

## *Love is strong as death.*

SONG OF SOLOMON 8:6

Whose love can this be that is as mighty as the conqueror of monarchs? Does it belong to the destroyer of the human race? Would it not sound like satire if it were applied to my poor, weak, and scarcely living love to Jesus my Lord? I do love Him, and perhaps by His grace I could even die for Him, but as for my love in itself, it can scarcely endure the scoffer's jest, much less a cruel death. Surely this is my Beloved's love that is spoken of here—the love of Jesus, the matchless lover of souls. His love was indeed stronger than the most terrible death, for it endured the trial of the cross triumphantly. It was a lingering death, but love survived the torment; a shameful death, but love despised the shame; a penal death, but love bore our iniquities; a forsaken, lonely death, from which the eternal Father hid His face, but love endured the curse and triumphed over all. There never was such love, never such a death. It was a desperate duel, but love bore the pain. What then, my heart? Have you no emotions stirred within you at the thought of such heavenly affection? Yes, my Lord, I long, I want to feel Your love flaming like a furnace within me. Come Yourself and excite the love of my spirit.

*For every drop of crimson blood*
*Thus shed to make me live,*
*O wherefore, wherefore have not I*
*A thousand lives to give?*

Why should I despair of loving Jesus with a love as strong as death? He deserves it: I desire it. The martyrs felt such love, and they were mere men and women, so why not I? They mourned their weakness, and yet out of weakness were made strong. Grace gave them their unflinching constancy—there is the same grace for me. Jesus, lover of my soul, shed abroad this love, even Your love, in my heart tonight.

## *Do not be conformed to this world.*

ROMANS 12:2

If there is any possibility of a Christian being saved while he conforms to this world, it can only be so as through fire. Such a bare salvation is almost to be dreaded as much as to be desired. Reader, would you like to leave this world in the darkness of a desponding deathbed and enter heaven like a shipwrecked sailor climbs the rocks of his native country? Then allow the world to squeeze you into its mold and refuse identity with Christ or to bear His reproach. Would you like to have a heaven below as well as a heaven above? Do you want to comprehend with all saints what are the heights and depths and to know the love of Christ that passes knowledge? Would you like to receive an abundant entry into heaven? Then do not live as a friend of the world. If you would attain the full assurance of faith, you cannot do so in communion with sinners. If you desire to be on fire for God, realize that your love will be dampened by the cold rain of a godless society. You cannot become a great Christian, you can never can be a mature believer in Christ Jesus while you give in to godless maxims and modes of life. It is incongruous for an heir of heaven to be a great friend with the heirs of hell. It has a bad look when the servant is too intimate with the king's enemies. Even small inconsistencies are dangerous. Just as small thorns make great blisters and little moths destroy fine clothes, so little frivolities and little indiscretions will rob your testimony of a thousand joys. Professing Christian on the fence, you do not know what you are losing by your conformity to the world. It cuts the tendons of your strength and makes you crawl when you ought to run. So for your own comfort's sake and for the sake of your growth in grace, if you are a Christian, be a Christian, and be a marked and distinct one.

### The firstborn of a donkey you shall redeem with a lamb, or if you will not redeem it you shall break its neck.

EXODUS 34:20

Every firstborn creature must be the Lord's; but since the donkey was unclean, it could not be presented in sacrifice. What then? Should it be allowed to go free from the universal law? By no means. God allows for no exceptions. The donkey is His due, but He will not accept it; He will not void the claim, but yet He cannot be pleased with the victim. As a result, no way of escape remained but redemption—the creature must be saved by the substitution of a lamb in its place; or if not redeemed, it must die. My soul, here is a lesson for you. That unclean animal is you. You are justly the property of the Lord who made you and preserves you, but you are so sinful that God will not, cannot, accept you; and it has come to this—the Lamb of God must stand in your place or you must die eternally. Let all the world know of your gratitude to that spotless Lamb who has already bled for you and so redeemed you from the fatal curse of the law. Sometimes it must have been a question for the Israelite which should die—the donkey or the lamb. Surely a good man would pause to estimate and compare. Without question there was no comparison between the value of the soul of man and the life of the Lord Jesus, and yet the Lamb dies, and man the donkey is spared. My soul, adore the boundless love of God to you and others of the human race. Worms are purchased with the blood of the Son of the Highest! Dust and ashes are redeemed with a price far above silver and gold! What a doom was mine if plentiful redemption had not been found! The breaking of the neck of the donkey was but a momentary penalty, but who will measure the wrath to come to which no limit can be imagined? Inestimably dear is the glorious Lamb who has redeemed us from such a doom.

## *For with you is the fountain of life.*

PSALM 36:9

There are times in our spiritual experience when human counsel or sympathy or religious ordinances fail to comfort or help us. Why does our gracious God permit this? Perhaps it is because we have been living too much without Him, and so He takes away everything upon which we have been in the habit of depending, so that He may drive us to Himself. It is a great blessing to live at the fountainhead. While our water bottles are full, we are content, like Hagar and Ishmael, to go into the wilderness; but when those are empty, nothing will serve us but God Himself. We are like the prodigal; we love the pig-swill and forget our Father's house. Remember, we can fashion pigsties and husks even out of the forms of religion; they are blessed things, but if we put them in the place of God, then they are of no value. Anything becomes an idol when it keeps us away from God: Even the brazen serpent is to be despised if we worship it instead of God. The prodigal was never safer than when he was driven to his father's home, because he could be sustained nowhere else. Our Lord favors us with a famine in the land so that it may make us seek after Himself even more. The best position for a Christian is living wholly and directly on God's grace—remaining where he stood at first—"having nothing, yet possessing everything."[1] Let us never for a moment think that our standing is in our sanctification, our mortification, our graces, or our feelings. But be sure of this, that because Christ offered a full atonement, therefore we are saved; for we are complete in Him. Having nothing of our own to trust in, but resting upon the merits of Jesus, His passion and holy life provide us with the only sure ground of confidence. Beloved, when we are brought to a thirsty condition, we are sure to turn eagerly to the fountain of life.

[1]2 Corinthians 6:10

## *He will gather the lambs in his arms.*

ISAIAH 40:11

Our Good Shepherd has in His flock a variety of experiences. Some are strong in the Lord, and others are weak in faith; but He is impartial in His care for all His sheep, and the weakest lamb is as dear to Him as the strongest in the flock. Lambs are prone to lag behind, to wander, and are apt to grow weary; but from all the danger of these infirmities the Shepherd protects them with His arm of power. He finds newborn souls, like young lambs, ready to perish—He nourishes them until life becomes vigorous. He finds weak minds ready to faint and die—He consoles them and renews their strength. All the little ones He gathers, for it is not the will of our heavenly Father that one of them should perish. What a quick eye He must have to see them all! What a tender heart to care for them all! What a far-reaching and powerful arm, to gather them all! In His lifetime on earth He was a great gatherer of the weaker sort, and now that He dwells in heaven, His loving heart extends to the meek and contrite, the timid and feeble, the fearful and fainting here below. How gently He gathered me to Himself, to His truth, to His blood, to His love, to His Church! With what effectual grace did He compel me to come to Himself! Since my conversion, He has frequently restored me from my wanderings and once again gathered me within the circle of His everlasting arms! The best of all is that He does it all Himself. He does not delegate the task of love but condescends Himself to rescue and preserve His most unworthy servant. How will I love or serve Him enough? I long to make His name great to the ends of the earth, but what can my feebleness do for Him? Great Shepherd, add to Your mercies this humble request: Grant me a heart to love You more truly as I ought.

## Behold, to obey is better than sacrifice.

1 SAMUEL 15:22

Saul had been commanded to completely wipe out all the Amalekites and their cattle. Instead of doing so, he preserved the king and allowed his people to take the best of the oxen and of the sheep. When called to account for this, he declared that he did it with a view to offering sacrifice to God; but Samuel met him at once with the assurance that sacrifices were no excuse for an act of direct rebellion. The sentence before us is worthy to be printed in letters of gold and to be displayed before the eyes of the present idolatrous generation, who are very fond of making a show of obedience but who utterly neglect the laws of God. Never forget that to keep strictly to the path of your Savior's command is better than any outward form of religion; and to pay attention to His precept is better than to bring animals or other precious things to lay upon His altar. If you are failing to keep the least of Christ's commands to His disciples, I urge you to be disobedient no longer. All the pretensions you make of attachment to your Master and all the devout actions that you may perform are no substitute for disobedience. "To obey," even in the slightest and smallest thing, "is better than sacrifice," however pompous. Forget the Gregorian chants, sumptuous robes, incense, and banners; the first thing that God requires of His child is obedience; and even if you gave your body to be burned and all your goods to feed the poor, if you did not listen to the Lord's commands, all your formalities would profit you nothing. It is a blessed thing to be teachable as a little child, but it is a much more blessed thing, when one has been taught the lesson, to carry it out to the letter. How many adorn their temples and decorate their priests, but refuse to obey the word of the Lord! My soul, do not share in their deceit.

## *God, my Maker, who gives songs in the night.*

JOB 35:10

Any man can sing during the day. When the cup is full, man draws inspiration from it. When money is in plentiful supply, any man can praise the God who provides an abundant harvest or sends home a loaded ship. It is easy enough for a tuneful harp to whisper music when the winds blow; the difficulty is for music to carry when no wind is stirring. It is easy to sing when we can read the notes by daylight; but it takes a skillful singer whose song springs forth when there is not a ray of light to read by. No man can make a song in the night by himself; he may attempt it, but he will find that a song in the night must be divinely inspired. Let everything go well, I can weave songs, fashioning them from the flowers that grow upon my path; but put me in a desert, where no green thing grows, and with what shall I frame a hymn of praise to God? How shall a mortal man make a crown for the Lord without jewels? Let this voice be clear and this body full of health, and I can sing God's praise: Silence my tongue, put me on a bed of suffering, and how will I then chant God's high praises, unless He Himself provides the song? No, it is not in man's power to sing when everything is against him, unless an altar-coal shall touch his lip. It was a divine song from Habakkuk that filled the night when he sang, "Though the fig tree should not blossom, nor fruit be on the vines, the produce of the olive fail and the fields yield no food, the flock be cut off from the fold and there be no herd in the stalls, yet I will rejoice in the LORD; I will take joy in the God of my salvation."[1] So, since our Maker gives "*songs in the night*," let us wait upon Him for the music. Chief musician, let us not remain songless because we face affliction, but tune our lips to the melody of thanksgiving.

[1]Habakkuk 3:17-18

## *Do not withhold.*

ISAIAH 43:6

Although this message was sent to the south and referred to the offspring of Israel, it may profitably be a summons to ourselves. We are naturally backward to all good things, and it is a lesson of grace to learn to go forward in the ways of God. Reader, are you unconverted, but do you desire to trust in the Lord Jesus? Then *do not withhold*. Love invites you; the promises assure you of success; the precious blood prepares the way. Do not let sin or fear hinder you, but come to Jesus just as you are. Do you long to pray? Would you like to pour out your heart before the Lord? Do not withhold. The mercy-seat is prepared for all who need mercy; a sinner's cries will prevail with God. You are invited—in fact, you are commanded—to pray; come therefore with boldness to the throne of grace.

Dear friend, are you already saved? Then *do not withhold* from union with the Lord's people. Do not neglect the ordinances of baptism and the Lord's Supper. You may be of a timid disposition, but you must fight against it, for fear that it will lead you into disobedience. There is a sweet promise made to those who confess Christ—do not miss it, in case you should come under the condemnation of those who deny Him. If you have talents, *do not withhold* from using them. Do not hoard your wealth; do not waste your time; do not let your abilities rust or your influence be unfelt. Jesus did not withhold; imitate Him by being head of the line in self-denials and self-sacrifices. *Do not withhold* from close communion with God, from boldly appropriating covenant blessings, from advancing in the divine life, from searching out the precious mysteries of the love of Christ. Do not, beloved friend, be guilty of keeping others back by your coldness, harshness, or suspicions. For Jesus' sake go forward yourself, and encourage others to do the same. Hell and the united bands of superstition and infidelity are ready for the fight. Soldiers of the cross, do not withhold!

## *Why are you troubled, and why do doubts arise in your hearts?*

LUKE 24:38

Why do you say, O Jacob, and speak O Israel, 'My way is hidden from the LORD, and my right is disregarded by my God?'"[1] The Lord cares for everything, and the smallest creatures share in His universal providence, but His particular providence is over His saints. "The angel of the LORD encamps around those who fear him."[2] "Precious is their blood in his sight."[3] "Precious in the sight of the LORD is the death of his saints."[4] "And we know that for those who love God all things work together for good, for those who are called according to his purpose."[5] Let the fact that He is the Savior of all men but is specially the Savior of those who believe cheer and comfort you. You are His peculiar care, His royal treasure that He guards as the apple of His eye, His vineyard over which He watches day and night. "Even the hairs of your head are all numbered."[6] Let the thought of His special love to *you* be a spiritual painkiller, a soothing balm to your woe: "I will never leave *you*, nor forsake *you*."[7] God says that just as much to you as to any saint of old. "Fear not . . . I am your shield; your reward shall be very great."[8] We lose much consolation by the habit of reading His promises for the whole Church instead of taking them directly home for ourselves. Believer, grasp the divine Word with a personal, appropriating faith. Imagine that you hear Jesus say, "I have prayed for you that your faith may not fail."[9] Imagine you see Him walking on the water of your trouble, for He is there, and He is saying, "Do not fear—it is I." These are sweet words of Christ! May the Holy Spirit make you feel them as if they were spoken to *you*; forget others for a while—accept the voice of Jesus as addressed to you and say, "Jesus whispers consolation; I cannot refuse it; I will sit under His shadow with great delight."[10]

[1]Isaiah 40:27  [2]Psalm 34:7  [3]Psalm 72:14  [4]Psalm 116:15  [5]Romans 8:28
[6]Matthew 10:30  [7]Hebrews 13:5  [8]Genesis 15:1  [9]Luke 22:32
[10]See Song of Solomon 2:3

## He will take what is mine and declare it to you.

JOHN 16:15

There are times when all the promises and doctrines of the Bible are of no help unless a gracious hand applies them to us. We are thirsty but too faint to crawl to the water-brook. When a soldier is wounded in battle, it is of little use for him to know that there are those at the hospital who can bind up his wounds and medicines to ease all the pains that he now suffers: What he needs is to be carried there and to have the remedies applied. It is the same with our souls, and to meet this need there is one, even the Spirit of truth, who takes the things of Jesus and applies them to us. Do not think that Christ has placed His joys on heavenly shelves so we may climb up and retrieve them for ourselves; rather He draws near and sheds His peace abroad in our hearts. Christian, if you are tonight struggling under deep distress, your Father does not give you promises and then leave you to draw them up from the Word like buckets from a well. The promises He has written in the Word He will write afresh on your heart. He will display His love to you and by His blessed Spirit dispel your cares and troubles. Let it be known to you, if you mourn, that it is God's prerogative to wipe every tear from the eyes of His people. The good Samaritan did not say, "Here is the wine, and here is the oil for you"; he actually poured in the oil and the wine. So Jesus not only gives you the sweet wine of His promise, but He holds the golden cup to your lips and pours the lifeblood into your mouth. The poor, sick, worn-out pilgrim is not merely strengthened to walk, but he is lifted up on eagles' wings. Glorious Gospel that provides everything for the helpless, that draws near to us when we cannot reach it ourselves—it brings us grace before we seek grace! There is as much glory in the giving as in the gift. Happy people who have the Holy Spirit to bring Jesus to them!

### *Why are you sleeping? Rise and pray that you may not enter into temptation.*

LUKE 22:46

When is the Christian most liable to sleep? Is it not *when his temporal circumstances are prosperous*? Have you not found it so? When you had daily troubles to take to the throne of grace, were you not more awake than you are now? Easy roads make sleepy travelers. Another dangerous time is *when all goes pleasantly in spiritual matters*. Christian did not fall asleep when lions were in the way or when he was wading through the river or when fighting with Apollyon. But when he had climbed halfway up the Hill Difficulty and came to a delightful spot, he sat down and promptly fell asleep, to his great sorrow and loss. The enchanted ground is a place of balmy breezes, filled with fragrant odors and soft influences, all of which tend to lull pilgrims to sleep. Remember Bunyan's description: "Then they came to an arbor, warm, and promising much refreshing to the weary pilgrims; for it was finely wrought above head, beautified with greens, and furnished with benches and settees. It also had in it a soft couch, where the weary might lean." "The arbor was called the Slothful's Friend, and was made on purpose to attract, if it might, some of the pilgrims to take their rest there when weary." Depend upon it—it is in easy places that men shut their eyes and wander into the dreamy land of forgetfulness. Old Erskine wisely remarked, "I like a roaring devil better than a sleeping devil." There is no temptation half so dangerous as not being tempted. The distressed soul does not sleep; it is after we enter into peaceful confidence and full assurance that we are in danger of slumbering. The disciples fell asleep after they had seen Jesus transfigured on the mountaintop. Take heed, joyful Christian, easy days are close neighbors to temptations: Be as happy as you will—only be watchful!

### *He . . . began to wash the disciples' feet.*
### *— John 13:5*

The Lord Jesus loves His people so much that every day He is still doing for them much that is analogous to washing their soiled feet. Their poorest actions He accepts; their deepest sorrow He feels; their slenderest wish He hears; and their every transgression He forgives. He is still their servant as well as their Friend and Master. He not only performs majestic deeds for them, when in all His priestly garb and function He stands up to plead for them, but He also humbly, patiently goes among His people with the basin and the towel. He does this when He puts away from us day by day our constant infirmities and sins. Last night when you bowed the knee, you mournfully confessed that much of your conduct was not worthy of your profession; and even tonight you must grieve again that you have fallen into the selfsame folly and sin from which special grace delivered you long ago. And yet Jesus displays great patience with you. He will hear your confession of sin; He will say, "I will—be clean!" He will again apply the blood of sprinkling and speak peace to your conscience and remove every spot. It is a great act of eternal love when Christ once for all absolves the sinner and places him in the family of God; but what condescending patience it is when the Savior with much long-suffering bears the repetitive follies of His wayward disciple, day by day and hour by hour washing away the multiplied transgressions of His erring but still much-loved child! To dry up a flood of rebellion is something marvelous, but to endure the constant dripping of repeated offenses, to bear with a perpetual trying of patience, this is truly divine! While we find comfort and peace in our Lord's daily cleansing, its legitimate influence upon us will be to increase our watchfulness and quicken our desire for holiness. Is that your experience?

**So she set out and went and gleaned in the field
after the reapers, and she happened to come to
the part of the field belonging to Boaz,
who was of the clan of Elimelech.**

RUTH 2:3

*She happened to come.* Yes, it seemed nothing but an accident, but it was divinely ruled over! Ruth had gone out with her mother-in-law's blessing, under the care of her mother-in-law's God, to humble but honorable work, and the providence of God was guiding her every step. Little did she know that among the sheaves she would find a husband, that he would make her the joint owner of all those broad acres, and that she, a poor foreigner, would become one of the ancestors of the great Messiah. God is very good to those who trust in Him and often surprises them with unexpected blessings. Little do we know what may happen to us tomorrow, but this sweet fact may cheer us—that no good thing will be withheld. Chance is banished from the faith of Christians, for they see the hand of God in everything. The trivial events of today or tomorrow may involve consequences of the highest importance. O Lord, deal as graciously with Your servants now as You did with Ruth.

How blessed would it be if, in wandering in the field of meditation tonight, we should happen to find ourselves in the place where the Lord Jesus will reveal Himself to us! O Spirit of God, guide us to Him. We would rather glean in His field than carry home the whole harvest from any other place. We would follow the footsteps of His flock, which would guide us to the green pastures where He dwells! This is a weary world when Jesus is away—we would survive easier without sun and moon than without Him—but how divinely fair all things become in the glory of His presence! Our souls know the virtue that lives in Jesus and can never be content without Him. We will wait in prayer tonight until we "happen" to come to a part of the field belonging to Jesus in which He will reveal Himself to us.

*October 26*

## *All streams run to the sea, but the sea is not full; to the place where the streams flow, there they flow again.*

ECCLESIASTES 1:7

Everything on earth is on the move; time knows nothing of rest. The solid earth is a rolling ball, and the great sun itself is a star obediently fulfilling its course around some greater luminary. Tides move the sea; winds stir the breezy ocean; friction wears the rock: Change and death rule everywhere. The sea is not a miser's storehouse for a wealth of waters, for as by one force the waters flow into it, by another they are lifted from it. Men are born to die: Everything is hurry, worry, and vexation of spirit. Friend of the unchanging Jesus, what a joy it is to reflect upon your change-less heritage, your sea of bliss that will be forever full since God Himself shall pour eternal rivers of pleasure into it. We seek an abiding city beyond the skies, and we shall not be disappointed. The passage before us should teach us to be grateful. The ocean is a great receiver, but it is also a generous distributor. What the rivers bring, it returns to the earth in the form of clouds and rain. The man who takes everything but makes no return is out of joint with the universe. To give to others is still sowing seed for ourselves. He who is so good a steward as to be willing to use his substance for his Lord shall be entrusted with more. Friend of Jesus, are you rendering to Him in proportion to the benefit you receive? Have you been given a great deal? Where is your fruit? Have you done all you might? Can you not do more? To be self-ish is to be wicked. Suppose the ocean gave up none of its watery treasure; it would bring ruin upon our race. God forbid that any of us should follow the ungenerous and destructive policy of liv-ing for ourselves. Jesus did not please Himself. All fullness dwells in Him, but from His fullness we have all received. Oh, to be like Jesus and no longer live for ourselves!

## *We have all become like one who is unclean.*

ISAIAH 64:6

The believer is a new creature; he belongs to a holy genera-tion and a peculiar people. The Spirit of God is in him, and in every respect he is far removed from the natural man. But for all that the Christian is still a sinner. He is so because of the imperfection of his nature, and he will continue as such to the end of his earthly life. The dirty fingers of sin leave marks on our cleanest clothes. Sin spoils our repentance, before the great Potter has finished it upon the wheel. Selfishness defiles our tears, and unbelief tampers with our faith. The best thing we ever did apart from the merit of Jesus only added to the number of our sins; for when we have been most pure in our own sight, still, like the heavens, we were not pure in God's sight; and as He charged His angels with folly, so He must charge us with it, even in our most angelic frames of mind. The song that seeks to emulate the angels' melodies has human discords in it. The prayer that moves the arm of God is still a bruised and battered prayer, and only moves that arm because the sinless One, the great Mediator, Jesus, has stepped in to take away the sin of our supplication. The most golden faith or the purest degree of sanctification to which a Christian ever attained on earth has still so much dross in it as to be only worthy of the flames. Every night we look in the mirror we see a sinner and need to confess, "We have become like one who is unclean, and all our righteous deeds are like a polluted garment." How precious then is the blood of Christ to hearts like ours! How priceless a gift is His perfect righteousness! And how bright is the hope of perfect holiness in heaven! Even now, though sin dwells in us, *its power is broken*. It remains, but it no longer reigns; we are in bitter conflict with it, but we are dealing with a vanquished foe. In a little while we will enter victoriously into the city where nothing defiles.

## *His head is the finest gold; his locks are wavy, black as a raven.*

SONG OF SOLOMON 5:11

Comparisons all fail to set forth the Lord Jesus, but the spouse uses the best she can find. *By the head of Jesus* we may understand His deity, "for the head of Christ is God";[1] and then the mold of purest gold is the best conceivable metaphor, but all too poor to describe one so precious, so pure, so dear, so glorious. Jesus is not a grain of gold, but a vast globe of it, a priceless mass of treasure such as earth and heaven cannot excel. The creatures are mere iron and clay—they will all perish like wood, hay, and stubble; but the ever living Head of the creation of God will shine on forever and ever. In Him is no mixture, nor smallest taint of alloy. He is forever infinitely holy and altogether divine. *The wavy locks* depict His manly vigor. There is nothing effeminate in our Lord. He is the manliest of men—bold as a lion, strong as an ox, swift as an eagle. Every conceivable and inconceivable beauty is to be found in Him, though He once was despised and rejected of men.

> *His head the finest gold;*
> *With secret sweet perfume,*
> *His curled locks hang all as black*
> *As any raven's plume.*

The glory of His head is not shorn away. He is eternally crowned with peerless majesty. *The black hair* indicates youthful freshness, for Jesus has the dew of His youth upon Him. Others grow weak with age, but He is forever a Priest like Melchizedek; others come and go, but He remains as God upon His throne, world without end. We will behold Him tonight and adore Him. Angels are gazing on Him—His redeemed must not turn their eyes away from Him. Where else is there such a Beloved? Oh, for an hour's fellowship with Him! Be gone, you intruding anxieties! Jesus draws me, and I run after Him.

[1] 1 Corinthians 11:3

## *But their eyes were kept from recognizing him.*

LUKE 24:16

The disciples ought to have known Jesus; they had heard His voice so often and gazed upon that marred face so frequently that it is incredible they did not discover Him. Yet is it not also with you? You have not seen Jesus lately. You have been to His table, and yet you have not met Him there. You are in a dark trouble this evening, and though He plainly says, "It is I, do not be afraid," yet you cannot discern Him. Sadly, our eyes are kept from seeing Him. We know His voice, we have looked into His face, we have leaned our head upon His shoulder, and yet, though Christ is very near us, we are saying, "I wish I knew where I could find Him!" We should know Jesus, for we have the Scriptures to reflect His image, and yet how possible it is for us to open that precious book and have no glimpse of our loving Lord! Dear child of God, are you in that state? Jesus feeds among the lilies of the Word, and you walk among those lilies, and yet you do not behold Him. He is accustomed to walking through the glades of Scripture and communing with His people, as the Father did with Adam in the cool of the day, and yet you are in the garden of Scripture but cannot see Him, although He is always there. And why do we not see Him? This must be ascribed in our case, as in the disciples', to unbelief. They evidently did not expect to see Jesus, and therefore they did not know Him. To a great extent in spiritual things we get what we expect from the Lord. Only faith can bring us to see Jesus. Make it your prayer, "Lord, open my eyes, that I may see my Savior present with me." It is a blessed thing to want to see Him; but it is far better to gaze upon Him. To those who seek Him He is kind; but to those who find Him, He is dear beyond expression!

### *O you who dwell in the gardens, with companions listening for your voice; let me hear it.*

SONG OF SOLOMON 8:13

My sweet Lord Jesus remembers well the garden of Gethsemane, and although He has left that garden, He now dwells in the garden of His church: There He discloses Himself to those who keep His blessed company. The voice of love with which He speaks to His beloved is more musical than the harps of heaven. There is a depth of melodious love within it that leaves all human music far behind. Tens of thousands on earth, and millions above, are consumed with its harmonious accents. Some whom I know well, and whom I greatly envy, are at this moment hearkening to the beloved voice. O that I were a partaker of their joys! It is true some of these are poor, others bedridden, and some near the gates of death; but, my Lord, I would cheerfully starve with them, pine with them, or die with them if I might simply hear Your voice. Once I heard it often, but I have grieved Your Spirit. Return to me in compassion and once again say to me, "I am your salvation." No other voice can content me. I know Your voice and cannot be deceived by another; let me hear it, I pray You. I do not know what You will say, nor do I make any condition, my Beloved; simply let me hear You speak, and if it be a rebuke I will bless You for it. Perhaps the cleansing of my dull ear will require a painful surgery, but let it cost me what it will, I have only one consuming desire—to hear Your voice. Pierce my ear with Your harshest notes, but do not allow me to remain deaf to Your calls. Tonight, Lord, grant Your unworthy servant his desire, for I am Yours, and You have bought me with Your blood. You have opened my eyes to see You, and the sight has saved me. Lord, open my ear. I have read Your heart; now let me hear from Your lips.

## *It was I who knew you in the wilderness, in the land of drought.*

HOSEA 13:5

Yes, Lord, You did indeed know me in *my fallen state*, and You did even then choose me for Yourself. When I was loathsome and self-abhorred, You received me as Your child, and You satisfied my longings. Blessed forever be Your name for this free, rich, abounding mercy. Since then, *my inward experience* has often been a wilderness; but You have kept me still as Your beloved and poured streams of love and grace into me to gladden me and make me fruitful. When *my outward circumstances* have been at the worst, and I have wandered in a land of drought, Your sweet presence has comforted me. Men have ignored me, and I have been scorned; but You have known my soul in adversities, for no affliction dims the luster of Your love. Most gracious Lord, I magnify You for all Your faithfulness to me in trying circumstances, and I deplore the fact that I have at times forgotten You and been proud of heart when I have owed everything to Your gentleness and love. Have mercy upon Your servant in this matter!

My soul, if Jesus acknowledged you in your lowly condition, be sure that you own both Himself and His cause now that you are in prosperity. Do not be puffed up by worldly successes, and do not be ashamed of the truth or of the poor church with which you have been associated. Follow Jesus into the wilderness: Bear the cross with Him when the persecution heats up. He owned you, O my soul, in your poverty and shame—never be so treacherous as to be ashamed of Him. Let me know more shame at the thought of being ashamed of my best Beloved! Jesus, my soul cleaves to You.

> *I'll turn to Thee in days of light,*
> *As well as nights of care,*
> *Thou brightest amid all that's bright!*
> *Thou fairest of the fair!*

> *. . . and they were unaware until the flood came,*
> *and swept them all away,*
> *so will be the coming of the Son of man.*

MATTHEW 24:39

The doom was universal. Neither rich nor poor escaped: the learned and the illiterate, the admired and the despised, the religious and the profane, the old and the young all sank in one common ruin. Some had doubtless ridiculed the preacher, but where were their merry jests now? Others had threatened Noah for his zeal, which they regarded as madness. What happened to their boastings and hard speeches? The critic who judged the old man's work drowns in the same sea that covers his sneering companions. Those who spoke patronizingly of the good man's faithfulness to his convictions, but did not share them, have sunk to rise no more, and the workers who for pay helped to build the wondrous ark are all lost also. The Flood swept them all away and made no single exception. Even so, outside of Christ, final destruction is sure to everyone; no rank, possession, or character will be enough to save a single soul who has not believed in the Lord Jesus. My soul, consider this widespread judgment and tremble at it.

How incredible was the general apathy! They were all eating and drinking, marrying and giving in marriage, until the awful morning dawned. There was not one wise individual upon earth outside of the ark. Folly duped the whole race, folly as to self-preservation—the most foolish of all follies. Folly in doubting the most true God—the most malignant foolishness. Is it not strange, my soul? All men are negligent of their souls until grace gives them reason; then they leave their madness and act like rational beings, but not until then.

*All*, blessed be God, were safe in the ark; no ruin entered there. From the huge elephant down to the tiny mouse all were safe. The timid hare was equally secure with the courageous lion, the helpless lamb as safe as the laborious ox. All are safe in Jesus. My soul, are you in Him?

321

### Hot indignation seizes me because of the wicked, who forsake your law.

PSALM 119:53

My soul, do you feel this holy trembling at the sins of others? For if you do not, you lack inward holiness. David's cheeks were wet with rivers of waters because of prevailing unholiness. Jeremiah desired eyes like fountains that he might lament the iniquities of Israel, and Lot was deeply troubled by the conduct of the men of Sodom. Those upon whom the mark was set in Ezekiel's vision were those who sighed and cried for the sins of Jerusalem. Gracious souls cannot help but be grieved to see what pains men take to go to hell. They know the evil of sin experimentally [experientially], and they are alarmed to see others flying like moths into its blaze. Sin makes the righteous shudder because it violates a holy law that it is in every man's highest interest to keep; it pulls down the pillars of the nation. Sin in others horrifies a believer because it makes him think of the baseness of his own heart: When he sees a transgressor he is reminded of his own frailty and vulnerability: "He fell today, and I may fall tomorrow." Sin to a believer is horrible because it crucified the Savior; he sees in every iniquity the nails and spear. How troubling it should be when the Christian learns to tolerate rather than shrink from it in disgust. Each of us must examine his heart. It is an awful thing to insult God to His face. The good God deserves better treatment; the great God claims it; the just God will have it or repay His adversary to his face. An awakened heart trembles at the audacity of sin and stands alarmed at the contemplation of its punishment. How monstrous a thing is rebellion! How dreadful a doom is prepared for the ungodly! My soul, never laugh at sin's fooleries, lest you begin to smile at sin itself. It is your enemy, and your Lord's enemy: Learn to detest it and to distance yourself from it, for only then can you give evidence of the possession of holiness, without which no one can see the Lord.

## Their prayer came to his holy habitation
## in heaven.

2 CHRONICLES 30:27

Prayer is the never-failing response of the Christian in any case, in every plight. When you cannot use your sword, you may take up the weapon of prayer. Your powder may be damp, your bowstring may be relaxed, but the weapon of prayer need never be out of order. Satan laughs at the javelin, but he trembles at prayer. Swords and spears need to be sharpened, but prayer never rusts; and when we think it most blunt, it cuts the best. Prayer is an open door that no one can shut. Devils may surround you on all sides, but the way upward is always open, and as long as that road is unobstructed, you will not fall into the enemy's hand. We can never be taken by siege or invasion as long as heavenly helps can come down to us and relieve us in the time of our necessities. Prayer is never out of season: In summer and in winter its merchandise is precious. Prayer gains audience with heaven in the dead of night, in the middle of business, in the heat of noonday, in the shades of evening. In every condition, whether poverty or sickness or obscurity or slander or doubt, your covenant God will welcome your prayer and answer it from His holy place. And prayer is never *futile*. True prayer is always true power. You may not always get what you ask, but you shall always have your real needs supplied. When God does not answer His children according to the letter, He does so according to the spirit. If you ask for cornmeal, will you be angry because He gives you fine flour? If you seek physical health, should you complain if instead He makes your sickness result in your spiritual health? Is it not better to have the cross sanctified than removed? This evening, my soul, do not forget to offer your petition and request, for the Lord is ready to grant your desires.

### *In your light do we see light.*

PSALM 36:9

No lips can tell the love of Christ to the heart until Jesus Himself shall speak within. Descriptions all fall flat and feeble unless the Holy Spirit fills them with life and power; until God makes Himself known to us, the soul does not see Him. If you would see the sun, would you gather together the common means of illumination and seek in that way to view its splendor? No; the wise man knows that the sun must reveal itself, and only by its own blaze can that mighty orb be seen. It is the same with Christ. "Blessed are you, Simon Bar-Jonah!" He said to Peter. "For flesh and blood has not revealed this to you."[1] Purify flesh and blood by any educational process you may select, elevate mental faculties to the highest degree of intellectual power, yet none of these can reveal Christ. The Spirit of God must come with power and overshadow the man with His wings, and then in that mystic holy of holies the Lord Jesus must display Himself to the sanctified eye, as He does not to the spiritually blind sons of men. Christ must be His own mirror. The great mass of this dim-sighted world can see nothing of the indescribable glories of Jesus. He stands before them without form or majesty, a root out of a dry ground, rejected by the vain and despised by the proud. Only where the Spirit has illumined the eye, quickened the heart with divine life, and educated the soul to a heavenly taste, only there is He understood. He is precious to the believer; He is the chief cornerstone, the Rock of your salvation, your all in all; but to others He is "a stone of stumbling, and a rock of offense."[2] Happy are those to whom our Lord reveals Himself, for His promise to such is that He will *make His home with them*. O Jesus, our Lord, our heart is open; come in, and never leave. Show Yourself to us now! Favor us with a glimpse of Your embracing loveliness.

[1]Matthew 16:17   [2]Romans 9:33

## *Give thanks to him; bless his name!*

PSALM 100:4

Our Lord would have all His people rich in high and happy thoughts concerning His blessed person. Jesus is not content that His brethren should think poorly of Him; it is His pleasure that His people should be delighted with His beauty. We are not to regard Him as a bare necessity, like bread and water, but as a luxurious delicacy, as a rare and ravishing delight. To this end He has revealed Himself as the "pearl of great price" in its peerless beauty, as the "bundle of myrrh"[1] in its refreshing fragrance, as the "rose of Sharon" in its lasting perfume, as the "lily" in its spotless purity.

As a help to high thoughts of Christ, remember the estimation that Christ has beyond the skies, where things are measured by the right standard. Think how God esteems the Only Begotten, His unspeakable gift to us. Consider what the angels think of Him, as they count it their highest honor to veil their faces at His feet. Consider what the blood-washed think of Him, as day without night they sing His well-deserved praises. High thoughts of Christ will enable us to act consistently in our relationship with Him. The more loftily we see Christ enthroned, and the more lowly we are when bowing before the foot of the throne, the more truly shall we be prepared to act our part toward Him. Our Lord Jesus desires us to think well of Him, that we may submit cheerfully to His authority. High thoughts of Him increase our love. Love and esteem go together. Therefore, believer, think much of your Master's excellencies. Study Him in His pre-incarnate glory, before He took upon Himself your nature! Think of the mighty love that drew Him from His throne to die upon the cross! Admire Him as He conquers all the powers of hell! See Him risen, crowned, glorified! Bow before Him as the Wonderful, the Counselor, the Mighty God, for only in this way will your love for Him be what it should.

[1]Song of Solomon 1:13, KJV

## *This is the blood of the covenant that God commanded for you.*

HEBREWS 9:20

There is a strange power in the very name of blood, and the sight of it is always moving. A kind heart cannot bear to see a sparrow bleed and, unless familiarized by use, turns away with horror at the slaughter of a beast. As to the blood of men, it is a consecrated thing: It is murder to shed it in anger; it is a dreadful crime to squander it in war. Is this solemnity occasioned by the fact that the blood is the life, and the shedding of it the token of death? We think so. When we rise to contemplate the blood of the Son of God, our awe is greater yet, and we shudder as we think of the guilt of sin and the terrible penalty that the Sin-bearer endured. Blood, always precious, is priceless when it streams from Immanuel's side. The blood of Jesus seals the *covenant* of grace and makes it certain forever. Covenants of old were made by sacrifice, and the everlasting covenant was ratified in the same manner. What comfort that our salvation rests upon the sure foundation of divine commitments that cannot be dishonored! Salvation by the works of the law is a frail and broken vessel whose shipwreck is sure; but the covenant vessel fears no storms, for the blood ensures the whole. The blood of Jesus made His *covenant* valid. Wills are of no power unless the testators die. In this light the soldier's spear is a blessed aid to faith, since it proved our Lord to be really dead. There can be no doubt about that matter, and we may boldly appropriate the legacies that He has left for His people. Happy are they who see their title to heavenly blessings assured to them by a dying Savior. But does this blood not speak to us? Does it not bid us sanctify ourselves unto Him by whom we have been redeemed? Does it not call us to newness of life and incite us to entire consecration to the Lord? O that the power of the blood might be known and felt in us tonight!

## *And you will be my witnesses.*

ACTS 1:8

In order to learn how to discharge your duty as a witness for Christ, look at His example. He is always witnessing—by the well of Samaria or in the temple of Jerusalem; by the sea of Galilee or on the mountainside. He is witnessing day and night; His mighty prayers are as vocal to God as His daily services. He witnesses under all circumstances. Scribes and Pharisees cannot shut His mouth; even before Pilate He witnesses a good confession. He witnesses so clearly and distinctly that there is no mistake in understanding Him. Christian, make your life a clear testimony. Be like the stream in which you can see every stone at the bottom—not like a muddy creek where you can only see the surface, but clear and transparent, so that your heart's love for God and man may be visible to all. You need not say, "I am true"; be true. Do not boast of integrity, but be upright. Then your testimony will be such that men cannot help seeing it. Never, on account of fear of feeble man, restrain your witness. Your lips have been warmed with a coal from off the altar; let them speak as heaven-touched lips should do. "In the morning sow your seed, and at evening withhold not your hand."[1] Do not watch the clouds or consult the wind; in season and out of season witness for the Savior, and if it transpires that for Christ's sake and the Gospel's you must endure suffering in any shape, do not shrink, but rejoice in the honor conferred upon you, that you are counted worthy to suffer with your Lord. And find joy also in this—that your sufferings, your losses, and persecutions shall make you a platform from which with more vigor and with greater power you will witness for Christ Jesus. Study your great example, and be filled with His Spirit. Remember that you need much teaching, much upholding, much grace, and much humility if your witnessing is to be to your Master's glory.

[1]Ecclesiastes 11:6

## *The teacher says, Where is my guest room, where I may eat the Passover with my disciples?*

MARK 14:14

Jerusalem at the time of the Passover was one great inn; each householder had invited his own friends, but no one had invited the Savior, and He had no dwelling of His own. It was by His own supernatural power that He found Himself an upper room in which to keep the feast. This is still the case today—Jesus is not received among the sons of men except when by His supernatural power and grace He makes the heart anew. All doors are open enough to the prince of darkness, but Jesus must clear a way for Himself or lodge in the streets. On account of the mysterious power exerted by our Lord, the householder raised no question but at once cheerfully and joyfully opened his guest room. Who he was and what he was we do not know, but he willingly accepted the honor that the Redeemer proposed to confer upon him. In similar fashion we can still discover who are the Lord's chosen and who are not, for when the Gospel comes to some, they fight against it and will not have it; but where men receive it, welcoming it, this is a sure indication that there is a secret work going on in the soul and that God has appointed them to eternal life. Are you willing, dear reader, to receive Christ? Then there is no difficulty in the way. Christ will be your guest; His own power is working with you, making you willing. What an honor to entertain the Son of God! The heaven of heavens cannot contain Him, and yet He condescends to find a house within our hearts! We are not worthy that He should come under our roof, but what an unutterable privilege when He condescends to enter! For then He makes a feast and causes us to feast with Him upon His royal provision; we sit at a banquet where the food is immortal and provides immortality to those who feed on it. Blessed among the sons of Adam is he who entertains the angels' Lord.

*His place of defense will be the fortress of rocks;*
*his bread will be given him;*
*his water will be sure.*

ISAIAH 33:16

Christian, do you doubt whether God will fulfill His promise? Will the fortresses of rock be swept away by a storm? Will the storehouses of heaven fail? Do you think that your heavenly Father, even though He knows that you need food and clothes, will forget you? When not a sparrow falls to the ground without your Father's knowledge, and the very hairs of your head are all numbered, will you mistrust and doubt Him? Perhaps your affliction will continue upon you until you dare to trust God, and then it will end. There have been many who have been tried and troubled until at last they have been driven in sheer desperation to exercise faith in God, and the moment of their faith has been the instant of their deliverance; they have seen whether God would keep His promise or not. So I urge you, doubt Him no longer! Do not please Satan, and do not trouble yourself by indulging any more those hard thoughts of God. Do not imagine that it is a small matter to doubt Jehovah. Remember, it is a sin; and not a little sin either, but in the highest degree criminal. The angels never doubted Him, nor the devils either: We alone, out of all the beings whom God has fashioned, dishonor Him by unbelief and tarnish His honor by mistrust. Shame on us for this! Our God does not deserve to be so poorly treated; in our past life we have proved Him to be true and faithful to His word, and with so many instances of His love and of His kindness as we have received and are daily receiving at His hands, it is base and inexcusable that we allow a doubt to lodge within our heart. From now on let us resolve to wage constant war against doubts of our God—enemies to our peace and to His honor—and with an unstaggering faith believe that what He has promised He will also perform. "I believe; help my unbelief!"[1]

[1] Mark 9:24

## *It is enough for the disciple to be like his teacher.*

MATTHEW 10:25

No one will dispute this statement, for it would not be proper for the pupil to be exalted above his Teacher. When our Lord was on earth, what was the treatment He received? Were His claims acknowledged, His instructions followed, His perfections worshiped by those whom He came to bless? No. "He was despised and rejected by men."[1] His place was outside the city: Cross-bearing was His occupation. Did the world provide Him with comfort and rest? "Foxes have holes, and birds of the air have nests, but the Son of man has nowhere to lay His head."[2] This inhospitable country provided Him no shelter: It cast Him out and crucified Him. If you are a follower of Jesus and maintain a consistent, Christlike walk and behavior, you must expect to experience persecution and rejection also. Your Christian testimony will be scrutinized and criticized. People will treat it as they treated the Savior—they will despise it. Do not imagine that pagans will admire you or that the more holy and the more Christlike you are, the more peaceably people will act toward you. If they did not prize the polished gem, do you think that they will esteem the rough cut jewel? If they have referred to Jesus as Satan, how much more will they denigrate the teacher's disciples? If we were more like Christ, we would be more hated by His enemies. It is a sad dishonor to a child of God to be the world's favorite. It is a very bad omen to hear a wicked world clap its hands and shout "Well done" to the Christian man. He may begin to look to his character and wonder whether he has been doing wrong when the unrighteous give him their approval. Let us be true to our Master and have no friendship with a blind and base world that scorns and rejects Him. Far be it from us to seek a crown of honor where our Lord found only a crown of thorns.

[1]Isaiah 53:3  [2]Matthew 8:20

## *He chose our heritage for us.*

PSALM 47:4

Believer, if your inheritance is meager, you should be satisfied with your earthly portion; for you may rest assured that it is best *for you*. Unerring wisdom ordained your lot and selected for you the safest and best condition. When a ship of large tonnage is to be brought up a river that has a large sandbank, if someone should ask, "Why does the captain steer through the deep part of the channel and deviate so much from a straight line?" his answer would be, "Because I could not get my ship into harbor at all if I did not keep to the deep channel." In the same way you would run aground and suffer shipwreck if your divine Captain did not steer you into the depths of affliction where waves of trouble follow each other in quick succession. Some plants die if they have too much sunshine. It may be that you are planted where you get only a little, but you are put there by the loving Farmer because only in that situation will you produce fruit unto perfection. Remember this: If any other condition had been better for you than the one in which you are, divine love would have put you there. You are placed by God in the most suitable circumstances, and if you could choose your lot, you would soon cry, "Lord, choose my heritage for me, for by my self-will I am pierced through with many sorrows." Be content with the things you have, since the Lord has ordered all things for your good. Take up your own daily cross; it is the burden best suited for your shoulder and will prove most effective to make you perfect in every good word and work to the glory of God. Busy self and proud impatience must be put down; it is not for them to choose, but for the Lord of Love!

> *Trials must and will befall—*
> *But with humble faith to see*
> *Love inscribed upon them all,*
> *This is happiness to me.*

## In these days he went out to the mountain to pray, and all night he continued in prayer to God.

LUKE 6:12

If ever a man might have lived without prayer, it was our spotless, perfect Lord, and yet no one ever prayed as much as He! His love for His Father was such that He loved to be in communion with Him. His love for His people was such that He desired to be regularly interceding for them. *The fact* that Jesus placed such importance on prayer is a lesson for us—He has given us an example that we may follow in His steps. *The time* He chose was admirable—it was the hour of silence when the crowd would not disturb Him, the time of inaction when everyone else had stopped work, and the season when sleep made men forget their difficulties and stop applying to Him for relief. While others found rest in sleep, He refreshed Himself with prayer. *The place* was also well selected. He was alone where none would intrude, where none would observe: And so He was free from Pharisaic ostentation and vulgar interruption. Those dark and silent hills provided a suitable prayer chapel for the Son of God. Heaven and earth in midnight stillness heard the groans and sighs of the mysterious Being in whom both worlds were blended. *The continuance* of His pleadings is remarkable: The passing hours were not too long; the cold wind did not chill His devotions; the grim darkness did not cloud His faith or loneliness prevent His persistence. We fail to watch with Him for one hour, but He never fails to watch for us night and day. The occasion for this prayer is notable; it was after His enemies had been enraged. Prayer was His refuge and solace; it was before He dispatched the twelve apostles. Prayer was the gate of His enterprise, the herald of His new work. Should we not learn from Jesus to resort to special prayer when we are under peculiar trial or considering new ventures for the Master's glory? Lord Jesus, teach us to pray.

# And he told them a parable to the effect that they ought always to pray.

LUKE 18:1

Jesus has sent His Church into the world on the same errand upon which He Himself came, and this mission includes intercession. What if I say that the Church is the world's priest? Creation is dumb, but the Church finds a mouth for it. It is the Church's high privilege to pray with acceptance. The door of grace is always open for her petitions, and they never return empty-handed. The curtain was torn *for her*; the blood was sprinkled upon the altar *for her*; God constantly invites her to bring her requests. Will she refuse the privilege that angels might envy? Is she not the bride of Christ? Can she not approach her King at any hour? Will she allow the precious privilege to be unused? The Church always needs to pray. There are always some among her who are declining or falling into open sin. There are lambs to be prayed for, that they may be carried in Christ's bosom; the strong, lest they grow presumptuous; and the weak, lest they become despairing. If we kept up prayer-meetings twenty-four hours a day all the days in the year, we might never be without a special subject for supplication. Is there ever a time when no one is sick or poor or afflicted or wavering? Is there ever a time when we do not seek the conversion of relatives, the reclaiming of backsliders, or the salvation of the lost? With congregations constantly gathering, with ministers always preaching, with millions of sinners lying dead in trespasses and sins—in a country over which the darkness of religious formalism is certainly descending—in a world full of idols, cruelties, devils—if the Church does not pray, how will she excuse her neglect of the commission of her loving Lord? Let the Church be constant in supplication; let every private believer give himself to the ministry of prayer.

> ### *Laban said, "It is not so done in our country, to give the younger before the firstborn."*
>
> GENESIS 29:26

We do not excuse Laban for his dishonesty, but we are wrong not to learn from the custom that he quoted as his excuse. There are some things that must be taken in order, and if we would win the second we must secure the first. The second may be the more lovely in our eyes, but the rule of the heavenly country must stand, and the elder must be married first. For instance, many men desire the beautiful and well-favored Rachel of joy and peace in believing, but they must first be married to the tender-eyed Leah of repentance. Everyone falls in love with happiness, and many would cheerfully work for fourteen years to enjoy it; but according to the rule of the Lord's kingdom, the Leah of real holiness must be loved in our soul before the Rachel of true happiness can be attained. Heaven stands not first but second, and only by persevering to the end can we win a portion in it. The cross must be carried before the crown can be worn. We must follow our Lord in His humiliation or we will never rest with Him in glory.

My soul, what do you say—are you so vain as to hope to be an exception to the heavenly rule? Do you hope for reward without work, or honor without endeavor? Dismiss the idle expectation, and be content with the despised things for the sake of the sweet love of Jesus, which will more than repay you. In such a spirit, working and suffering, you will find afflictions grow sweet and hard things easy. Like Jacob, your years of service will seem like only a few days on account of the love you have for Jesus; and when the dear hour of the wedding feast shall come, all your toils will be as though they never happened—an hour with Jesus will make up for years of pain and toil.

*Jesus, to win Thyself so fair,*
*Thy cross I will with gladness bear:*
*Since so the rules of heaven ordain,*
*The first I'll wed the next to gain.*

### *Summon your power, O God, the power, O God, by which you have worked for us.*

PSALM 68:28

It is wise, as well as necessary, to beseech God continually to strengthen what He has worked in us. Failure to do so finds many Christians blaming themselves for those trials and afflictions of spirit that arise from unbelief. It is true that Satan seeks to flood the fair garden of the heart and make it a scene of desolation, but it is also true that many Christians leave open the floodgates themselves and let in the dreadful deluge as a result of carelessness and lack of prayer to their strong Helper. We often forget that the Author of our faith must be the Preserver of it also. The lamp that was burning in the temple was never allowed to go out, but it had to be replenished every day with fresh oil; in the same way, our faith can only live by being sustained with the oil of grace, and we can only obtain this from God Himself. We will fail if we do not secure the needed sustenance for our lamps. He who built the world upholds it, or it would fall in one tremendous crash. He who made us Christians must maintain us by His Spirit, or our ruin will be speedy and final. So let us, then, evening by evening, go to our Lord for the grace and strength we need. We have a strong argument to plead, for it is *His own work of grace* that we ask Him to strengthen—"*the power . . . by which you have worked for us.*" Do you think He will fail to protect and provide that? Let your faith simply take hold of His strength, and all the powers of darkness, led by the master fiend of hell, cannot cast a cloud or shadow over your joy and peace. Why faint when you can be strong? Why suffer defeat when you may conquer? Take your wavering faith and faltering graces to Him who can revive and replenish them, and earnestly pray, "Summon your power, O God . . . by which you have worked for us."

### *Your eyes will behold the king in his beauty.*

ISAIAH 33:17

The more you know about Christ, the less will you be satisfied with superficial views of Him; and the more deeply you study His transactions in the eternal covenant, His engagements on your behalf as the eternal Security, and the fullness of His grace that shines in all His offices, the more truly will you see the King in His beauty. Learn to look at Him this way. Long increasingly to see Jesus. *Meditation and contemplation* are often like windows of gold and gates of silver through which we behold the Redeemer. Meditation puts the telescope to the eye and enables us to see Jesus in a better fashion than we could have seen Him if we had lived in the days of His earthly sojourn. Our conversation ought to be more in heaven, and we should be more taken up with the person, the work, the beauty of our incarnate Lord. More meditation, and the beauty of the King would flash upon us with more splendor. Beloved, it is very probable that we will have such a sight of our glorious King as we never had before *when we come to die.* Many saints in dying have looked up from amidst the stormy waters and have seen Jesus walking on the waves of the sea and heard Him say, "It is I—do not be afraid." Yes, when the building begins to shake, and the mortar falls away, we will see Christ through the studs, and between the rafters the sunlight of heaven will come streaming in. But if we want to see the King face to face in all His beauty, *we must go to heaven* for the sight or the King must come here in person. If only He would come on the wings of the wind! He is our Husband, and we are widowed by His absence; He is our fair and faithful Brother, and we are lonely without Him. Thick veils and clouds hang between our souls and their true life: When will the day break and the shadows run away? Let the long-expected day begin!

## *He who splits logs is endangered by them.*

ECCLESIASTES 10:9

Oppressors may enforce their will on poor and needy men just as easily as they can split logs of wood, but they better be careful, for it is a dangerous business, and a splinter from a tree has often killed the woodsman. Jesus is persecuted in every injured saint, and He is strong to avenge His loved ones. Success in treading down the poor and needy is a thing to be trembled at: If the persecutors do not face immediate danger, they will face great danger in the end.

*To split logs is a common everyday business*, and yet it has its dangers. So then, reader, there are dangers connected with your calling and daily life that it will be good for you to be aware of. We do not refer to hazards by flood and field or by disease and sudden death, but to perils of a spiritual sort. Your occupation may be as humble as log splitting, and yet the devil can tempt you in it. You may be a domestic servant, a farm laborer, or a mechanic, and you may be greatly shielded from temptations to the bigger vices, and yet some secret sin may undo you. Those who live at home and do not mingle with the rough world may still be endangered by their very seclusion. The one who thinks himself safe is safe nowhere! Pride may enter a poor man's heart; greed may reign in a cottager's bosom; uncleanness may venture into the quietest home; and anger and envy and malice may insert themselves into the most rural dwelling. Even in speaking a few words to a doorman we may sin; a small purchase at a shop may be the first link in a chain of temptations; the mere looking out of a window may be the beginning of evil. Lord, how exposed we are! How shall we be saved! To keep ourselves is a work too hard for us: Only You Yourself are able to preserve us in such an evil world. Spread Your protection over us, and we, like little chickens, will cower down beneath You and feel ourselves safe!

## *You are from everlasting.*

PSALM 93:2

Christ is *everlasting*. Of Him we may sing with David, "Your throne, O God, is forever and ever."[1] Rejoice, believer, in Jesus Christ, the same yesterday, today, and forever. Jesus always *was*. The Baby born in Bethlehem was united to the Word, which was in the beginning, by whom all things were made. The title by which Christ revealed Himself to John in Patmos was, "[Him] who is and who was and who is to come."[2] If He was not God from everlasting, we could not love Him so devoutly; we could not feel that He had any share in the eternal love that is the fountain of all covenant blessings. But since He was from all eternity with the Father, we trace the stream of divine love to Himself equally with His Father and the blessed Spirit. As our Lord always *was*, so also He is forevermore. Jesus is not dead; "he always lives to make intercession for them."[3] Resort to Him in all your times of need, for He is always waiting to bless you. Furthermore, Jesus our Lord ever *shall be*. If God should spare your life to fulfill your full course of threescore years and ten, you will find that His cleansing fountain is still opened, and His precious blood has not lost its power; you will find that the Priest who filled the healing fount with His own blood lives to purge you from all iniquity. When only your last battle remains to be fought, you will find that the hand of your conquering Captain has not grown feeble—the living Savior shall cheer the dying saint. When you enter heaven you shall find Him there bearing the dew of His youth; and through eternity the Lord Jesus will still remain the perennial spring of joy and life and glory to His people. You may draw living waters from this sacred well! Jesus always was, He always is, He always shall be. He is eternal in all His attributes, in all His offices, in all His might and willingness to bless, comfort, guard, and crown His chosen people.

[1]Psalm 45:6 [2]Revelation 1:8 [3]Hebrews 7:25

## *Oh, that I knew where I might find him.*

JOB 23:3

In Job's extremely trying circumstances, he cried for the Lord. The longing desire of an afflicted child of God is to see his Father's face once more. His first prayer is not "Oh, that I might be healed of the disease that now spreads through my body!" nor even "Oh, that I might see my children restored from the jaws of the grave, and my property returned to me from the hand of the thief!" The first and foremost cry is, "Oh, that I knew where I might find Him, who is my God, that I might come even to His seat!" God's children run home when the storm comes. It is the heaven-born instinct of a gracious soul to seek shelter from all ills beneath the wings of Jehovah. "He who has made God his refuge" might serve as the title of a true believer. A hypocrite, when afflicted by God, resents the infliction and, like a slave, would run from the Master who has scourged him; but not so the true heir of heaven, who kisses the hand that struck him and seeks shelter from the rod in the heart of the God who frowned upon him. Job's desire to commune with God was intensified by the failure of all other sources of consolation. The patriarch turned away from his sorry friends and looked up to the heavenly throne, just as a traveler turns from his empty water jug and makes a beeline for the well. He bids farewell to earthborn hopes and cries, "Oh, that I knew where I might find my God!" Nothing teaches us about the preciousness of the Creator as much as when we learn the emptiness of everything else. Turning away with bitter scorn from earth's hives, where we find no honey, but many sharp stings, we rejoice in Him whose faithful word is sweeter than honey or the honeycomb. In every trouble we should first seek to realize God's presence with us. Only let us enjoy His smile, and then we can bear our daily cross with a willing heart for His dear sake.

### *The rock badgers are a people not mighty, yet they make their homes in the cliffs.*

PROVERBS 30:26

Conscious of their own natural defenselessness, the rock badgers resort to burrows in the rocks and are secure from their enemies. My heart, be willing to learn a lesson from these feeble folk. You are as weak and as exposed to peril as the timid badger; be as wise to seek a shelter. My best security is within the fortress of an unchanging Jehovah, where His unalterable promises stand like giant walls of rock. It will be well with you, my heart, if you can always hide yourself in the bulwarks of His glorious attributes, all of which are guarantees of safety for those who put their trust in Him. Blessed be the name of the Lord, I have so done and have found myself like David in the cave, safe from the cruelty of my enemy. I do not have to wonder how blessed it is to trust in the Lord, for long ago, when Satan and my sins pursued me, I fled to the cleft of the rock Christ Jesus, and in His wounded side I found a delightful resting-place. My heart, run to Him afresh tonight, whatever your present grief may be. Jesus feels for you; Jesus consoles you; Jesus will help you. No king in his impregnable fortress is more secure than the rock badger in his cliff home. The master of ten thousand chariots is not one bit better protected than the little dweller in the mountain's cleft. In Jesus the weak are strong, and the defenseless safe; they could not be more strong if they were giants or more safe if they were in heaven. Faith gives to men on earth the protection of the God of heaven. They cannot need any more and need not wish for more. The badgers cannot build a castle, but they avail themselves of what is there already. I cannot make myself a refuge, but Jesus has provided it, His Father has given it, His Spirit has revealed it, and here again tonight I enter it and am safe from every foe.

# Lazarus was one of those reclining with him at the table.

JOHN 12:2

*He is to be envied.* It was fine to be Martha and serve, but better to be Lazarus and enjoy. There are times for each purpose, and each is fitting in its season, but none of the trees of the garden yield such clusters as the vine of fellowship. To sit with Jesus, to hear His words, to mark His acts and receive His smiles was such a favor as must have made Lazarus as happy as the angels. When it has been our happy privilege to feast with our Beloved in His banqueting-hall, we would not have given half a sigh for all the kingdoms of the world, if so much breath could have bought them.

*He is to be imitated.* It would have been a strange thing if Lazarus had not been at the table where Jesus was, for he had been dead, and Jesus had raised him. For the risen one to be absent when the Lord who gave him life was at his house would have been dreadfully ungrateful. We too were once dead, yes, and like Lazarus bound in the grave of sin. Jesus raised us, and by His life we live. Can we be content to live at a distance from Him? Do we fail to remember Him at His table, where He deigns to feast with His brethren? This is cruel! It behooves us to repent and do as *He* has bidden us, for His least wish should be law to us. To have lived without constant fellowship with Jesus, who loved him so dearly, would have been disgraceful to Lazarus. Is it then excusable in us whom Jesus has loved with an everlasting love? To have been cold to Him who wept over his lifeless corpse would have shown a lack of feeling in Lazarus. What does it say of us over whom the Savior has not only wept but bled? Come, brethren, who read this portion; let us return to our heavenly Bridegroom and ask for His Spirit, that we may be on terms of closer intimacy with Him and never miss the opportunity to sit at the table with Him.

*November 22*

## The power of his resurrection.

PHILIPPIANS 3:10

The doctrine of a risen Savior is exceedingly precious. The resurrection is the cornerstone of the entire building of Christianity. It is the keystone of the arch of our salvation. It would take a volume to set out all the streams of living water that flow from this one sacred source, the resurrection of our dear Lord and Savior, Jesus Christ. But to *know* that He has risen, and to have fellowship with Him as such—communing with the risen Savior by possessing a risen life—seeing Him leave the tomb by leaving the tomb of worldliness ourselves—this is even more precious still. The doctrine is the basis of the experience, but as the flower is more lovely than the root, so is the experience of fellowship with the risen Savior more lovely than the doctrine itself. I would have you *believe* that Christ rose from the dead so as to sing of it and derive all the consolation that it is possible for you to extract from this well-affirmed and well-witnessed fact; but I beseech you, do not rest contented even there. Though you cannot, like the disciples, see Him visibly, yet I urge you to aspire to see Christ Jesus by the eye of faith; and though, like Mary Magdalene, you may not touch Him, yet you may be privileged to converse with Him and to know that He is risen, you yourselves being risen in Him to newness of life. To know a crucified Savior as having crucified all my sins is a high degree of knowledge; but to know a risen Savior as having justified me, and to realize that He has bestowed upon me new life, having made me a new creature through His own newness of life—this is a noble style of experience. Short of it, none should rest satisfied. May you both "know him and the power of his resurrection." Why should souls who are made alive with Jesus wear the grave-clothes of worldliness and unbelief? Rise, for the Lord is risen.

## *Get you up to a high mountain.*

ISAIAH 40:9

Each believer should be thirsting for God, for the living God, and longing to climb the hill of the Lord and see Him face to face. We should not rest content in the mists of the valley when the summit of the mountain beckons us. My soul thirsts to drink deeply of the cup that is reserved for those who reach the mountain's peak and bathe their brows in heaven. How pure are the dews of the hills; how fresh is the mountain air; how abundant is the provision of the dwellers aloft, whose windows look into the New Jerusalem! Many saints are content to live like men in coal mines, who do not see the sun; they eat dust like the serpent when they might taste the food of angels; they are content to wear the miner's garb when they might put on king's robes; tears disfigure their faces when they might anoint them with celestial oil. I am convinced that many a believer pines in a dungeon when he might walk on the palace roof and view the goodly land. Rouse yourself, believer, from your low condition! Discard your laziness, your lethargy, your coldness, or whatever interferes with your sincere and pure love for Christ, your soul's Husband. Make Him the source, the center, and the circumference of your soul's whole range of delight. What fully enchants you to remain in a pit when you may sit on a throne? Do not live in the lowlands of bondage now that mountain liberty is conferred upon you. Do not be satisfied any longer with your tiny attainments, but press forward to things more sublime and heavenly. Aspire to a higher, a nobler, a fuller life. Upward to heaven! Nearer to God!

> *When will Thou come unto me, Lord?*
> *Oh come, my Lord most dear!*
> *Come near, come nearer, nearer still,*
> *I'm blest when Thou art near.*

> *A little sleep, a little slumber, a little folding of the hands to rest, and poverty will come upon you like a robber, and want like an armed man.*

PROVERBS 24:33-34

The worst of sluggards only ask for a little slumber; they would be indignant if they were accused of complete laziness. A little folding of the hands to rest is all they desire, and they have a host of reasons to show that this indulgence is entirely legitimate. Yet by these "littles" the day runs out, and the time for work is all gone, and the field is overgrown with thorns. It is by little procrastinations that men ruin their souls. They do not intend to delay for years—a few months, they say, will bring the more convenient season—tomorrow they will attend to serious things; but the present hour is so occupied and so unsuitable that they beg to be excused. Like sands from an hourglass, time passes; life is wasted by driblets, and seasons of grace lost by little slumbers. Oh, to be wise, to catch the fleeting hour, to use the passing moments! May the Lord teach us this sacred wisdom, because otherwise a poverty of the worst kind awaits us—eternal poverty that will want even a drop of water and beg for it in vain. Like a robber steadily pursuing his victim, poverty overtakes the lazy, and ruin overthrows the undecided: Each hour brings the dreaded pursuer nearer; he doesn't pause on the way, for he is on his master's business and must not delay. As an armed man enters with authority and power, in similar fashion want will come to the idle, and death to the impenitent, and there will be no escape. O that men would become wise and would diligently seek the Lord Jesus, before the solemn day will dawn when it will be too late to plow and to sow, too late to repent and believe. In harvest, it is useless to lament that the seedtime was neglected. As of now, there is still time for faith and holy decision. May we obtain them tonight.

## *For he says to Moses, "I will have mercy on whom I have mercy, and I will have compassion on whom I have compassion."*

ROMANS 9:15

In these words the Lord in the plainest manner claims the right to give or to withhold His mercy according to His own sovereign will. As the prerogative of life and death is vested in the monarch, so the Judge of all the earth has a right to spare or condemn the guilty, as may seem best in His sight. Men by their sins have forfeited all claim upon God; they deserve to perish for their sins—and if they all do so, they have no ground for complaint. If the Lord steps in to save any, He may do so if the ends of justice are not thwarted; but if He judges it best to leave the condemned to suffer the righteous sentence, none may call Him to account. All those discourses about the rights of men being placed on the same footing are foolish and impudent and ignorant; worse still are the arguments against discriminating grace, which are just the rebellions of proud human nature against God's rule. When we are brought to see our own utter ruin, and the justice of the divine verdict against sin, we no longer scoff at the truth that the Lord is not bound to save us; we do not murmur if He chooses to save others, as though He were doing us an injury, but feel that if He deigns to look upon us, it will be His own free act of undeserved goodness, for which we will forever bless His name.

How will those who are the subjects of divine election sufficiently adore the grace of God? They have no room for boasting, for sovereignty most effectually excludes it. The Lord's will alone is glorified, and the very notion of human merit is cast out to everlasting contempt. There is no more humbling doctrine in Scripture than that of election, none more deserving of gratitude, and consequently none more sanctifying. Believers should not be afraid of it but adoringly rejoice in it.

## For whoever has despised the day of small things shall rejoice, and shall see the plumb line in the hand of Zerubbabel.

ZECHARIAH 4:10

Small things marked the beginning of the work in the hand of Zerubbabel, but none should despise it, for the Lord had raised up one who would persevere until the work was completed with shouts of joy. The plumb line was in good hands. Here is the comfort of every believer in the Lord Jesus. Let the work of grace be ever so small in its beginnings, *the plumb line is in good hands.* A master builder greater than Solomon has undertaken to raise the heavenly temple, and He will not fail nor be discouraged till the pinnacle shall be raised. If the plumb line were in the hand of any merely human being, we might fear for the building, but the pleasure of the Lord will prosper in Jesus' hand. The works did not proceed irregularly and without care, for *the master's hand carried a good instrument.* If the walls had been built in a hurry without proper supervision, they might have been out of line; but the plumb line was used by the chosen overseer. Jesus is always watching the construction of His spiritual temple, to ensure that it is built securely and well. We are for speed, but Jesus is for judgment. He will use the plumb line, and that which is out of line must come down, every stone of it. This explains the failure of many a flattering work, the overthrow of many a glittering profession. It is not for us to judge the Lord's Church, since Jesus has a steady hand and a true eye and can use the plumb line well. Do we not rejoice to see judgment left to Him?

*The plumb line was in active use*—it was in the builder's hand, a sure indication that he meant to bring the work to completion. Lord Jesus, how glad we would be to see You at Your great work. O Zion, the beautiful, your walls are still in ruins! Rise, glorious Builder, and make her desolations to rejoice at Your coming.

## The forgiveness of our trespasses, according to the riches of his grace.

EPHESIANS 1:7

Could there be a sweeter word in any language than that word "forgiveness" when it sounds in a guilty sinner's ear, like the joyful notes of liberation to the captive Israelite? Blessed, forever blessed, be the dear star of pardon that shines into the condemned cell and gives the perishing a gleam of hope amid the midnight of despair! Can it be possible that sin, such sin as mine, can be forgiven, forgiven altogether and forever? Hell is my portion as a sinner—there is no possibility of my escaping from it while sin remains upon me. Can the load of guilt be lifted, the crimson stain removed? Can the unbreakable stones of my prison-house ever be loosed from their mortices, or the doors be lifted from their hinges? Jesus tells me that I may still be cleared. Forever blessed be the revelation of atoning love that not only tells me that pardon is possible, but that it is secured to all who trust in Jesus. I have believed in the atoning sacrifice, even Jesus crucified, and therefore my sins are at this moment and forever forgiven by virtue of His substitutionary pains and death. What joy is this! What unimagined bliss to be a perfectly pardoned soul! My soul dedicates all her powers to Him who by His own unpurchased love became my Savior and provided for me redemption through His blood. What riches of grace does free forgiveness exhibit! To forgive at all, to forgive fully, to forgive freely, to forgive forever—here is a panorama of wonders. And when I think of how great my sins were, how dear were the precious drops that cleansed me from them, and how gracious was the method by which pardon was sealed home to me, I am in a maze of wondering, worshiping affection. I bow before the throne that absolves me, I clasp the cross that delivers me, and all my days I give to serve the Incarnate God, through whom I am this night a pardoned soul.

## *He sought the welfare of his people.*

ESTHER 10:3

Mordecai was a true patriot, and so when he was promoted to the highest position under Ahasuerus, he used his eminence to promote the prosperity of Israel. In this he was a type of Jesus who, upon His throne of glory, does not seek His own but spends His power for His people. It would be beneficial if every Christian would be a Mordecai to the Church, striving according to his ability for its prosperity. Some are placed in positions of affluence and influence; let them honor their Lord in the high places of the earth and testify for Jesus before great men. Others have what is far better, namely, close fellowship with the King of kings. Let them be sure to pray daily for the weak among the Lord's people, the doubting, the tempted, and the comfortless. It will redound to their honor if they make much intercession for those who are in darkness and dare not draw close to the mercy-seat. Instructed believers may serve their Master greatly if they offer their talents for the general good and impart their wealth of heavenly learning to others by teaching them the things of God. The very least in our churches may seek the welfare of God's people; and such a desire, if they can give no more, will be acceptable. It is at once the most Christlike and the most happy course for a believer to stop living for himself. He who blesses others cannot fail to be blessed himself. On the other hand, to seek our own personal greatness is a wicked and unhappy plan of life; its way will be grievous, and its end will be fatal.

Here is the place to ask you, my friend, whether you are to the best of your power seeking the best for the Church in your neighborhood. I trust you are not doing the Church mischief by bitterness and scandal, nor weakening it by your neglect. Friend, unite with the Lord's poor, bear their cross, do them all the good you can, and you will not miss your reward.

## *Spices for the anointing oil.*

EXODUS 35:8

Much use was made of this anointing oil under the law, and that which it represents is of primary importance under the Gospel. The Holy Spirit, who anoints us for all holy service, is indispensable to us if we would serve the Lord acceptably. Without His help our religious services are just an empty show, and our inward experience is a dead thing. Whenever our ministry is without unction, what miserable stuff it becomes! And the prayers, praises, meditations, and efforts of private Christians are no better. A holy anointing is the soul and life of godly devotion, its absence the most serious of all calamities. To go before the Lord without anointing would be like a common Levite thrusting himself into the priest's role—his religious services would be sins, not sacrifices. May we never embark upon holy tasks without sacred anointings. They fall upon us from our glorious Head; from His anointing we who are but the skirts of His garments receive a generous unction. Choice spices were mixed with great skill and care to form the anointing oil, to let us see how rich are all the influences of the Holy Spirit. All good things are found in the divine Comforter. Matchless consolation, infallible instruction, immortal quickening, spiritual energy, and divine sanctification are all mixed with other excellencies in the heavenly anointing oil of the Holy Spirit. It imparts a delightful fragrance to the character and person of the one upon whom it is poured. Nothing like it can be found in all the treasures of the wealthy or the secrets of the wise. It is not to be imitated. It only comes from God, and it is freely given, through Jesus Christ, to every waiting soul. Let us seek it, for we may have it, even this very evening. O Lord, anoint Your servants.

> ## ... *Michael and his angels fighting against the dragon. And the dragon and his angels fought back.*
>
> REVELATION 12:7

War always will rage between the two great sovereignties until one or the other is crushed. Peace between good and evil is an impossibility; to pretend otherwise would signal a victory for the powers of darkness. *Michael will always fight*; his holy soul is vexed with sin and will not endure it. Jesus will always be the dragon's foe, and not in any quiet sense but actively, vigorously, with full determination to exterminate evil. All His servants, whether angels in heaven or messengers on earth, will and must fight; they are born to be warriors. At the cross they enter into a covenant never to make a truce with evil; they are a warlike company, firm in defense and fierce in attack. The duty of every soldier in the army of the Lord is every day, with all his heart and soul and strength, to fight against the dragon.

*The dragon and his angels will fight back*; they are incessant in their onslaughts, prepared to use every kind of weaponry. We are foolish to expect to serve God without opposition: The more zealous we are, the more we can expect to be attacked by the ruffians of hell. The church may become lazy, but her great antagonist does not; his restless spirit never allows the war to pause; he hates the woman's seed and would happily devour the Church if he could. The servants of Satan share a great deal of the old dragon's energy and are usually an active crew. War rages all around, and to dream of peace is dangerous and futile.

Glory be to God, we know the end of the war. The great dragon will be cast out and forever destroyed, while Jesus and those who are with Him will receive the crown. So let us sharpen our swords tonight, and ask the Holy Spirit to make us ready for the conflict. Battle was never so important, and the crown never so glorious. Every one to their positions as warriors of the cross, and may the Lord tread Satan under your feet shortly!

# *Let them thank the LORD for his steadfast love,*
# *for his wondrous works to the children of men!*

PSALM 107:8

If we complained less and were more thankful, we would be happier, and God would be more glorified. Every day thank God for *ordinary mercies*—we refer to them as ordinary, and yet they are so priceless that without them we are ready to perish. Let us thank God for our eyes with which we see the sun, for the health and strength to walk around, for the bread we eat, for the clothes we wear. Let us thank Him that we are not among the hopeless or confined among the guilty; let us thank Him for liberty, for friends, for family associations and comforts. Let us praise Him, in fact, for everything that we receive from His generous hand, for although we deserve little, He provides an abundance. The sweetest and the loudest note in our thankful songs should be of *redeeming love*. God's redeeming acts toward His chosen are forever the favorite themes of their praise. If we know what redemption means, let us not withhold our hymns of thanksgiving. We have been redeemed from the power of our corruptions, lifted from the depth of sin in which we were naturally plunged. We have been led to the cross of Christ—our shackles of guilt have been removed. We are no longer slaves, but children of the living God, and can anticipate the time when we will be presented before the throne without spot or wrinkle or any such thing. Even now by faith we wrap ourselves in the fair linen that is to be our everlasting array and rehearse our unceasing thankfulness to the Lord our Redeemer. Child of God, can you remain silent? Stir yourselves with thoughts of your inheritance, and lead your captivity captive, crying with David, "Bless the LORD, O my soul, and all that is within me, bless his holy name."[1] Let this new month begin with new songs.

[1]Psalm 103:1

## *Behold, all is vanity.*

ECCLESIASTES 1:14

Nothing can satisfy the entire man but the Lord's love and the Lord's own self. Some have tried to anchor in other harbors, but they have been driven out of such fatal refuges. Solomon, the wisest of men, was permitted to make experiments for us all, and to do for us what we should not attempt ourselves. Here is his testimony in his own words: "So I became great and surpassed all who were before me in Jerusalem. Also my wisdom remained with me. And whatever my eyes desired I did not keep from them. I kept my heart from no pleasure, for my heart found pleasure in all my toil, and this was my reward for all my toil. Then I considered all that my hands had done and the toil I had expended in doing it, and behold, all was vanity and a striving after wind, and there was nothing to be gained under the sun."[1] "Vanity of vanities, all is vanity."[2] What! The whole of it vanity? Is there nothing in all the wealth of kings? Nothing in that vast territory reaching from the river to the sea? Nothing in those glorious palaces? Nothing in the riches of the forests of Lebanon? In all your music and dancing and wine and luxury is there nothing? "Nothing," he says, "but sorrow, and his work is a vexation." This was his verdict when he had experimented on the paths of apparent pleasure. To embrace the Lord Jesus, to rest in His love and be fully assured of union with Him—this is all in all. Dear reader, you do not need to try these empty paths to find out whether they are better than the Christian's. If you roam the universe, you will not find another friend like Jesus; if you could have all the comforts of life but lost your Savior, you would be wretched; but if you win Christ, then you could rot in a dungeon and even there find peace. If you live in obscurity or die hungry, you will still be satisfied with favor and will be full of the goodness of the Lord.

[1]Song of Solomon 2:9-11  [2]Song of Solomon 1:2

## The LORD, mighty in battle!

PSALM 24:8

God is glorious in the eyes of His people, since He has worked such wonders for them, in them, and by them. *For them,* the Lord Jesus upon Calvary defeated every foe, breaking all the weapons of the enemy in pieces by His finished work of satisfactory obedience; by His triumphant resurrection and ascension He completely overturned the hopes of hell, leading captivity captive, making a show of our enemies openly, triumphing over them by His cross. Every arrow of guilt that Satan might have shot at us is broken, for who can lay anything to the charge of God's elect? Vain are the sharp swords of infernal malice and the perpetual battles of the serpent's seed, for among God's people the lame take the prey, and the feeblest warriors are crowned.

Believers will also worship the Lord Jesus for His conquests *in them,* since the arrows of their natural hatred are snapped, and the weapons of their rebellion are broken. What victories grace has won in our evil hearts! How glorious is Jesus when the will is subdued and sin dethroned! As for our remaining corruptions, they will sustain an equally sure defeat, and every temptation and doubt and fear will be completely destroyed. In the sanctuary of our peaceful hearts, the name of Jesus is great beyond compare: He has won our love, and He shall wear it. In equal measure we may look for victories *by us.* We are more than conquerors through Him who loved us. We will cast down the powers of darkness that are in the world by our faith and zeal and holiness; we will win sinners to Jesus; we will overturn false systems; we will convert nations. For God is with us, and none shall stand against us. This evening let the Christian warrior sing the war song and prepare for tomorrow's fight. Greater is He who is in us than he who is in the world.

## *We ourselves . . . groan inwardly as we wait eagerly for adoption as sons, the redemption of our bodies.*

ROMANS 8:23

This groaning is common among God's people: To a greater or lesser extent we all feel it. It is not the groan of murmuring or complaint: It is a note of desire rather than of distress. Having received a deposit, we desire the rest of our portion; we are sighing that our entire manhood, in its trinity of spirit, soul, and body, may be set free from the last trace of the Fall; we long to discard the rags of corruption, weakness, and dishonor and to be clothed with incorruption, immortality, glory—the spiritual body that the Lord Jesus will bestow upon His people. We long for the manifestation of our adoption as the children of God. "We . . . groan," but it is *"inwardly."* It is not the hypocrite's groan, by which he would make men believe that he is a saint because he is wretched. Our sighs are sacred things, too holy and too personal for us to broadcast. We keep our longings for our Lord to ourselves. Then the apostle says we *"wait,"* by which we learn that we are not to be petulant, like Jonah or Elijah when they said, "Let me die"; nor are we to whimper and sigh for the end of life because we are tired of work or wish to escape from our present sufferings till the will of the Lord is done. We are to groan for glorification, but we are to wait patiently for it, knowing that what the Lord appoints is best. Waiting implies being ready. We are to stand at the door expecting the Beloved to open it and take us away to Himself. This groaning is a test. You can learn a lot about a man by what he groans after. Some men groan after wealth—they worship money; some groan continually under the troubles of life—they are merely impatient. But the man who sighs after God, who is uneasy until he is made like Christ—that is the blessed man. May God help us to groan for the coming of the Lord and the resurrection that He will bring to us.

## *Then the LORD showed me four craftsmen.*

ZECHARIAH 1:20

In the vision described in this chapter, the prophet saw four terrible horns. They were pushing this way and that way, dashing down the strongest and the mightiest; and the prophet asked, "What are these?" The answer was, "These are the horns that have scattered Judah." He saw before him a representation of those powers that had oppressed the Church of God. There were four horns, for the church is attacked from all quarters. The prophet had good reason to feel dismayed; but suddenly there appeared before him "four craftsmen." He asked, "What are these coming to do?" These were the men whom God had found to break those horns in pieces. *God will always find men for His work*, and He will find them at the right time. The prophet did not see the craftsmen at first, when there was nothing to do, but first the "horns" and then the "craftsmen." The Lord always finds enough men. He did not find three craftsmen, but four; there were four horns, and there must be four workmen. God finds *the right men*—not four men with pens to write, not four architects to draw plans, but four craftsmen to do the work. Rest assured, you who tremble for the Church of God, that when the "horns" grow troublesome, the "craftsmen" will be found. You need not worry about the weakness of the Church of God at any moment; there may be growing up in obscurity the valiant reformer who will shake the nations. Chrysostoms may come forth from our Ragged Schools, and Augustines from the thickest darkness of London's poverty. The Lord knows where to find His servants. He has in ambush a multitude of mighty men, and at His word they will take to the battle; "for the battle is the LORD's,"[1] and He will get to Himself the victory. So let us remain faithful to Christ, and He, in the right time, will raise up for us a defense, whether it be in the day of our personal need or in the season of peril to His Church.

[1] 1 Samuel 17:47

## *. . . with a golden sash around his chest.*

REVELATION 1:13

One like "a son of man" appeared to John in Patmos, and the beloved disciple noticed that He wore "a golden sash." A sash, for Jesus was never unprepared while on earth, but always stood ready for service; and now before the eternal throne He continues His ministry as our great High Priest. It is good for us that He has not ceased to fulfill His offices of love, since it is one of our choicest safeguards that He ever lives to make intercession for us. Jesus is never lazy; His garments are never loose as though His offices were ended; He diligently carries on the cause of His people. A *golden* sash, to declare the superiority of His service, the royalty of His person, the dignity of His state, the glory of His reward. He no longer cries out of the dust, but He pleads with authority, a King as well as a Priest. Our cause is safe enough in the hands of our enthroned Redeemer.

Our Lord presents all His people with an example. We must never unbind our sashes. This is not the time for lying down to rest; it is the season of service and warfare. We need to bind the sash of truth more and more tightly around us. It is a golden sash, and as such it will be our richest ornament. And we greatly need it, for a heart that is not well braced up with the truth as it is in Jesus and with the faithfulness that is fashioned by the Spirit will be easily entangled with the things of this life and tripped up by the snares of temptation. We possess the Scriptures in vain unless we bind them around us like a sash, surrounding our entire nature, keeping each part of our character in order, and giving compactness to our whole being. If in heaven Jesus does not remove the sash, neither should we upon earth. Stand, therefore, having fastened on the belt of truth.

## *I have become all things to all people, that by all means I might save some.*

1 CORINTHIANS 9:22

Paul's great object was not merely to instruct and to improve, but to save. Anything short of this would have disappointed him; he desired to see men renewed in heart, forgiven, sanctified, in fact saved. Have our Christian efforts been aimed at anything below this great objective? Then let us correct our ways, for what good will it be at the last great day to have taught and moralized men if they appear before God unsaved? If through life we have sought inferior objects and forgotten that men needed to be saved, then we will be held accountable. Paul knew the ruin of man's natural state and did not try to educate him, but to save him; he saw men sinking to hell and did not talk of refining them, but of saving from the wrath to come. To accomplish their salvation, he gave himself up with untiring zeal to spreading the Gospel, to warning and beseeching men to be reconciled to God. His prayers were persistent and his labors incessant. His consuming passion, his ambition, his calling was to save souls. He became a servant to all men, working for them, feeling a woe within him if he did not preach the Gospel. He laid aside his preferences to prevent prejudice; he submitted his will in things indifferent, and if men would just receive the Gospel, he raised no questions about forms or ceremonies. The Gospel was the one all-important business with him. If he might save some, he would be content. This was the crown for which he extended himself, the sole and sufficient reward of all his labors and self-denials. Dear reader, have you and I lived to win souls to this extent? Are we possessed with the same all-absorbing desire? If not, why not? Jesus died for sinners. Can we not live for them? Where is our tenderness? Where is our love for Christ, if we do not seek His honor in the salvation of men? Lord Jesus, saturate us through and through with an undying zeal for the souls of men.

## *In your goodness, O God,*
## *you have provided for the needy.*

PSALM 68:10

All God's gifts are prepared gifts laid away to meet wants He has foreseen. He anticipates our needs; and out of the fullness that He has treasured up in Christ Jesus, He provides from His goodness for the poor. You may trust Him for all the necessities you may face, for He has infallibly foreknown every one of them. He can say of us in all conditions, "I knew that you would be this and that." A man takes a journey across the desert, and when he has completed a day and pitched his tent, he discovers that he wants many comforts and necessities that he has not brought in his baggage. "Ah!" he says. "I did not foresee this. If I had this journey to do again, I would bring these things with me—they are necessary to my comfort." But God is already aware of all the requirements of His poor, wandering children, and when those needs occur, supplies are ready. It is goodness that He has prepared for the poor in heart, goodness and goodness only. "My grace is sufficient for you."[1] "As your days, so shall your strength be."[2]

Reader, is your heart heavy this evening? God knew it would be; the comfort that your heart requires is treasured in the sweet assurance of this text. You are poor and needy, but He has thought upon you and has the exact blessing that you require in store for you. Plead the promise; believe it and obtain its fulfillment. Do you feel that you never were so consciously sinful as you are now? Behold, the crimson fountain is open still, with all its former efficacy, to wash your sin away. You will never come into such a position that Christ cannot help you. You will never arrive at a place in your spiritual affairs in which Jesus Christ will not be equal to the emergency, for your history has all been foreknown and provided for in Jesus.

[1]2 Corinthians 12:9   [2]Deuteronomy 33:25

## *My people will abide in a peaceful habitation.*

ISAIAH 32:18

Peace and rest do not belong to the unregenerate; they are the peculiar possession of the Lord's people, and of them only. The God of Peace gives perfect peace to those whose hearts are fixed upon Him. Before the Fall, God gave man the Garden of Eden as his quiet resting-place; sadly, how quickly sin spoiled the fair abode of innocence. In the day of universal wrath when the Flood swept away a guilty race, the chosen family was quietly secured in the resting-place of the ark, which floated them from the old condemned world into the new earth of the rainbow and the covenant, symbolizing Jesus, the ark of our salvation. Israel rested safely beneath the blood-sprinkled dwellings of Egypt when the destroying angel smote the firstborn; and in the wilderness the shadow of the pillar of cloud and the flowing rock gave the weary pilgrims sweet repose. Today we rest in the promises of our faithful God, knowing that His words are full of truth and power; we rest in the doctrines of His Word, which are consolation itself; we rest in the covenant of His grace, which is a haven of delight. We are more highly favored than David in the cave or Jonah beneath his plant, for no one can invade or destroy our shelter. The person of Jesus is the quiet resting-place of His people, and when we draw near to Him in the breaking of the bread, the hearing of the Word, the searching of the Scriptures, prayer, or praise, we find that any form of approach to Him brings peace to our spirits.

> *I hear the words of love, I gaze upon the blood,*
> *I see the mighty sacrifice, and I have peace with God.*
> *'Tis everlasting peace, sure as Jehovah's name,*
> *'Tis stable as His steadfast throne, forevermore the same:*
> *The clouds may go and come, and storms may sweep my sky,*
> *This blood-sealed friendship changes not, the cross is ever nigh.*

## The Lord opened her heart.

ACTS 16:14

In Lydia's conversion there are many points of interest. It was brought about by *providential circumstances*. She was a seller of purple goods, from the city of Thyratira, but at just the right time for hearing Paul we find her at Philippi; providence, which is the servant of grace, led her to the right spot. Again, *grace was preparing her soul for the blessing*—grace preparing for grace. She did not know the Savior, but as a Jewess she knew many truths that were excellent stepping-stones to a knowledge of Jesus. Her conversion took place in the use of the means. On the Sabbath she went to a place of prayer, and there prayer was answered. Never neglect the means of grace. God *may* bless us when we are not in His house, but we have more reason to expect that He will when we are in fellowship with His people. Observe the words, "*The Lord opened her heart.*" She did not open her own heart. Her prayers did not do it; Paul did not do it. The Lord Himself must open the heart to receive the things that make for our peace. He alone can put the key into the door and open it and gain entry for Himself. He is the heart's Master just as He is the heart's Maker. The first outward evidence of the opened heart was *obedience*. As soon as Lydia had believed in Jesus, she was baptized. It is a sweet sign of a humble and broken heart when the child of God is willing to obey a command that is not essential to his salvation, that is not forced upon him by a selfish fear of condemnation, but is a simple act of obedience and communion with his Master. The next evidence was *love*, displaying itself in acts of grateful kindness to the apostles. Love for the saints has always been a mark of the true convert. Those who do nothing for Christ or His church provide no evidence of an "opened" heart. Lord, grant to us the blessing of opened hearts always!

## You are serving the Lord Christ.

COLOSSIANS 3:24

To what special group was this word spoken? To kings who proudly boast a divine right? No! Too often they serve themselves or Satan and forget God who patiently permits them to wear their majestic crowns for a little while. Is the apostle speaking to those so-called "right reverend fathers in God," the bishops or "the venerable archdeacons"? No; in fact, Paul knew nothing of these man-made titles. This word was not spoken even to pastors and teachers or to the wealthy and highly regarded among believers, but to servants and to slaves. Among the toiling multitudes—the journeymen, the day laborers, the domestic servants, the drudges of the kitchen—the apostle found, as we still find, some of the Lord's chosen, and he says to them, "Whatever you do, work heartily, as for the Lord and not for men, knowing that from the Lord you will receive the inheritance as your reward. You are serving the Lord Christ." This saying grants significance to the weary routine of earthly employments and sheds a halo around the most humble occupations. To wash feet may be servile, but to wash *His* feet is royal work. To untie sandals is poor employment, but to unloose the Master's shoe is a princely privilege. The shop, the barn, the kitchen, and the workbench become temples when men and women do all to the glory of God! Then divine service does not take place for a few hours and in a few places, but all life becomes holiness to the Lord, and every place and thing as consecrated as the tabernacle and its contents.

> *Teach me, my God and King, in all things Thee to see;*
> *And what I do in anything to do it as to Thee.*
> *All may of Thee partake, nothing can be so mean,*
> *Which with this tincture, for Thy sake,*
>    *will not grow bright and clean.*
> *A servant with this clause makes drudgery divine;*
> *Who sweeps a room, as for Thy laws, makes that*
>    *and the action fine.*

## They have dealt faithlessly with the Lord.

HOSEA 5:7

Believer, here is a sad truth! You are the beloved of the Lord, redeemed by blood, called by grace, preserved in Christ Jesus, accepted in the Beloved, on your way to heaven, and yet you "have dealt faithlessly" with God, your best friend; faithlessly with Jesus, to whom you belong; faithlessly with the Holy Spirit, by whom you have been born again to life eternal! How faithless you have been in the matter of vows and promises. Do you remember your love in the early days, that happy time, the springtime of your spiritual life? How closely you held to your Master then, saying, "He will never charge me with indifference; my feet will never grow slow in the way of His service; I will not allow my heart to wander after other loves; in Him is blessing I could ever enjoy. I give up everything for my Lord Jesus' sake." Has it been so? Sadly if conscience speaks, it will say, "He who promised so much has performed so little. Prayer has frequently been slurred—it has been short but not sweet, brief but not fervent. Communion with Christ has been forgotten. Instead of a heavenly mind, there have been earthly preoccupations, foolish vanities, and evil thoughts. Instead of service, there has been disobedience, instead of fervency lukewarmness, instead of patience petulance, instead of faith self-reliance; and as a soldier of the cross there has been cowardice, disobedience, and desertion, to a very shameful degree." "They have dealt faithlessly." Faithless to Jesus! What words shall be used in denouncing this? Words are cheap: Let our penitent thoughts condemn the sin that is so surely in us. Faithless to Your sacrifice, O Jesus! Forgive us, and let us not sin again! How shameful to be faithless to Him who never forgets us, but who to this day stands with our names engraven on His breastplate before the eternal throne.

## *Give me children, or I shall die.*

GENESIS 30:1

The cry of Rachel for physical children should be more than matched by the believer's longing for spiritual children. Our great object in living is to glorify God, and we mainly achieve this end by the winning of souls. We *must* see souls born unto God. If we do not win souls, we should mourn as the farmer who sees no harvest, as the fisherman who returns to his cottage with an empty net, or as the hunter who has roamed in vain over hill and dale. Ours should be Isaiah's language uttered with many a sigh and groan—"who has believed what they heard from us, and to whom has the arm of the Lord been revealed?"[1] As ambassadors of peace we should not cease to weep bitterly until sinners weep for their sins. If we intensely desire to see others believing in the Lord Jesus, we must act in accordance with the principle and pattern of Scripture. We must depend entirely upon the Spirit of God. His place as God is on the throne, and in all our enterprises He must be the beginning, the middle, and the end; we are instruments in His hand and nothing more.

We must be most of all clear upon the great soul-saving doctrine of the Atonement. "He made him to be sin who knew no sin, so that in him we might become the righteousness of God."[2] This truth that Christ died in the place of sinners gives rest to the conscience by showing how God can be just and the justifier of whoever believes. We must declare the love of God in Christ Jesus. Always keep Hs abounding mercy connected to His unerring justice. Never exalt one attribute at the expense of another. Let boundless mercy be seen in calm consistency with stern justice and unlimited sovereignty. Believer, are you longing to see spiritual offspring? Do not let the sun set on this day without imploring God to show Himself strong in this regard. Beseech Him, "Give me children, or I shall die."

*Editor's note: This meditation replaces Spurgeon's original devotional, on Isaiah 54:12 and was adapted from Charles Spurgeon's Lectures to Students, page 375.*

[1]John 12:38  [2]2 Corinthians 5:21

## *I have been crucified with Christ.*

GALATIANS 2:20

The Lord Jesus Christ acted in what He did as a great public representative person, and His dying upon the cross was the virtual dying of all His people. In Him all His people rendered justice its due and made an expiation to divine vengeance for all their sins. The apostle of the Gentiles delighted to think that as one of Christ's chosen people, he died upon the cross in Christ. He did more than believe this doctrinally—he accepted it confidently, resting his hope upon it. He believed that by virtue of Christ's death, he had satisfied divine justice and found reconciliation with God. Beloved, what a blessed thing it is when the soul can, as it were, stretch itself upon the cross of Christ and feel, "I am dead; the law has killed me, and I am therefore free from its power, because in Christ I have borne the curse, and in the person of my Substitute all that the law could do by way of condemnation has been executed upon me, for I am crucified with Christ."

But Paul meant even more than this. He not only believed in Christ's death and trusted in it, but he actually felt its power in himself causing the crucifixion of his old corrupt nature. When he saw the pleasures of sin, he said, "I cannot enjoy these: I am dead to them." Such is the experience of every true Christian. Having received Christ, he is to this world as one who is utterly dead. Yet, while conscious of death to the world, he can at the same time exclaim with the apostle, "I live." He is fully alive to God. The Christian's life is a matchless riddle. The unconverted cannot comprehend it; even the believer himself cannot understand it. Dead, yet alive! Crucified with Christ, and yet at the same time risen with Christ in newness of life! Union with the suffering, bleeding Savior and death to the world and sin are soul-cheering things. May we learn to live evermore in the enjoyment of them!

## And lay your foundations with sapphires.

ISAIAH 54:11

Not only what is seen in the Church of God but also what is unseen is fair and precious. Foundations are out of sight, and as long as they are firm, it is not expected that they should be valuable. But in God's work everything is of the same value— nothing devalued, nothing irrelevant. The deep foundations of the work of grace are as precious as sapphires; no human mind is able to measure their glory. We build upon the *covenant of grace*, which is stronger than steel and as enduring as diamonds and upon which age makes no impact. Sapphire foundations are eternal, and the covenant remains throughout the lifetime of the Almighty. Another foundation is *the person of the Lord Jesus*, clear and spotless, as everlasting and beautiful as the sapphire, combining the deep blue of earth's ever-rolling ocean and the azure of its all-embracing sky. At one time our Lord might have been compared to the ruby as He stood covered with His own blood, but now we see Him radiant with the soft blue of love—love abounding, deep, eternal. Our eternal hopes are built upon *the justice and the faithfulness of God*, which are as clear and cloudless as the sapphire. We are not saved by a compromise, by mercy defeating justice or law suspending its operations; no, we defy the eagle's eye to detect a flaw in the groundwork of our confidence: Our foundation is of sapphire and will endure the fire.

The Lord Himself has laid the foundation of His people's hopes. It is a subject for serious inquiry whether our hopes are built upon such a basis. Good works and ceremonies are not a foundation of sapphires, but of wood, hay, and stubble; neither are they laid by God but by our own conceit. Foundations will all be tested before long: Woe to him whose lofty tower will come down with a crash because it was built on sand. The one who is built on sapphires may face storm or fire with confidence, for he will pass the test.

> **You have never heard, you have never known,**
> **from of old your ear has not been opened.**
>
> ISAIAH 48:8

It is painful to remember that to a certain degree this accusation may be laid at the door of *believers*, who too often are in some measure *spiritually insensitive*. We may well bemoan the fact that we do not hear the voice of God as we should: "You have never heard." There are gentle motions of the Holy Spirit in the soul that are unheeded by us: There are whisperings of divine command and of heavenly love that are equally unobserved by our dull minds. Sadly, we have been *carelessly ignorant*—"You have never known." There are spiritual matters that we ought to have seen, corruptions that have been allowed to develop unnoticed, tender affections that are being harmed like flowers in the frost, untended by us, glimpses of the Lord that we might have perceived if we had not barricaded the windows of our soul. But we "have never known." As we think of this we are truly and deeply humbled. How we must adore the grace of God as we realize from the context that all of our folly and ignorance *was foreknown by God*, and notwithstanding that foreknowledge, He has still been pleased to deal with us in mercy! Ponder and admire the marvelous sovereign grace that could have chosen us in the sight of all this! Wonder at the price that was paid for us when Christ knew what we would be! He who hung upon the cross foresaw us as unbelieving, backsliding, cold of heart, indifferent, careless, lax in prayer, and yet He said, "I am the Lord your God, the Holy One of Israel, your Savior. Because you are precious in My eyes and honored, and I love you, I give men in return for you, peoples in exchange for your life." How wonderful and glorious is this redemption when we think how sinful we are! Holy Spirit, give us from now on a hearing ear and an understanding heart!

### I am the door. If anyone enters by me, he will be saved and will go in and out and find pasture.

JOHN 10:9

Jesus, the great I AM, is the entrance into the true Church and the way of access to God Himself. He gives to the one who comes to God by Him four choice privileges.

1. *He will be saved.* The fugitive entered the gate of the city of refuge and was safe. Noah entered the door of the ark and was secure. None can be lost who take Jesus as the door of faith to their souls. Entrance through Jesus into peace is the guarantee of entrance by the same door into heaven. Jesus is the only door, an open door, a wide door, a safe door; and blessed is he who rests all his hope of admission to glory upon the crucified Redeemer.

2. *He will go in.* He will be privileged to go in among the divine family, sharing the children's food and participating in all their honors and enjoyments. He will go into the rooms of communion, to the banquets of love, to the treasures of the covenant, to the storehouses of the promises. He will go in to the King of kings in the power of the Holy Spirit, and the secret of the Lord will be with him.

3. *He will go out.* This blessing is much forgotten. We go out into the world to work and suffer, but what a mercy to go in the name and power of Jesus! We are called to bear witness to the truth, to cheer the disconsolate, to warn the careless, to win souls, and to glorify God. And as the angel said to Gideon, "Go in this might of yours,"[1] even so the Lord would have us proceed as His messengers in His name and strength.

4. *He will find pasture.* He who knows Jesus will never lack. Going in or out will be equally helpful to him: In fellowship with God he will grow, and in watering others he will be watered. Having made Jesus his all, he will find all in Jesus. His soul will be like a watered garden and like a well of water that never runs dry.

[1]Judges 6:14

## Know well the condition of your flocks,
## and give attention to your herds.

PROVERBS 27:23

Every wise businessman will occasionally hold a stock-taking, when he will examine his accounts, consider what he has on hand, and determine clearly whether his trade is prosperous or declining. Every man who is wise in the kingdom of heaven will cry, "Search me, O God . . . Try me";[1] and he will frequently set apart special seasons for self-examination, to discover whether things are right between God and his soul. The God whom we worship is a great heart-searcher; and in the past His servants referred to Him as "I am he who searches mind and heart, and I will give to each of you as your works deserve."[2] Let me encourage you in His name to diligently search and solemnly test your spiritual state, for fear you should come short of the promised rest. This is what every wise man does, and what God Himself does with us all. I exhort you to do the same yourself this evening. Let the oldest saint examine the basics of his piety, for gray heads may cover evil hearts: And the young professor should not despise the word of warning, for the greenness of youth may accompany the rottenness of hypocrisy. Every now and then a spiritual giant falls. The enemy still continues to sow tares among the wheat. It is not my aim to introduce doubts and fears to your mind; I rather hope that the rough wind of self-examination may help to drive them away. It is not security but fleshly security that we would kill, not confidence but carnal confidence that we would overthrow, not peace but false peace that we would destroy. By the precious blood of Christ, which was not shed to make you a hypocrite, but rather that sincere souls might declare His praise, I urge you to search and look, for fear that in the end it will be said of you, "Tekel, you have been weighed in the balances and found wanting."[3]

[1]Psalm 139:23   [2]Revelation 2:23   [3]Daniel 5:27

## *The sea was no more.*

### REVELATION 21:1

We could scarcely rejoice at the thought of losing the glorious old ocean: The new heavens and the new earth are not attractive to our imagination if in fact there is literally going to be no great and wide sea with its gleaming waves and sandy shores. Should the text not be read as a metaphor tinged with the prejudice with which the oriental mind universally regarded the sea in the olden times? A real physical world without a sea is a sad idea; it would be an iron ring without the sapphire that made it precious. There must be a spiritual meaning here. In the new dispensation there will be no *division*—the sea separates nations and divides peoples from each other. To John in Patmos the deep waters were like prison walls, shutting him out from his brethren and his work: There will be no such barriers in the world to come. Leagues of rolling billows lie between us and family members whom tonight we prayerfully remember, but in the bright world to which we go there will be unbroken fellowship for all the redeemed family. In this sense there shall be no more sea. The sea is the emblem of change; with its ebbs and flows, its glassy smoothness and its mountainous billows, its gentle murmurs and its tumultuous roarings, it is never the same for very long. It is a slave of the fickle winds and the changing moon, and its instability is proverbial. In this earthly journey we have too much of this; earth is constant only in her inconstancy. But in our heavenly state all mournful change will be unknown, and with it every fear of storms that would wreck our hopes and drown our joys. The sea of glass glows with splendor unbroken by a wave. No tempest howls along the peaceful shores of paradise. Soon we will reach that happy land where partings and changes and storms shall be ended! Jesus will guide us there. Are we in Him or not? This is the grand question.

## Call the laborers and pay them their wages.

MATTHEW 20:8

G od is a good Master; He pays His servants while they work and also when their work is done. One of His payments is this: *an easy conscience*. If you have spoken faithfully of Jesus to one person, when you go to bed at night you feel happy, thinking, "I have today discharged my conscience of that man's blood." There is a great *comfort in doing something for Jesus*. What a happiness to place jewels in His crown and allow Him to see of the travail of His soul! There is also great reward in watching *the first buddings of conviction in a soul*! To say of that girl in the class, "She has a tender heart—I do hope that the Lord is at work in her." To go home and pray over that boy who said something in the afternoon that made you think he must know more of divine truth than you had feared! Oh, the joy of hope! But as for *the joy of success*—it is unspeakable! This joy, overwhelming as it is, is a hungry thing—you pine for more of it. To be a soul-winner is the happiest thing in the world. With every soul you bring to Christ, you get a new heaven on earth. But who can conceive of the bliss that awaits us above! How sweet is the sentence, "Enter into *the joy of your master!*"[1] Do you know what the joy of Christ is over a saved sinner? This is the very joy that we are to possess in heaven. Yes, when He ascends the throne, you shall ascend with Him. When the heavens ring with "Well done, well done," you will have a part in the reward. You have worked with Him; you have suffered with Him; you will now reign with Him. You have sown with Him; you will reap with Him. Your face was covered with sweat like His, and your soul, like His, was grieved for the sins of men; now your face will be bright with heaven's splendor as is His countenance, and now your soul will be filled with heavenly joys just as His soul is.

[1] Matthew 25:21, 23

## *I clothed you also with embroidered cloth and shod you with fine leather. I wrapped you in fine linen and covered you with silk.*

EZEKIEL 16:10

Consider the matchless generosity with which the Lord provides for His people's apparel. They are arrayed in this way so that the divine skill is seen producing an unrivaled "*embroidered cloth*," in which every attribute takes its part and every divine beauty is revealed. There is no art like the art displayed in our salvation, no skillful workmanship like that seen in the righteousness of the saints. Justification has engrossed learned pens in every age of the church and will be the theme of admiration in eternity. In all this splendor there is utility and durability, comparable to our being "*shod . . . with fine leather*." This skin covered the tabernacle and formed one of the finest and strongest leathers known. The righteousness that is of God by faith endures forever, and he who is shod with this divine preparation will walk through the desert in safety. The purity and dignity of our holy vestments are brought out in "*fine linen*." When the Lord sanctifies His people, they are clothed as priests in pure white; the snow itself does not excel them. They are in the eyes of men and angels fair to look upon, and even in the Lord's eyes they are without spot. Meanwhile the royal apparel is delicate and rich as "*silk*." No expense is spared, no beauty withheld, no grandeur denied.

What, then? Can we infer nothing from this? Surely there is gratitude to be felt and joy to be expressed. Come, my heart, do not refuse your evening hallelujah! Tune your pipes! Touch your chords!

> *Strangely, my soul, art thou arrayed*
> *By the Great Sacred Three!*
> *In sweetest harmony of praise*
> *Let all your powers agree.*

## *The sheep follow him, for they know his voice.*

JOHN 10:4

What is it that provides the infallible evidence that you are a child of God? It is a foolish presumption to answer this by our own judgment; but God's Word reveals it to us, and we may walk confidently when we have revelation as our guide. We are told concerning our Lord, "to all who did *receive him*, who believed in his name, he gave the right to become children of God."[1] So if I have received Christ Jesus into my heart, I am a child of God. That reception is described in the same verse as *believing in the name of Jesus Christ.* If, then, I believe on Jesus Christ's name—that is, simply from my heart entrust myself to the crucified but now exalted Redeemer—I am a member of the family of the Most High. Whatever else I may not have, if I have this, I have the privilege of becoming a child of God. The Lord Jesus puts it in another way: "The sheep follow him, for they know his voice." Here is the matter in a nutshell. Christ appears as a shepherd to His own sheep, not to others. As soon as He appears, His own sheep perceive Him—they trust Him, they are prepared to follow Him. He knows them, and they know Him; there is a mutual knowledge—there is a constant connection between them. And so the evidence, the infallible mark of regeneration and adoption, is a hearty faith in the appointed Redeemer. Reader, are you in doubt, are you uncertain about whether you are one of God's children? Then do not let an hour pass until you have said, "Search me, O God, and know my heart."[2] Do not linger here, I warn you! If you must linger anywhere, let it be about some secondary matter—your health, if you wish, or the title deeds of your home. But about your soul, your never-dying soul and its eternal destiny, I urge you to be in earnest. Make certain of this eternal issue.

[1]John 1:12  [2]Psalm 139:23

## *Yours is the day, yours also the night.*

PSALM 74:16

Lord, You do not abdicate Your throne when the sun goes down, nor do You leave the world during all those long wintry nights to be the prey of evil. Your eyes watch us like the stars, and Your arms surround us as the band of planets belts the sky. The benefit of kindly sleep and all the influences of the moon are in Your hand, and the alarms and solemnities of night are equally with You. This is very sweet to me when walking in the midnight hours or tossing to and fro in anguish. There are precious fruits supplied by the moon as well as by the sun: May my Lord make me a favored partaker in them. The night of affliction is just as much under the arrangement and control of the Lord of Love as the bright summer days when all is bliss. Jesus is in the tempest. His love wraps the night about itself like a cloak, but to the eye of faith the sable robe is scarcely a disguise. From the first watch of the night even to the break of day the eternal Watcher observes His saints and overrules the shades and shadows of midnight for His people's highest good. We believe in no rival deities of good and evil contending for mastery, but we hear the voice of Jehovah saying, "I form light and create darkness . . . I am the LORD, who does all these things."[1] Gloomy seasons of religious indifference and social sin are not exempted from the divine purpose. When the altars of truth are defiled, and the ways of God forsaken, the Lord's servants weep with bitter sorrow, but they need not despair, for even the darkest eras are governed by the Lord and will come to an end at His command. What seems defeat to us may be victory to Him.

> *Though enwrapt in gloomy night,*
> *We perceive no ray of light;*
> *Since the Lord Himself is here,*
> *'Tis not fitting we should fear.*

[1] Isaiah 45:7

### And the glory of the LORD shall be revealed, and all flesh shall see it together.

ISAIAH 40:5

We anticipate the happy day when every knee will bow before Christ; when the gods of the heathen shall be cast to the moles and the bats; when empty religion will be exploded, and the crescent of Mohammed will topple, never again to cast its harmful rays upon the nations; when kings shall worship before the Prince of Peace, and all nations shall call the Redeemer blessed. Some despair of this. They look on the world as a ship breaking up and going to pieces, never to float again. We know that the world and all that is in it will one day be burned up, and afterwards we look for new heavens and for a new earth; but we cannot read our Bibles without the conviction that—

*Jesus shall reign where'er the sun*
*Doth his successive journeys run.*

We are not discouraged by the length of His delays; we are not disheartened by the long period that He assigns to the church in which to struggle with little success and much defeat. We believe that God will never tolerate this world, which has once seen Christ's blood shed upon it, remaining as the devil's stronghold. Christ came here to deliver this world from the detested sway of the powers of darkness. What a shout that will be when men and angels unite to cry "Hallelujah! For the Lord our God Almighty reigns"[1] What a satisfaction it will be in that day to have had a part in the fight, to have helped to break the arrows of the bow, and to have shared in winning the victory for our Lord! Happy are those who entrust themselves to this conquering Lord, and who fight side by side with Him doing their part in His name and by His strength! How unhappy are those on the side of evil! It is a losing side, and it is a matter in which to lose is to lose and to be lost forever. On whose side are you?

[1]Revelation 19:6

> *And when the days of the feast had run their*
> *course, Job would send and consecrate them,*
> *and he would rise early in the morning and offer*
> *burnt offerings according to the number of them*
> *all. For Job said, "It may be that my children*
> *have sinned, and cursed God in their hearts."*
> *Thus Job did continually.*

JOB 1:5

What Job did early in the morning, after the family festivities, it will be good for the believer to do for himself before he rests tonight. Amid the cheerfulness of household gatherings it is easy to slide into sinful frivolity and to forget our declared character as Christians. It ought not to be so, but sadly it is, that our days of feasting are very seldom days of sanctified enjoyment but too frequently degenerate into unholy amusement. It is possible to experience joy as pure and sanctifying as a dip in the rivers of Eden: Holy gratitude should be just as purifying an element as grief. Sadly for our poor hearts, facts prove that the house of mourning is better than the house of feasting. Come, believer, how have you sinned today? Have you been forgetful of your high calling? Have you been like others in using empty words and unguarded speech? Then confess the sin, and flee to the sacrifice. The sacrifice sanctifies. The precious blood of the Lamb removes the guilt and purges the defilement of our sins of ignorance and carelessness. This is the best ending of a Christmas day—to wash anew in the cleansing fountain. Believer, come to this sacrifice continually; if it is good tonight, it is good every night. To live at the altar is the privilege of the royal priesthood; to them sin, bad as it is, is nevertheless no cause for despair, since they draw near once more to the sin-atoning victim, and their conscience is purged from dead works.

> *Gladly I close this festive day,*
> *Grasping the altar's hallow'd horn;*
> *My slips and faults are washed away,*
> *The Lamb has all my trespass borne.*

## *I am with you always.*

MATTHEW 28:20

The Lord Jesus is among His people; He walks between the golden candlesticks; His promise is, "I am with you always." He is as surely with us now as He was with the disciples at the lake when they saw coals of fire and fish being prepared for breakfast. Not physically, but still in reality, Jesus is with us. And an important truth this is, for where Jesus is, *love becomes passionate*. Of all the things in the world that can set the heart burning, there is nothing like the presence of Jesus! A glimpse of Him is so overwhelming that we are ready to say, "Turn away Your eyes from me, for they have overcome me." Even the fragrance of the aloes and the myrrh and the cinnamon, which linger on His perfumed garments, causes the sick and the faint to grow strong. A moment's leaning of the head upon that gracious chest, welcoming His divine love into our poor cold hearts, and suddenly we are no longer cold but shine like seraphs, equal to every task and capable of bearing every suffering. If we know that Jesus is with us, *every power will be heightened*, and every grace will be strengthened, and we will cast ourselves into the Lord's service with heart and soul and strength; therefore the presence of Christ is to be desired above all things. *His presence will be realized most by those who are most like Him.* If you desire to see Christ, you must grow in conformity to Him. Bring yourself, by the power of the Spirit, into union with Christ's desires and motives and plans of action, and you are likely to be favored with His company. Remember, *His presence may be enjoyed*. His promise is as true as ever. He delights to be with us. If He does not come, it is because we hinder Him by our indifference. He will reveal Himself to our sincere prayers and graciously allow Himself to be detained by our cries and by our tears, for these are the golden chains that bind Jesus to His people.

## *And the L*ORD *will guide you continually.*

ISAIAH 58:11

The Lord will guide you." Not an angel, but the Lord will guide you. He said He would not go through the wilderness before His people, but an angel would go before them to lead them in the way; but Moses said, "If your presence will not go with me, do not bring us up from here."[1] Christian, God has not left you in your earthly pilgrimage to be guided by an angel: He Himself leads the procession. You may not see the cloudy, fiery pillar, but the Lord will never forsake you. Notice the word *will*—"The Lord *will* guide you." This makes it certain! We may be sure that God will not forsake us! His precious shalls and wills are better than men's promises. "I will never leave you nor forsake you."[2] Then observe the adverb *"continually."* We are not merely being led sometimes, but we have a perpetual guide; not occasionally left to our own understanding, and so to wander, but continually hearing the guiding voice of the Great Shepherd; and if we keep close to His heels, we will not drift but will be led by a right way to our eternal dwelling. If you have to change your position in life, if you have to emigrate to another country, if it should happen that you are poverty-stricken or suddenly promoted to a more responsible position than the one you now occupy, if you are thrown among strangers or cast among foes, don't tremble, for "the Lord will guide you continually." There are no dilemmas out of which you will not be delivered if you live near to God and your heart is kept warm with holy love. You will not go astray in the company of God. Like Enoch, walk with God, and you cannot miss your road. You have infallible wisdom to direct you, unchangeable love to comfort you, and eternal power to defend you. "The Lord"—mark the word—"the Lord will guide you continually."

[1]Exodus 33:15  [2]Hebrews 13:5

## *I have not come to bring peace,*
## *but a sword.*

MATTHEW 10:34

The Christian will be sure to make enemies. It will be one of his objects to make none; but if doing what is right and believing what is true should cause him to lose every earthly friend, he will regard it as a small loss, since his great Friend in heaven will be even more friendly and will reveal Himself to him more graciously than ever. You who have taken up His cross, don't you know what your Master said? "I have come to set a man against his father, and a daughter against her mother . . . And a person's enemies will be those of his own household." Christ is the great Peacemaker; but before peace, He brings war. Where the light comes, the darkness must vanish. Where truth is, the lie must flee; or if it remains, there must be a stern conflict, for the truth cannot and will not lower its standard, and the lie must be trampled underfoot. If you follow Christ, you will have all the dogs of the world yelping at your heels. If you live in such a manner as to stand the test of the last judgment, you can depend upon it that the world will not speak well of you. He who has the friendship of the world is an enemy to God; but if you are true and faithful to the Most High, men will resent your uncompromising commitment, since it is a testimony against their iniquities. You must do the right and not fear the consequences. You will need the courage of a lion to pursue a course that turns your best friend into your fiercest foe; but for the love of Jesus you must take your stand. To risk reputation and affection for the truth's sake is so demanding that to do it constantly you will need a degree of moral principle that only the Spirit of God can work in you. Do not turn your back like a coward, but play the man. Follow boldly in your Master's steps, for He has made this rough journey before you. Better a brief warfare and eternal rest than false peace and everlasting torment.

## *What do you think about the Christ?*

MATTHEW 22:42

The great test of your soul's health is, *What do you think about Christ?* Is He the best of friends—"distinguished among ten thousand"[1]—your all in all? When Christ is held in such esteem, all the faculties of the spiritual man are energized. I can gauge your piety by this standard: Does Christ take a high or low position with you? If you have thought little of Christ, if you have been content to live without His presence, if you have cared only slightly for His honor, if you have neglected His laws, then I know that your soul is sick—God grant that it may not be a sickness leading to death! But if the first thought of your spirit has been, *How can I honor Jesus?*—if the daily desire of your soul has been, "O that I knew where I might find him!"[2] I tell you that you may face a thousand infirmities, and even hardly know whether you are a child of God at all, and yet I am persuaded beyond a doubt that you are safe, since Jesus is great in your esteem. I'm not concerned about your rags—what do you think of *His* royal apparel? I'm not concerned about your wounds, though they bleed profusely—what do you think of *His* wounds? Are they like glittering rubies in your esteem? I think none the less of you, though you lie like Lazarus on the refuse pile, and the dogs lick you—I do not judge you by your poverty: What do you think of the King in His beauty? Does He sit enthroned in your heart? Would you set Him higher if you could? Would you be willing to die if you could add another trumpet to the melody that proclaims His praise? Then it is well with you. Whatever you may think of yourself, if Christ is great to you, you will be with Him in the end.

> *Though all the world my choice deride,*
> *Yet Jesus shall my portion be;*
> *For I am pleased with none beside,*
> *The fairest of the fair is He.*

[1]Song of Solomon 5:10   [2]Job 23:3

### *Do you not know that the end will be bitter?*

2 SAMUEL 2:26

Reader, if you are merely a professor and not a possessor of the faith that is in Christ Jesus, the following lines are a true sketch of your end.

You are a respectable attender at a place of worship; you go because others go, not because your heart is right with God. This is your beginning. I will suppose that for the next twenty or thirty years you will be spared to continue in this way, professing religion by an outward attendance upon the means of grace, but having no heart in the matter. Tread softly, for I must show you the deathbed of someone just like you. Let us gaze upon him gently. A clammy sweat is on his brow, and he wakes up crying, "O God, it is hard to die. Did you send for my pastor?" "Yes, he is coming." The pastor comes. "Sir, I fear that I am dying!" "Have you any hope?" "I cannot say that I have. I fear to stand before my God. Oh, pray for me." The prayer is offered for him with sincere earnestness, and the way of salvation is for the ten-thousandth time put before him, but before he has grasped the rope, I see him sink. I may put my finger upon those cold eyelids, for they will never see anything here again. But where is the man, and where are the man's true eyes? It is written, "In Hades, being in torment, he lifted up his eyes."[1] Why did he not lift up his eyes before? Because he was so accustomed to hearing the Gospel that his soul slept under it. If you should lift up your eyes in hell, how bitter will be your wailings. Let the Savior's own words reveal the woe: "Father Abraham, have mercy on me, and send Lazarus to dip the end of his finger in water, and cool my tongue, for I am in anguish in this flame."[2] There is a frightful meaning in those words. May you never have to spell it out by the red light of God's wrath!

[1] Luke 16:23   [2] Luke 16:24

# The harvest is past, the summer is ended, and we are not saved.

JEREMIAH 8:20

*N*ot saved! Dear reader, is this your sorry condition? Warned of the judgment to come, invited to escape for your life, and yet at this moment *not saved*! You know the way of salvation, you read it in the Bible, you hear it from the pulpit, it is explained to you by friends, and still you neglect it, and therefore you are *not saved*. You will be without excuse when the Lord shall execute judgment. The Holy Spirit has blessed the Word that has been preached in your hearing, and times of refreshing have come from the divine presence, and yet you are still without Christ. All these hopeful seasons have come and gone—your summer and your harvest have past—and still you are *not saved*. Years have followed one another into eternity, and your last year will soon be here: Youth has gone, manhood is going, and still you are not saved. Let me ask you—*will you ever be saved?* Is there any likelihood of it? Already the most favorable seasons have left you unsaved. Will other occasions alter your condition? Every means has failed with you—the best of means, used perseveringly and with the utmost affection. What more can be done for you? Affliction and prosperity have equally failed to impress you; tears and prayers and sermons have been wasted on your barren heart. Are not the probabilities dead against your ever being saved? Is it not more than likely that you will stay as you are till death forever bars the door of hope? Do you recoil from this idea? Yet it is a most reasonable one: He who is not washed in so many waters will in all probability go filthy to his end. The convenient time never has come—why should it ever come? It is logical to fear that it will never arrive and that like Felix you will find no convenient occasion until you are in hell. Think carefully about hell and of the dreadful probability that you will soon be there!

Reader, suppose you should die unsaved—no words can picture your doom. Write out your dreadful predicament in tears and blood; talk of it with groans and gnashing of teeth: You will be punished with everlasting destruction and banished from the glory of the Lord and from the glory of His power. Allow my words to startle you into serious thought. Be wise, be wise in time, and before another year begins believe in Jesus, who is able to save you completely. Consecrate these last hours to lonely thought, and if you are brought to deep repentance, it will be well; and if it leads to a humble faith in Jesus, it will be best of all. See to it that this year does not pass away with you still unforgiven. Do not let the new year's midnight bells sound upon a joyless spirit! Now, *now*, NOW believe and live.

> *ESCAPE FOR THY LIFE;*
> *LOOK NOT BEHIND THEE,*
> *NEITHER STAY THOU*
> *IN THE PLAIN;*
> *ESCAPE TO THE MOUNTAIN,*
> *LEST THOU BE CONSUMED.*